D0024339

WATER LAW
IN A NUTSHELL
THIRD EDITION

By

DAVID H. GETCHES
Raphael J. Moses Professor of Natural Resources Law
University of Colorado School of Law
Boulder, Colorado

ST. PAUL, MINN.
WEST PUBLISHING CO.
1997

Nutshell Series, In a Nutshell, the Nutshell Logo and the West Group symbol are registered trademarks used herein under license.

TEXT IS PRINTED ON 10% POST CONSUMER RECYCLED PAPER

3rd Reprint — 2003

FOREWORD TO THE THIRD EDITION

When the first edition of this book appeared in 1984, there was a dearth of current supplemental sources available to students or lawyers to assist them in gaining a basic understanding of water law. That changed with the appearance in 1988 of the treatise by A. Dan Tarlock entitled *Law of Water Rights and Resources* and a thorough revision of the multi-volume work *Water and Water Rights* edited by Robert E. Beck. Because of favorable response from practicing lawyers as well as students, this edition continues to address the fundamentals of water law in a way that will be useful to both sets of readers. Deeper treatment can be provided by the two treatises.

Over one hundred case citations have been added to this edition of the *Nutshell*. It is current through the summer of 1996. As in the previous edition, an effort was made to include virtually every principal case found in the three leading law school casebooks: Tarlock, Corbridge & Getches, *Water Resources Management* (Fourth Edition, 1993), Gould & Grant, *Water Law* (Fifth Edition, 1995), and Sax, Abrams & Thompson, *Legal Control of Water Resources* (Second Edition, 1991).

This third edition of *Water Law in a Nutshell* has been revised to capture the latest developments in this fast-moving field. Competition for water in the western United States has always been keen. Now, shortages and conflicting uses are felt more frequently in the East as a result of urbanization and population growth. The competition for water is compounded as the value of water flowing in streams for recreation and for ecological integrity increases.

State laws reflect the pressures for accommodating diverse and expanding water uses. Courts, agencies, and legislatures are beginning to weigh issues of public interest and environmental considerations in water decisions. To cope with rising demands, states are tightening their administration of water rights, insisting on greater efficiency and conservation, and many are adjudicating all the rights in a river basin to ensure more certainty and to cull out unused and over-stated rights. The law of surface use continues to change in response to recreational demands. States are also turning more to the conjunctive management of groundwater and surface water to get optimum use out of their available water resources. The basic principles of riparian and appropriation law have not changed greatly. Indeed, today they are less often determinative of disputes than regulatory and administrative requirements of permit statutes. One exception is the doctrine of beneficial use in prior appropriation law which is slowly evolving to reflect a changing concept of the kinds of water uses that are "beneficial" to society.

The role of federal law is more pervasive than ever in deciding the extent to which water can be allocated and used for particular purposes. Because states typically have been slow to incorporate environmental and other public concerns in their water laws, federal laws have filled some of the gaps. Not only water quality protection under the Clean Water Act, but provisions that protect wetlands and waterways from being filled in or drained, and laws like the Endangered Species Act, profoundly influence how and where water is used. Meanwhile, the predominant federal role in financing and building water projects through most of this century has faded in relative importance.

I am greatly indebted to my student research assistants at the University of Colorado School of Law for their excellent support. Christopher Wirth (Class of '97) was careful and untiring in searching out new developments in the law and contributed to the organization and editing of the book. Morgan Word (Class of '97) did solid research work and Scott Miller (Class of '98) assisted in the editing.

DHG

Boulder, Colorado
August, 1996

*

FOREWORD TO THE SECOND EDITION

Water law has been an especially active field since the first edition of *Water Law in a Nutshell*. There have been court decisions in hundreds of cases and statutory changes in several states. In addition, scholarship in the field has been expanding. There are now three water law casebooks in use in law schools and a new treatise entitled *Law of Water Rights and Resources* by Professor A. Dan Tarlock. More law review articles are being written than ever before in water law.

This second edition represents a revision of the first in light of changes in the law through late 1989. Citations appear at relevant places to nearly all of the principal cases appearing in Meyers, Tarlock, Corbridge, and Getches, *Water Resource Management* (Third Edition, 1988), Trelease and Gould, *Water Law* (4th Edition, 1986), Sax and Abrams, *Legal Control of Water Resources* (1986). And a new chapter has been added on surface use of waters in light of the increased importance of public recreational water uses. Throughout this edition, wherever appropriate, information has been expanded on instream flow protection, water quality and public interest concerns in water use and water allocation. This reflects the growing interest in those matters throughout the country. For thorough treatment of water pollution control, however, readers are urged to look to other sources, including *Environmental Law in a Nutshell.*

I am indebted to research assistants from the University of Colorado School of Law for their work in making this edition possible. Ellen Ostheimer Creagar and Michael James Grode spent many hours to ensure the accuracy and currency of this edition and edited the manuscript with care. I am also grateful to Elizabeth Thomas and John S. Hajdik for their assistance earlier in the project.

DHG

Escazu, Costa Rica
April, 1990

FOREWORD TO THE FIRST EDITION

In spite of all its interesting issues and its great practical importance, water law is a field in which there is a dearth of supplemental sources that are useful to students. A few voluminous treatises are available to aid the practitioner in finding answers to difficult questions. But there is no basic source. This book is a modest effort at providing a supplemental source for the student of water law. It also should serve as an orientation device for lawyers who do not regularly practice in the field and for non-lawyers who need a background in the subject.

The study of water is complicated by the widely differing systems that exist in the several states. No attempt is made here to draw together and explicate the complete law of any particular state. This book states the general rules that apply within major systems of water law and attempts to give examples of special rules applicable in particular states. Generally, the statutory and case law of the states is current through 1982, and relevant United States Supreme Court cases is current through July, 1983.

This book owes its existence to many people. A number of student research assistants at the University of Colorado School of Law worked on its preparation. Mark Cohen, Esq. worked diligently and made an important imprint on Chapters Two and Four. Richard Cauble, Esq. devoted many hours and made a fine, professional contribution to Chapters Five, Six, Eight, and Nine. George Jent, Esq., Stephen Ellis, Esq., Sharon Nelson, Esq. and Dary James all assisted with parts of Chapter Three.

The author is greatly indebted to Ann Amundson, Esq. for her splendid editorial assistance with the manuscript. My colleagues Professor Charles Wilkinson and Professor James Corbridge were kind enough to review portions of the draft manuscript and made important suggestions on how to improve it. I am very grateful to Anne Guthrie who typed and retyped successive drafts of the manuscript. Finally, I thank my wife Ann and my children on whose time this book was written.

DHG

Boulder, Colorado
February, 1984

OUTLINE

	Page
FOREWORD TO THE THIRD EDITION	III
FOREWORD TO THE SECOND EDITION	VII
FOREWORD TO THE FIRST EDITION	IX
TABLE OF CASES	XXIX

Chapter One. Overview and Introduction to Water Law ... 1
I. The Study of Water Law ... 1
II. Legal Systems for Water Allocation ... 3
    A.   Riparian Rights ... 4
    B.   Prior Appropriation ... 6
    C.   Hybrid Systems ... 7
III. Special Types of Water ... 8
    A.   Groundwater ... 8
    B.   Diffused Surface Water ... 10
IV. Public Rights ... 11
V. Intergovernmental Problems ... 12
    A.   Reserved Rights ... 12
    B.   Federal Actions Affecting State Water Rights ... 13
    C.   Interstate Problems ... 14
VI. Water Institutions ... 14

Chapter Two. Riparian Rights ... 15
I. History of the Riparian Doctrine ... 15
    A.   European Precedents ... 15
        1. France ... 16
        2. England ... 17

OUTLINE

Page

I. History of the Riparian Doctrine—Continued
   B.   Early Development in the Eastern
        United States 18
   C.   Repudiation and Recognition in the
        American West 20
   D.   Riparian Law Today 22
II. Riparian Lands 23
   A.   Contiguity to Source 23
   B.   Types of Watercourses 23
      1. Streams 24
      2. Lakes and Ponds 24
      3. Springs and Other Natural Water Bodies 26
      4. Underground Watercourses 26
      5. Foreign Waters 27
      6. Artificially Created Watercourses 27
   C.   Extent 29
      1. Watershed Limitation 29
      2. Divisions of Riparian Land 30
         a. Unity of Title Rule 30
         b. Source of Title Rule 31
III. Nature of Riparian Rights 33
   A.   Rights of Riparian Proprietors 34
      1. Preference for "Natural" Uses.. 34
      2. Irrigation, Industrial, and Mining Uses 35
      3. Municipal Uses 36
         a. Common Law 36
         b. Statutory and Charter Provisions 37
      4. Storage Rights 38
      5. Water Power 39
         a. Waterwheels, Mills, etc. 39

OUTLINE

Page

III. Nature of Riparian Rights—Continued
           b. Hydroelectric Generation..... 40
           6. Recovery of Gravel 41
           7. Discharge of Waste................. 42
    B.   Rights in the Surface of Waterways 44
           1. Reciprocal Rights Among Ripar-
              ians............................... 44
           2. Rights of the Public.............. 45
              a. Navigable Waters 45
              b. Other Waterways 46
IV. Limits on Riparian Rights 47
    A.   Reasonable Use Limitation 47
    B.   Non-Riparian Uses 51
           1. Use Limited to Riparian Land... 51
           2. Use Limited to Watershed 51
           3. Limitations on Rules Prevent-
              ing Non-Riparian Use 52
              a. Restatement Rule 52
              b. Requirement of Actual
                Harm........................... 53
              c. Permit and Hybrid States 54
              d. Prescription.................... 54
              e. Economic Solutions 55
V. Permit Systems................................. 56
    A.   Applicability of Permit Require-
        ments 56
    B.   Permit Criteria...................... 57
    C.   Permit Provisions 58
VI. Transfers of Riparian Rights................... 59
    A.   Appurtenance 59
    B.   Grants and Reservations.............. 59

		Page
VII.	Loss of Riparian Rights	66
A.	Effect of Non–Use	67
B.	Avulsion and Accretion	68
C.	Prescription	69
D.	Legislation	72
	1. Statutes Modifying Water Rights	72
	a. Permit Systems	72
	b. Hybrid Systems	72
	2. Forfeiture Statutes	73

Chapter Three. Prior Appropriation 74

I.	General Description	74
II.	Development of Prior Appropriation Doctrine	77
A.	Federal Statutes	79
	1. 1866 Mining Act	79
	2. 1870 Amendment to Mining Act	80
	3. 1877 Desert Land Act	80
B.	Development of Modern Systems	81
III.	Appropriative Water Rights as Property	82
A.	No Individual Ownership of Flowing Water	82
B.	State Constitutional and Statutory Provisions	85
C.	Statutes Limiting Riparian Rights	85
IV.	Elements of Appropriation	88
A.	Intent	89
B.	Diversion	92
	1. Types of Diversions	93
	2. Due Diligence Requirement and Conditional Rights	93

Page

IV. Elements of Appropriation—Continued
  3. Exceptions to the Diversion Requirement 95
  C. Beneficial Use 97
V. Priority: Linchpin of the Appropriative Right 101
  A. Priority 101
  B. Qualifications of the Senior's Right   102
  C. Enforcement of Priorities 103
  D. Preferences 104
VI. Waters Subject to Appropriation 106
  A. Watercourses 106
    1. Streams 107
    2. Lakes and Ponds 109
    3. Springs 109
  B. Waters Made Available by Human Effort 110
    1. Foreign and Developed Water ... 110
    2. Salvaged Water Distinguished ... 112
  C. Withdrawals From Appropriation ... 113
    1. Maintenance of Instream Flows   113
    2. Reservations for Future Uses 116
VII. Extent of the Appropriative Right 117
  A. Measure of the Right: Beneficial Use 118
  B. Beneficial Use as a Limit 120
    1. "Duty of Water" Limitations 122
    2. Reasonably Efficient Means of Diversion 123
    3. The Expanding Concept of Beneficial Use 128
  C. Recapture and Reuse 129

		Page
VII.	Extent of the Appropriative Right—Continued	
	1. Total Use Must Not Exceed Water Right	130
	2. Reuse Limited to Original Land	132
VIII.	Procedures for Perfecting and Administering Rights	135
A.	Early Systems	135
	1. Prestatutory Period (1840–1870)	135
	2. Early Statutes	136
	3. Problems With Early Statutes	137
B.	Current Permit Systems	138
	1. Purpose	138
	2. Constitutionality	138
	a. Source of Authority	138
	b. Separation of Powers	139
	3. Permitting Procedures	141
	a. Filing	141
	b. Notice	142
	c. Hearing	142
	d. Issuance of Permit	143
	4. Statutory Criteria	144
	5. Public Interest Considerations	145
C.	Adjudication	149
	1. General Stream Adjudications	149
	2. Validation or Review of Agency Permit Decisions	150
	3. Conflicts Among Water Users	150
D.	Regulation of Water Distribution	151
E.	The Colorado System	152
IX.	Transfers and Changes of Water Rights	155
A.	Transfers Generally	156

Page

IX. Transfers and Changes of Water Rights—Continued
   B. State Restrictions on Transfers Apart From the Land ---------------- 156
   C. Restrictions on Transbasin Diversions ----------------------------------- 158
   D. Changes In Use ------------------------ 161
      1. No Harm Rule ---------------------- 161
      2. Procedures ------------------------- 162
      3. Types of Changes ------------------ 164
         a. Change in Point of Diversion 168
         b. Change in Place of Use -------- 168
         c. Change in Purpose of Use ---- 169
         d. Change in Time of Use ------- 170
         e. Change in Point of Return --- 171
      4. Limits on Changed Use ----------- 173
         a. Historical Consumptive Use 173
         b. Permitted or Decreed Diversion Right--------------------- 175
         c. Other Restrictions ------------ 175
X. Loss of Water Rights ----------------------- 176
   A. Abandonment --------------------------- 176
   B. Forfeiture------------------------------- 178
   C. Adverse Possession -------------------- 179
XI. Access to Water Sources---------------------- 180
   A. Across Public Lands-------------------- 180
   B. Across Private Lands ------------------ 182
      1. Status of Trespassing Appropriators ----------------------------- 182
      2. Purchase of Rights–Of–Way------ 183
      3. Condemnation of Rights–Of–Way --------------------------------- 184

Page

XI. Access to Water Sources—Continued
   C.   Appurtenancy of Ditch Rights to
       Water Rights................................ 185

XII. Storage 185
   A.   Acquisition of Storage Rights 186
       1. Storage Water Rights.................. 186
       2. Permission to Construct Stor-
          age Facilities 187
   B.   Use of Storage Rights...................... 187
   C.   Limits on Storage 188

**Chapter Four. Hybrid Systems and Oth-
   er Variations** 190
 I. Development of Hybrid Systems.............. 191
   A.   California's Early Recognition of
       Both Appropriative Rights and
       Riparian Rights 192
   B.   Federal Recognition of Appropria-
       tive Rights 193
   C.   Limitations on Riparian Rights...... 196
 II. Modifications of Riparian Rights in Hy-
   brid Systems... 197
   A.   Reasonable Use Limitations 197
   B.   Extinguishment of Unused Ripari-
       an Rights..................................... 198
   C.   Constitutional Challenges 198
III. Administration of Hybrid Systems.......... 201
   A.   Resolving Disputes Among Water
       Users 202
   B.   Adjudication of Unused Riparian
       Rights 203
   C.   Prescription 204

Page

IV. Other Water Law Variations 206
  A.   Hawaiian Water Law 206
  B.   Water Law in Louisiana 212
  C.   Pueblo Water Rights 214

Chapter Five.   Rights to Use the Surface of Waterways 217
  I. Public Rights in Navigable Waters 218
     A.   Definitions of Navigability 219
          1. Federal Definition of Navigability for Title 219
          2. State Definitions of Navigability 222
     B.   Rights of the Public to Use the Surface of Navigable Waters 223
  II. The Public Trust Doctrine 224
  III. State–Recognized Public Rights of Surface Use of "Non-navigable" Waters 226
  IV. Access to Waterways for Lawful Surface Use 229
     A.   Condemnation 230
     B.   Implied Rights of Access 230
          1. Custom 230
          2. Implied Dedication 232
          3. Prescription 232
          4. Public Trust 232
          5. Police Power Regulation 233
  V. Reciprocal Rights of Riparian Owners 233

Chapter Six.   Groundwater 237
  I. Basic Hydrology 237
     A.   How Groundwater Occurs 237
          1. Permeability of Rock Formations 237

Page

I. Basic Hydrology—Continued
   2. Zones of Groundwater Occurrence 238
   3. Aquifers 239
   4. Underground Streams Distinguished 241
   B. How Wells Work 242
   1. Drilling and Pumping 242
   2. Effects of Well Use 243
      a. Cone of Influence 243
      b. Effects of Depletion 243
   3. Optimum Yield 245
II. Allocating Rights in Groundwater 247
   A. Nature of Rights 247
   1. Rights Based on Land Ownership 248
      a. Absolute Ownership Doctrine 248
      b. Correlative Rights 249
   2. Rights by Prior Appropriation ... 251
   3. Groundwater as a Public Resource 253
   B. Rules of Liability 254
   1. No Liability Rule 254
   2. Prior Appropriation—"Junior-Liable" Rule 255
   3. Reasonable Use Doctrine 255
   4. Restatement (Second) of Torts § 858 256
   5. "Economic Reach" Rule 258
   C. Economic Effects of Rules 259
   D. Permits 262

Page

II. Allocating Rights in Groundwater—Continued
        1. Well Permits 264
        2. Permits Evidencing a Water Right 264
   E. Statutory Limits on Pumping 265
        1. Protection of Existing Rights 266
        2. Legislative Schedules for Groundwater Mining 267
        3. Critical Area Legislation 269
III. Conjunctive Use 271
   A. Regulation of Groundwater Connected With Surface Sources 272
        1. Interaction of Groundwater and Surface Water 272
        2. Definition of Hydrologically Connected ("Tributary") Groundwater 274
        3. Conjunctive Use Management ... 275
        4. Regulation of Tributary Groundwater: The Colorado Example 278
   B. Imported Supplies and Intensive Management: The California Example 280
IV. Groundwater Storage 281
V. Controlling Groundwater Contamination 285
   A. Regulation of Groundwater Pumping 285
   B. Regulation of Polluting Activities ... 286
        1. State Regulation 286
        2. Federal Regulation 287
   C. State Judicial Remedies 289

Page

Chapter Seven. Diffused Surface Waters 291
I. Watercourses and Diffused Surface Waters Distinguished 292
   A. Watercourses 292
   B. Diffused Surface Waters 293
II. Protection From Damage by Surface Flows 293
   A. Common Enemy Doctrine 295
   B. Civil Law Doctrine 297
   C. Reasonable Use Doctrine 299
   D. Public Control of Surface Drainage 301
     1. Public Drainage Projects 301
     2. Public Restrictions on Draining Wetlands 302
III. Use of Diffused Surface Waters 303
   A. Right to Capture Diffused Surface Waters 303
   B. State Control of Use of Diffused Surface Waters 304

Chapter Eight. Federal and Indian Reserved Rights 308
I. Reserved Rights Doctrine 308
   A. Origin of the Doctrine—*Winters v. United States* 308
   B. Application to Federal (Non–Indian) Lands 311
   C. Federal Power 313
     1. Constitutional Bases 313
     2. Exercise by Congress or the Executive 314
   D. Relationship to State Water Law.... 315

OUTLINE

Page

I. Reserved Rights Doctrine—Continued
    1. Prior Appropriation 316
    2. Riparian Rights 317
II. Priority of Reserved Rights 318
    A. Date of Reservation 318
    B. Early Priorities Based on Aboriginal Indian Rights......................... 319
III. Quantity 319
    A. Purposes of the Reservation 319
        1. Limitation on Quantity Reserved 319
        2. Determining Purposes 320
        3. Indian Reservations: Practicably Irrigable Acreage 321
    B. Use for Other Than Original Purposes 322
IV. Waters Reserved 323
    A. Waters Bordering on or Traversing Reservations 323
    B. Waters Beyond Reservation Boundaries 324
    C. Groundwater 325
V. Transfers of Reserved Rights 326
    A. Users of Public and Indian Lands .. 326
    B. Individual Indian Allotments......... 327
    C. Uses Outside Indian Reservations .. 329
VI. Quantification 330
    A. Adjudication 332
        1. Suits by the United States......... 332
        2. Joinder of the United States in State Court Actions—McCarran Amendment..................... 334

Page

VI. Quantification—Continued
  B. Other Methods of Quantification 338
  C. Regulatory Authority 339
    1. Preemptive Power of the Federal Government........................ 340
    2. Tribal Self–Government............ 341
VII. "Non–Reserved" Federal Water Rights .. 344

Chapter Nine. Federal Control of Water and Water Development 346
  I. Federal Powers 346
  A. Navigability and Congressional Power 347
    1. Historically 347
    2. Modern Importance of the Navigation Power 348
    3. Navigability for Title 350
  B. The Navigation Servitude 351
    1. Basis of the Navigation Servitude 352
    2. Extent of the Navigation Servitude 353
      a. Obstructions to Navigation .. 353
      b. Damage to Property in Navigable Waterway................. 354
      c. Project on Navigable Stream Causing Damage to Property Rights on Non–Navigable Tributaries.............. 355
      d. Waters Rendered Navigable by Private Effort 356
    3. Measure of Damages for Condemnation............................... 357

Page

I. Federal Powers—Continued
          a. Value of Water Power 357
          b. Site Value............................. 358
          c. Water Rights Created Under
             State Law............................ 361
II. Federal Licensing of Water Power Projects 363
  A. Federal Power Act 363
  B. Conflict With State Law 365
  C. Protection for Fish and Wildlife..... 368
III. Federal Reclamation Projects................... 371
  A. Purposes 371
  B. Congressional Powers..................... 373
  C. Limitations on Beneficiaries of
      Projects... 373
      1. Background and Policy 373
      2. Acreage Limitation.................... 373
  D. Conflicts With State Water Law..... 376
IV. Environmental Legislation 379
  A. The Clean Water Act...................... 379
      1. NPDES Permitting System 380
      2. Water Quality Standards........... 382
      3. Planning Requirements 384
      4. Non-point Source Controls 384
      5. Dredge and Fill Permits............ 386
  B. Impact on State–Created Water
      Rights... 389
      1. Wallop Amendment.................... 389
      2. Regulatory Takings 389
      3. Effects on Common Law Remedies... 390
  C. Fish and Wildlife Coordination Act 391

Page

IV. Environmental Legislation—Continued
    D.   Wild and Scenic Rivers Act   391
V. International Treaties............................   392
    A.   Examples of International Treaties   393
        1. Mexico.................................   393
        2. Canada   395
    B.   Supremacy of Treaties Over State
        Water Law..................................   396

Chapter Ten.   Interstate Allocation   397
  I. Adjudication..   397
    A.   Litigation Between Private Parties   397
        1. Personal Jurisdiction   398
        2. Subject Matter Jurisdiction   398
        3. Applicable Law   399
        4. Parens Patriae Suits................   400
        5. Enforcement   401
    B.   Litigation Between States   402
        1. Original Jurisdiction of Supreme Court...........................   402
        2. Justiciability   403
        3. Sources of Law: The Doctrine of Equitable Apportionment ..   404
  II. Formation of Compact   407
    A.   Constitutional Authority.................   407
    B.   Administration and Enforcement of Compacts   409
    C.   Legal Effect of Compacts   409
        1. Limitations on Private Water Users   409
        2. Effect of Congressional Ratification.................................   410
    D.   Interpretation of Compacts   411

		Page
III.	Legislative Allocation	412
IV.	State Restrictions on Water Export	415

Chapter Eleven. Water Service and Supply Organizations — 418

I. Private Organizations — 420
- A. Water Utilities — 420
- B. Mutual Water Companies — 421
- C. Carrier Ditch Companies — 421
- D. Mutual Ditch and Irrigation Companies — 422
  1. Financing — 424
  2. Ownership of Rights — 424
  3. Transfers — 425
  4. Priorities — 426
  5. Regulation — 426

II. Public Organizations — 427
- A. Regulatory and Planning Bodies — 427
- B. Municipalities — 427
- C. Irrigation Districts — 429
  1. Formation of Districts — 430
  2. Benefits of Districts — 430
  3. Ownership of Water Rights — 431
  4. Election of Boards — 432
  5. Financial Aspects — 433
  6. Functions — 434
- D. Municipal Water Districts — 435

INDEX — 437

*

TABLE OF CASES

References are to Pages

A–B Cattle Co. v. United States, 196 Colo. 539, 589 P.2d 57 (Colo.1978), *126*

Ackerman v. City of Walsenburg, 171 Colo. 304, 467 P.2d 267 (Colo.1970), *186*

Acton v. Blundell, 12 Mees. & W. 324, 152 Eng.Rep. 1223 (Eng.1843), *248*

Adair, United States v., 723 F.2d 1394 (9th Cir.1983), cert. denied Oregon v. United States, 467 U.S. 1252, 104 S.Ct. 3536, 82 L.Ed.2d 841 (1984), *311*

Adams v. Greenwich Water Co., 138 Conn. 205, 83 A.2d 177 (Conn.1951), *38*

Adams v. Grigsby, 152 So.2d 619 (La.App. 2 Cir.1963), writ denied 244 La. 662, 153 So.2d 880 (La.1963), *213, 214*

Adams v. Lang, 553 So.2d 89 (Ala.1989), *255*

Adjudication of Guadalupe River Basin, In re, 642 S.W.2d 438 (Tex.1982), *88, 141*

Akers, United States v., 785 F.2d 814 (9th Cir.1986), *387*

Alameda County Water Dist. v. Niles Sand & Gravel Co., Inc., 37 Cal.App.3d 924, 112 Cal.Rptr. 846 (Cal.App. 1 Dist.1974), cert. denied Niles Sand & Gravel Co., Inc. v. Alameda County Water District, 419 U.S. 869, 95 S.Ct. 128, 42 L.Ed.2d 108 (1974), *283*

Alamosa-La Jara Water Users Protection Ass'n v. Gould, 674 P.2d 914 (Colo.1983), *127, 280*

Albuquerque, City of v. Reynolds, 71 N.M. 428, 379 P.2d 73 (N.M.1962), *276*

Almo Water Co. v. Darrington, 95 Idaho 16, 501 P.2d 700 (Idaho 1972), *169*

Altus, Okl., City of v. Carr, 255 F.Supp. 828 (W.D.Tex.1966), *416*

Anderson v. Bell, 433 So.2d 1202 (Fla.1983), *235*

TABLE OF CASES

Anderson, United States v., 736 F.2d 1358 (9th Cir.1984), *344*

Apfelbacher, State v., 167 Wis. 233, 167 N.W. 244 (Wis.1918), *63*

Appalachian Elec. Power Co., United States v., 311 U.S. 377, 61 S.Ct. 291, 85 L.Ed. 243 (1940), *350*

Nebraska Game and Parks Comm'n v. 25 Corporation, Inc., 236 Neb. 671, 463 N.W.2d 591 (Neb.1990), *96*

Application of (see name of party)

Central Nebraska Public Power & Irrig. Dist. v. Abrahamson, 226 Neb. 594, 413 N.W.2d 290 (Neb.1987), *283*

Argyelan v. Haviland, 435 N.E.2d 973 (Ind.1982), *297*

Arizona v. California, 460 U.S. 605, 103 S.Ct. 1382, 75 L.Ed.2d 318 (1983), *333*

Arizona v. California, 439 U.S. 419, 99 S.Ct. 995, 58 L.Ed.2d 627 (1979), *323*

Arizona v. San Carlos Apache Tribe of Arizona, 463 U.S. 545, 103 S.Ct. 3201, 77 L.Ed.2d 837 (1983), *337*

Arizona Center For Law In Public Interest v. Hassell, 172 Ariz. 356, 837 P.2d 158 (Ariz.App. Div. 1 1991), *225*

Arizona Public Service Co. v. Long, 160 Ariz. 429, 773 P.2d 988 (Ariz.1989), *131, 172*

Arizona, State of v. State of Cal., 373 U.S. 546, 83 S.Ct. 1468, 10 L.Ed.2d 542 (1963), *311, 315, 321, 324, 332, 333, 362, 377, 378, 379, 404, 412*

Arizona, State of v. State of California, 298 U.S. 558, 56 S.Ct. 848, 80 L.Ed. 1331 (1936), *312, 414*

Arizona, State of v. State of California, 283 U.S. 423, 51 S.Ct. 522, 75 L.Ed. 1154 (1931), *313, 349*

Arkansas v. McIlroy, 268 Ark. 227, 595 S.W.2d 659 (Ark.1980), cert. denied McIlroy v. Arkansas, 449 U.S. 843, 101 S.Ct. 124, 66 L.Ed.2d 51 (1980), *223*

Arkansas v. Oklahoma, 503 U.S. 91, 112 S.Ct. 1046, 117 L.Ed.2d 239 (1992), *404*

Ashwander v. Tennessee Valley Authority, 297 U.S. 288, 56 S.Ct. 466, 80 L.Ed. 688 (1936), *347*

Attica, City of v. Mull Drilling Co., Inc., 9 Kan.App.2d 325, 676 P.2d 769 (Kan.App.1984), *290*

Attorney General v. Thomas Solvent Co., 146 Mich.App. 55, 380 N.W.2d 53 (Mich.App.1985), *290*

Bach v. Sarich, 74 Wash.2d 575, 445 P.2d 648 (Wash.1968), *235*

Baeth v. Hoisveen, 157 N.W.2d 728 (N.D.1968), *86*

Baker v. Ore–Ida Foods, Inc., 95 Idaho 575, 513 P.2d 627 (Idaho 1973), *259, 270*

Ball v. James, 451 U.S. 355, 101 S.Ct. 1811, 68 L.Ed.2d 150 (1981), *432, 433, 434*

Bank of American Nat. Trust & Sav. Ass'n v. State Water Resources Control Bd., 42 Cal.App.3d 198, 116 Cal.Rptr. 770 (Cal.App. 3 Dist.1974), *143*

Basey v. Gallagher, 87 U.S. 670, 22 L.Ed. 452 (1874), *187*

Basin Elec. Power Co-op. v. State Bd. of Control, 578 P.2d 557 (Wyo.1978), *174*

Bassett v. Salisbury Mfg. Co., 43 N.H. 569 (N.H.1862), *248, 299*

Baugh v. Criddle, 19 Utah 2d 361, 431 P.2d 790 (Utah 1967), *178*

Bealey v. Shaw, 6 East 208, 102 Eng.Rep. 1266 (Eng.1805), *17*

Bean v. Morris, 221 U.S. 485, 31 S.Ct. 703, 55 L.Ed. 821 (1911), *400, 402*

Beaver Park Water, Inc. v. City of Victor, 649 P.2d 300 (Colo. 1982), *176*

Bell, United States v., 724 P.2d 631 (Colo.1986), *338*

Belle Fourche Irr. Dist. v. Smiley, 84 S.D. 701, 176 N.W.2d 239 (S.D.1970), *87*

Bessemer Irrigating Ditch Co. v. Woolley, 32 Colo. 437, 76 P. 1053 (Colo.1904), *155*

Biddix v. Henredon Furniture Industries, Inc., 76 N.C.App. 30, 331 S.E.2d 717 (N.C.App.1985), *390*

Bjornestad v. Hulse, 229 Cal.App.3d 1568, 281 Cal.Rptr. 548 (Cal.App. 3 Dist.1991), *433*

Bliss, State ex rel. v. Dority, 55 N.M. 12, 225 P.2d 1007 (N.M. 1950), *249*

Board of County Com'rs v. Rocky Mountain Water Co., 102 Colo. 351, 79 P.2d 373 (Colo.1938), *187*

Board of County Com'rs of Arapahoe County v. Denver Bd. of Water Com'rs, 718 P.2d 235 (Colo.1986), *428*

Board of County Com'rs of County of Arapahoe v. United States, 891 P.2d 952 (Colo.1995), *92*

Board of Water Supply, City and County of Honolulu, Hawaii v. Nakata, 471 U.S. 1014, 105 S.Ct. 2016, 85 L.Ed.2d 298 (1985), *209*

Bollinger v. Henry, 375 S.W.2d 161 (Mo.1964), *28, 50*

Bonham v. Morgan, 788 P.2d 497 (Utah 1989), *163*

Borough of (see name of borough)

TABLE OF CASES

Bott v. Michigan Dept. of Natural Resources, 415 Mich. 45, 327 N.W.2d 838 (Mich.1982), *223*

Botton v. State, 69 Wash.2d 751, 420 P.2d 352 (Wash.1966), *37, 236*

Boulder, City of v. Boulder & Left Hand Ditch Co., 192 Colo. 219, 557 P.2d 1182 (Colo.1976), *172, 426*

Bower v. Big Horn Canal Ass'n, 77 Wyo. 80, 307 P.2d 593 (Wyo.1957), *135*

Branch v. Oconto County, 13 Wis.2d 595, 109 N.W.2d 105 (Wis.1961), *230*

Brighton Ditch Co. v. City of Englewood, 124 Colo. 366, 237 P.2d 116 (Colo.1951), *173*

Broadbent v. Ramsbotham, 11 Ex. 602, 156 Eng.Rep. 971 (Eng. 1856), *304*

Brooks v. United States, 119 F.2d 636 (9th Cir.1941), cert. denied 313 U.S. 594, 61 S.Ct. 1116, 85 L.Ed. 1548 (1941), *399*

Brown v. Chase, 125 Wash. 542, 217 P. 23 (Wash.1923), *198*

Bryant v. Yellen, 447 U.S. 352, 100 S.Ct. 2232, 65 L.Ed.2d 184 (1980), *375, 431*

Bubb, Application of, 200 Colo. 21, 610 P.2d 1343 (Colo.1980), *183*

Burkart v. City of Fort Lauderdale, 168 So.2d 65 (Fla.1964), *68*

Byrd, United States v., 609 F.2d 1204 (7th Cir.1979), *386*

Cache LaPoudre Water Users Ass'n v. Glacier View Meadows, 191 Colo. 53, 550 P.2d 288 (Colo.1976), *278*

California v. F.E.R.C., 495 U.S. 490, 110 S.Ct. 2024, 109 L.Ed.2d 474 (1990), *366, 367, 379*

California v. United States, 438 U.S. 645, 98 S.Ct. 2985, 57 L.Ed.2d 1018 (1978), *341, 345, 367, 377, 378, 379*

California Oregon Power Co. v. Beaver Portland Cement Co., 295 U.S. 142, 55 S.Ct. 725, 79 L.Ed. 1356 (1935), *80, 196, 315, 346*

California, State of, United States v., 332 U.S. 19, 67 S.Ct. 1658, 91 L.Ed. 1889 (1947), *220*

California, State Water Resources Control Bd., State of, United States v., 694 F.2d 1171 (9th Cir.1982), *377*

Cappaert v. United States, 426 U.S. 128, 96 S.Ct. 2062, 48 L.Ed.2d 523 (1976), *312, 319, 325*

Carter v. Territory, 24 Haw. 47 (Hawai'i 1917), *208, 209*

Cartwright v. Public Service Co. of N.M., 66 N.M. 64, 343 P.2d 654 (N.M.1958), *214, 216*

Cary, State ex rel. v. Cochran, 138 Neb. 163, 292 N.W. 239 (Neb.1940), *104*

CF & I Steel Corp. v. Rooks, 178 Colo. 110, 495 P.2d 1134 (Colo.1972), *175*

CF & I Steel Corp. in Las Animas County, In re, 183 Colo. 135, 515 P.2d 456 (Colo.1973), *177*

Chandler–Dunbar Water Power Co., United States v., 229 U.S. 53, 33 S.Ct. 667, 57 L.Ed. 1063 (1913), *349, 357, 358*

Chemehuevi Tribe of Indians v. Federal Power Commission, 420 U.S. 395, 95 S.Ct. 1066, 43 L.Ed.2d 279 (1975), *365*

Chicago, M., St. P. & P. R. Co., United States v., 312 U.S. 592, 313 U.S. 543, 61 S.Ct. 772, 85 L.Ed. 1064 (1941), *355, 356*

Chino Valley, Town of v. City of Prescott, 131 Ariz. 78, 638 P.2d 1324 (Ariz.1981), *253*

City and County of (see name of city)

City of (see name of city)

Clark v. Nash, 198 U.S. 361, 25 S.Ct. 676, 49 L.Ed. 1085 (1905), *184*

Cleaver v. Judd, 238 Or. 266, 393 P.2d 193 (Or.1964), *132*

Cochran, State ex rel. Cary v., 138 Neb. 163, 292 N.W. 239 (Neb.1940), *104*

Coffin v. Left Hand Ditch Co., 6 Colo. 443 (Colo.1882), *158*

Collens v. New Canaan Water Co., 155 Conn. 477, 234 A.2d 825 (Conn.1967), *44*

Colorado v. New Mexico, 467 U.S. 310, 104 S.Ct. 2433, 81 L.Ed.2d 247 (1984), *406*

Colorado v. New Mexico, 459 U.S. 176, 103 S.Ct. 539, 74 L.Ed.2d 348 (1982), *406*

Colorado Mill. & Elevator Co. v. Larimer & Weld Irr. Co., 26 Colo. 47, 56 P. 185 (Colo.1899), *173*

Colorado River Water Conservation Dist. v. Municipal Subdistrict, Northern Colorado Water Conservancy Dist., 198 Colo. 352, 610 P.2d 81 (Colo.1979), *160*

Colorado River Water Conservation Dist. v. Rocky Mountain Power Co., 174 Colo. 309, 486 P.2d 438 (Colo.1971), cert. denied 405 U.S. 996, 92 S.Ct. 1245, 31 L.Ed.2d 465 (1972), *90*

Colorado River Water Conservation Dist. v. United States (Akin case), 424 U.S. 800, 96 S.Ct. 1236, 47 L.Ed.2d 483 (1976), *336, 337*

Colorado River Water Conservation Dist. v. Vidler Tunnel Water Co., 197 Colo. 413, 594 P.2d 566 (Colo.1979), *91*

Colorado Springs, City of v. Bender, 148 Colo. 458, 366 P.2d 552 (Colo.1961), *258, 259*

Colville Confederated Tribes v. Walton, 647 F.2d 42 (9th Cir. 1981), *344*

Colville Confederated Tribes v. Walton, 647 F.2d 42 (9th Cir. 1981), cert. denied 454 U.S. 1092, 102 S.Ct. 657, 70 L.Ed.2d 630 (1981), *328, 329*

Committee To Save Mokelumne River v. East Bay Mun. Utility Dist., 13 F.3d 305 (9th Cir.1993), *382*

Commonwealth of (see name of Commonwealth)

Comstock v. Ramsay, 55 Colo. 244, 133 P. 1107 (Colo.1913), *134*

Conant v. Deep Creek & Curlew Val. Irr. Co., 23 Utah 627, 66 P. 188 (Utah 1901), *398*

Consolidated People's Ditch Co. v. Foothill Ditch Co., 205 Cal. 54, 269 P. 915 (Cal.1928), *425*

Cook v. Evans, 45 S.D. 31, 185 N.W. 262 (S.D.1921), modified 45 S.D. 43, 186 N.W. 571 (S.D.1922), *195*

Coryell v. Robinson, 118 Colo. 225, 194 P.2d 342 (Colo.1948), *179*

Crandall v. Woods, 8 Cal. 136 (Cal.1857), *192*

Crawford Co. v. Hathaway, 67 Neb. 325, 93 N.W. 781 (Neb.1903), overruled on other grounds Wasserburger v. Coffee, 180 Neb. 149, 141 N.W.2d 738 (Neb.1966), *140*

Cress, United States v., 243 U.S. 316, 37 S.Ct. 380, 61 L.Ed. 746 (1917), *355, 356*

Crockett v. Jones, 42 Idaho 652, 249 P. 483 (Idaho 1926), *166*

Crowley, State ex rel. v. District Court, 108 Mont. 89, 88 P.2d 23 (Mont.1939), *124, 125*

Current Creek Irr. Co. v. Andrews, 9 Utah 2d 324, 344 P.2d 528 (Utah 1959), *255*

Daniel Ball, The, 77 U.S. 557, 19 L.Ed. 999 (1870), *221, 350*

Danielson, People ex rel. v. City of Thornton, 775 P.2d 11 (Colo.1989), *177*

Day v. Armstrong, 362 P.2d 137 (Wyo.1961), *228*

De Beque, Town of v. Enewold, 199 Colo. 110, 606 P.2d 48 (Colo.1980), *95*

Denver, City and County of v. Fulton Irrigating Ditch Co., 179 Colo. 47, 506 P.2d 144 (Colo.1972), *111*

Denver, City and County of v. Sheriff, 105 Colo. 193, 96 P.2d 836 (Colo.1939), *94, 100*

Denver, City and County of, United States v., 656 P.2d 1 (Colo. 1982), *320*

Department of Ecology v. United States Bureau of Reclamation, 118 Wash.2d 761, 827 P.2d 275 (Wash.1992), *135*

Diana Shooting Club v. Husting, 156 Wis. 261, 145 N.W. 816 (Wis.1914), *224*

Dimmock v. City of New London, 157 Conn. 9, 245 A.2d 569 (Conn.1968), *37*

District Court In and For County of Eagle, United States v., 401 U.S. 520, 91 S.Ct. 998, 28 L.Ed.2d 278 (1971), *335, 337*

District Court, State ex rel. Crowley v., 108 Mont. 89, 88 P.2d 23 (Mont.1939), *124, 125*

District 10 Water Users Ass'n v. Barnett, 198 Colo. 291, 599 P.2d 894 (Colo.1979), *275*

Dolan v. City of Tigard, 512 U.S. 374, 114 S.Ct. 2309, 129 L.Ed.2d 304 (1994), *233*

Donich v. Johnson, 77 Mont. 229, 250 P. 963 (Mont.1926), *187*

Dontanello v. Gust, 86 Wash. 268, 150 P. 420 (Wash.1915), *71*

Duckworth v. Watsonville Water & Light Co., 158 Cal. 206, 110 P. 927 (Cal.1910), *63*

Dugan v. Rank, 372 U.S. 609, 83 S.Ct. 999, 10 L.Ed.2d 15 (1963), *336*

Dyer, State ex rel. v. Sims, 341 U.S. 22, 71 S.Ct. 557, 95 L.Ed. 713, 44 O.O. 364 (1951), *407, 408, 410*

East Bay Municipal Utility Dist. v. Department of Public Works, 1 Cal.2d 476, 35 P.2d 1027 (Cal.1934), *105, 143*

East Jordan Irr. Co. v. Morgan, 860 P.2d 310 (Utah 1993), *423*

Elgin v. Weatherstone, 123 Wash. 429, 212 P. 562 (Wash.1923), *112*

Elk–Rifle Water Co. v. Templeton, 173 Colo. 438, 484 P.2d 1211 (Colo.1971), *92*

El Paso v. Reynolds, 597 F.Supp. 694 (D.C.N.M.1984), *417*

Emery, State ex rel. v. Knapp, 167 Kan. 546, 207 P.2d 440 (Kan.1949), *199*

Emmert, People v., 198 Colo. 137, 597 P.2d 1025 (Colo.1979), *228*

Empire Water & Power Co. v. Cascade Town Co., 205 F. 123 (8th Cir.1913), *96, 99*

Enlarged Southside Irr. Ditch Co. v. John's Flood Ditch Co., 120 Colo. 423, 210 P.2d 982 (Colo.1949), *168*

Enterprise Irr. Dist. v. Willis, 135 Neb. 827, 284 N.W. 326 (Neb.1939), *123*

Environmental Defense Fund, Inc. v. East Bay Municipal Utility Dist., 52 Cal.App.3d 828, 125 Cal.Rptr. 601 (Cal.App. 1 Dist. 1975), *128*

Erickson v. Queen Val. Ranch Co., 22 Cal.App.3d 578, 99 Cal. Rptr. 446 (Cal.App. 3 Dist.1971), *124*

Erickson, State ex rel. v. McLean, 62 N.M. 264, 308 P.2d 983 (N.M.1957), *119*

Estate of (see name of party)

Evans v. Merriweather, 4 Ill. 492 (Ill.1842), *38*

Fallbrook Irr. Dist. v. Bradley, 164 U.S. 112, 17 S.Ct. 56, 41 L.Ed. 369 (1896), *430*

Farmers Highline Canal & Reservoir Co. v. City of Golden, 129 Colo. 575, 272 P.2d 629 (Colo.1954), *102, 161*

Farm Inv. Co. v. Carpenter, 9 Wyo. 110, 61 P. 258 (Wyo.1900), *140*

Farrell v. Richards, 30 N.J.Eq. 511 (N.J.Ch.1879), *19*

F. Arthur Stone & Sons v. Gibson, 230 Kan. 224, 630 P.2d 1164 (Kan.1981), *87*

Federal Land Bank v. Morris, 112 Mont. 445, 116 P.2d 1007 (Mont.1941), *186*

Federal Power Commission v. State of Or. (Pelton Dam case), 349 U.S. 435, 75 S.Ct. 832, 99 L.Ed. 1215 (1955), *312*

Federal Power Commission v. Union Elec. Co., 381 U.S. 90, 85 S.Ct. 1253, 14 L.Ed.2d 239 (1965), *364*

Fellhauer v. People, 167 Colo. 320, 447 P.2d 986 (Colo.1968), *278, 279*

First Iowa Hydro–Elec. Co-op. v. Federal Power Com'n, 328 U.S. 152, 66 S.Ct. 906, 90 L.Ed. 1143 (1946), *366*

Forbell v. City of New York, 164 N.Y. 522, 58 N.E. 644 (N.Y. 1900), *256*

Fort Lyon Canal Co. v. Catlin Canal Co., 642 P.2d 501 (Colo. 1982), *426*

Fort Morgan Land & Canal Co. v. South Platte Ditch Co., 18 Colo. 1, 30 P. 1032 (Colo.1892), *118*

Fort Morgan Reservoir & Irrigation Co. v. McCune, 71 Colo. 256, 206 P. 393 (Colo.1922), *133*

Franco–American Charolaise, Ltd. v. Oklahoma Water Resources Bd., 855 P.2d 568 (Okla.1990), *88, 200, 201*

TABLE OF CASES

Fresno, City of v. California, 372 U.S. 627, 83 S.Ct. 996, 10 L.Ed.2d 28 (1963), *377, 378, 379*

Friendswood Development Co. v. Smith–Southwest Industries, Inc., 576 S.W.2d 21 (Tex.1978), *244*

Fulghum v. Town of Selma, 238 N.C. 100, 76 S.E.2d 368 (N.C. 1953), *429*

Fundingsland v. Colorado Ground Water Commission, 171 Colo. 487, 468 P.2d 835 (Colo.1970), *267*

Fuss v. Franks, 610 P.2d 17 (Wyo.1980), *133*

General Adjudication of All Rights to Use Water in Big Horn River System, In re, 899 P.2d 848 (Wyo.1995), *329*

Gerlach Live Stock Co., United States v., 339 U.S. 725, 70 S.Ct. 955, 94 L.Ed. 1231 (1950), *349, 362, 373*

Gibbons v. Ogden, 22 U.S. 1, 6 L.Ed. 23 (1824), *348*

Gila River System, In re, 175 Ariz. 382, 857 P.2d 1236 (Ariz. 1993), *273*

Gion v. Santa Cruz, 84 Cal.Rptr. 162, 465 P.2d 50 (Cal.1970), *232*

Glenn Dale Ranches, Inc. v. Shaub, 94 Idaho 585, 494 P.2d 1029 (Idaho 1972), *126*

Grand River Dam Authority, United States v., 363 U.S. 229, 80 S.Ct. 1134, 4 L.Ed.2d 1186 (1960), *356*

Green v. Chaffee Ditch Co., 150 Colo. 91, 371 P.2d 775 (Colo. 1962), *174*

Greisinger v. Klinhardt, 321 Mo. 186, 9 S.W.2d 978 (Mo.1928), *29*

Grey v. United States, 21 Cl.Ct. 285 (Cl.Ct.1990), *328*

Gustin v. Harting, 20 Wyo. 1, 121 P. 522 (Wyo.1912), *184*

Hallenbeck v. Granby Ditch & Reservoir Co., 160 Colo. 555, 420 P.2d 419 (Colo.1966), *177*

Hamp v. State, 19 Wyo. 377, 118 P. 653 (Wyo.1911), *152*

Handy Ditch Co. v. Greeley & Loveland Irr. Co., 86 Colo. 197, 280 P. 481 (Colo.1929), *186*

Haney v. Neace–Stark Co., 109 Or. 93, 216 P. 757 (Or.1923), *165*

Hansen v. City of San Buenaventura, 233 Cal.Rptr. 22, 729 P.2d 186 (Cal.1986), *429*

Harris v. Harrison, 93 Cal. 676, 29 P. 325 (Cal.1892), *50*

Harvey Land and Cattle Co. v. Southeastern Colorado Water Conservancy Dist., 631 P.2d 1111 (Colo.1981), *90*

Hawaiian Commercial & Sugar Co. v. Wailuku Sugar Co., 15 Haw. 675 (Hawai'i 1904), *208*

Hay, State ex rel. Thornton v., 254 Or. 584, 462 P.2d 671 (Or.1969), *231*

Hayes v. Adams, 109 Or. 51, 218 P. 933 (Or.1923), *242*

Hays, State ex rel. Meek v., 246 Kan. 99, 785 P.2d 1356 (Kan. 1990), *228*

Hazard Powder Co. v. Somersville Mfg. Co., 78 Conn. 171, 61 A. 519 (Conn.1905), *40*

Heine v. Reynolds, 69 N.M. 398, 367 P.2d 708 (N.M.1962), *164*

Heise v. Schulz, 167 Kan. 34, 204 P.2d 706 (Kan.1949), *38*

Henderson v. Kirby Ditch Co., 373 P.2d 591 (Wyo.1962), *424*

Henderson v. Wade Sand and Gravel Co., Inc., 388 So.2d 900 (Ala.1980), *245*

Herminghaus v. Southern California Edison Co., 200 Cal. 81, 252 P. 607 (Cal.1926), *198*

Herminghaus v. Southern California Edison Co., 200 Cal. 81, 252 P. 607 (Cal.1926), cert. dismissed Southern California Edison Co. v. Herminghaus, 275 U.S. 486, 48 S.Ct. 27, 72 L.Ed. 387 (1927), *197*

Herriman Irr. Co. v. Keel, 25 Utah 96, 69 P. 719 (Utah 1902), *242*

Hiber, State v., 48 Wyo. 172, 44 P.2d 1005 (Wyo.1935), *108*

Higday v. Nickolaus, 469 S.W.2d 859 (Mo.App.1971), *256*

Hinderlider v. La Plata River & Cherry Creek Ditch Co., 304 U.S. 92, 58 S.Ct. 803, 82 L.Ed. 1202 (1938), *408, 409, 411*

Hoefs v. Short, 114 Tex. 501, 273 S.W. 785 (Tex.1925), *108, 305*

Hough v. Porter, 51 Or. 318, 95 P. 732 (Or.1908), Supp. op. 51 Or. 318, 98 P. 1083 (Or.1909), *195, 199*

Hough v. Porter, 51 Or. 318, 95 P. 732 (Or.1908), *196*

Howell v. Johnson, 89 F. 556 (C.C.Mont.1898), *400*

Hudson County Water Co. v. McCarter, 209 U.S. 349, 28 S.Ct. 529, 52 L.Ed. 828 (1908), *416*

Hudson River Fisherman's Ass'n v. Williams, 139 A.D.2d 234, 531 N.Y.S.2d 379 (N.Y.A.D. 3 Dept.1988), *38*

Hughes v. Washington, 389 U.S. 290, 88 S.Ct. 438, 19 L.Ed.2d 530 (1967), *221*

Hutchinson v. Stricklin, 146 Or. 285, 28 P.2d 225 (Or.1933), overruled on other gournds Rencken v. Young, 300 Or. 352, 711 P.2d 954 (Or.1985), *170*

Idaho Conservation League, Inc. v. State, 128 Idaho 155, 911 P.2d 748 (Idaho 1995), *149*

TABLE OF CASES

Idaho, United States v., 508 U.S. 1, 113 S.Ct. 1893, 123 L.Ed.2d 563 (1993), *338*

Illinois Cent. R. Co. v. State of Illinois, 146 U.S. 387, 13 S.Ct. 110, 36 L.Ed. 1018 (1892), *225*

Imperial Irr. Dist. v. State Water Resources Control Bd., 225 Cal.App.3d 548, 275 Cal.Rptr. 250 (Cal.App. 4 Dist.1990), *121*

In re (see name of party)

Intake Water Co. v. Yellowstone River Compact Com'n, 590 F.Supp. 293 (D.C.Mont.1983), affirmed 769 F.2d 568 (9th Cir.1985), cert. denied 476 U.S. 1163, 106 S.Ct. 2288, 90 L.Ed.2d 729 (1986), *410*

International Paper Co. v. Ouellette, 479 U.S. 481, 107 S.Ct. 805, 93 L.Ed.2d 883 (1987), *391*

Irwin v. Phillips, 5 Cal. 140 (Cal.1855), *192*

Ivanhoe Irr. Dist. v. McCracken, 357 U.S. 275, 78 S.Ct. 1174, 2 L.Ed.2d 1313 (1958), *377, 378, 379*

Jacobucci v. District Court, 189 Colo. 380, 541 P.2d 667 (Colo. 1975), *424*

Jenkins v. State, Dept. of Water Resources, 103 Idaho 384, 647 P.2d 1256 (Idaho 1982), *178*

Jensen v. Department of Ecology, 102 Wash.2d 109, 685 P.2d 1068 (Wash.1984), *283*

Jesse, United States v., 744 P.2d 491 (Colo.1987), *321*

Johnson v. Seifert, 257 Minn. 159, 100 N.W.2d 689 (Minn.1960), *234*

Johnson, State v., 265 A.2d 711 (Me.1970), *302*

Jones v. Warmsprings Irr. Dist., 162 Or. 186, 91 P.2d 542 (Or.1939), *133*

Joslin v. Marin Municipal Water Dist., 67 Cal.2d 132, 60 Cal. Rptr. 377, 429 P.2d 889 (Cal.1967), *41, 42*

Just v. Marinette County, 56 Wis.2d 7, 201 N.W.2d 761 (Wis. 1972), *302*

Kahookiekie v. Keanini, 8 Haw. 310 (Hawai'i 1891), *208*

Kaiser Aetna v. United States, 444 U.S. 164, 100 S.Ct. 383, 62 L.Ed.2d 332 (1979), *348, 356, 357*

Kaiser Steel Corp. v. W. S. Ranch Co., 81 N.M. 414, 467 P.2d 986 (N.M.1970), *184*

Kansas City Life Ins. Co., United States v., 339 U.S. 799, 70 S.Ct. 885, 94 L.Ed. 1277 (1950), *353, 356*

TABLE OF CASES

Kansas, State of v. State of Colo., 206 U.S. 46, 27 S.Ct. 655, 51
    L.Ed. 956 (1907), *373, 401, 405*
Katz v. Walkinshaw, 141 Cal. 116, 74 P. 766 (Cal.1903), *249, 250*
Kearney Lake, Land & Reservoir Co. v. Lake DeSmet Reservoir
    Co., 475 P.2d 548 (Wyo.1970), *188*
Kelley v. Carlsbad Irr. Dist., 76 N.M. 466, 415 P.2d 849 (N.M.
    1966), *284*
Keys v. Romley, 64 Cal.2d 396, 50 Cal.Rptr. 273, 412 P.2d 529
    (Cal.1966), *301*
Kiwanis Club Foundation, Inc., of Lincoln v. Yost, 179 Neb. 598,
    139 N.W.2d 359 (Neb.1966), *28*
Knapp, State ex rel. Emery v., 167 Kan. 546, 207 P.2d 440
    (Kan.1949), *199*
Knight v. Grimes, 80 S.D. 517, 127 N.W.2d 708 (S.D.1964), *200*
Kootenai Environmental Alliance, Inc. v. Panhandle Yacht Club,
    Inc., 105 Idaho 622, 671 P.2d 1085 (Idaho 1983), *225*
Kray v. Muggli, 84 Minn. 90, 86 N.W. 882 (Minn.1901), *28, 29*
Kuiper v. Well Owners Conservation Ass'n, 176 Colo. 119, 490
    P.2d 268 (Colo.1971), *280*

Langenegger v. Carlsbad Irr. Dist., 82 N.M. 416, 483 P.2d 297
    (N.M.1971), *276*
Las Vegas, City of, State ex rel. Martinez v., 118 N.M. 257, 880
    P.2d 868 (N.M.App.1994), *216*
Lawrie v. Silsby, 76 Vt. 240, 56 A. 1106 (Vt.1904), *63*
League to Save Lake Tahoe v. Tahoe Regional Planning Agency,
    507 F.2d 517 (9th Cir.1974), cert. denied Raley v. League to
    Save Lake Tahoe, 420 U.S. 974, 95 S.Ct. 1398, 43 L.Ed.2d 654
    (1975), *412*
Lemmon v. Hardy, 95 Idaho 778, 519 P.2d 1168 (Idaho 1974), *89*
Letford, People ex rel. Rogers v., 102 Colo. 284, 79 P.2d 274
    (Colo.1938), *430*
Lewis Blue Point Oyster Cultivation Co. v. Briggs, 229 U.S. 82,
    33 S.Ct. 679, 57 L.Ed. 1083 (1913), *355*
Lindsey v. McClure, 136 F.2d 65 (10th Cir.1943), *169, 401*
Little Blue Natural Resources Dist. v. Lower Platte North Natu-
    ral Resources Dist., 206 Neb. 535, 294 N.W.2d 598 (Neb.
    1980), *160*
Lockary v. Kayfetz, 917 F.2d 1150 (9th Cir.1990), *428*
Long v. Louisiana Creosoting Co., 137 La. 861, 69 So. 281
    (La.1915), *212*

TABLE OF CASES

Lonoaea v. Wailuku Sugar Co., 9 Haw. 651 (Hawai'i 1895), *208*

Loosli v. Heseman, 66 Idaho 469, 162 P.2d 393 (Idaho 1945), *294*

Los Angeles, City of v. Aitken, 10 Cal.App.2d 460, 52 P.2d 585 (Cal.App.1935), *45*

Los Angeles, City of v. City of San Fernando, 123 Cal.Rptr. 1, 537 P.2d 1250 (Cal.1975), *215, 251, 282*

Los Angeles Department of Water & Power, City of v. National Audubon Society, 464 U.S. 977, 104 S.Ct. 413, 78 L.Ed.2d 351 (1983), *148, 226*

Lower Colorado River Authority v. Texas Dept. of Water Resources, 689 S.W.2d 873 (Tex.1984), *145*

Lucas v. South Carolina Coastal Council, 505 U.S. 1003, 112 S.Ct. 2886, 120 L.Ed.2d 798 (1992), *231, 351, 390*

Lux v. Haggin, 69 Cal. 255, 10 P. 674 (Cal.1886), *67, 193, 197, 202*

Lynah, United States v., 188 U.S. 445, 23 S.Ct. 349, 47 L.Ed. 539 (1903), *354, 355*

Mack, People v., 19 Cal.App.3d 1040, 97 Cal.Rptr. 448 (Cal.App. 3 Dist.1971), *223*

Marks v. Whitney, 98 Cal.Rptr. 790, 491 P.2d 374 (Cal.1971), *226*

Martha Lake Water Co. No. 1, In re, 152 Wash. 53, 277 P. 382 (Wash.1929), *109*

Martin v. Bigelow, 16 Am.Dec. 696 (Vt.1827), *70*

Martinez, State ex rel. v. City of Las Vegas, 118 N.M. 257, 880 P.2d 868 (N.M.App.1994), *216*

Mason v. Hill, 110 Eng.Rep. 692 (Eng.1833), *18*

Matador Pipelines, Inc. v. Oklahoma Water Resources Bd., 742 P.2d 15 (Okla.1987), *287*

Mathers v. Texaco, Inc., 77 N.M. 239, 421 P.2d 771 (N.M.1966), *267*

Matthews v. Bay Head Imp. Ass'n, 95 N.J. 306, 471 A.2d 355 (N.J.1984), *232*

McBryde Sugar Co., Ltd. v. Robinson, 54 Haw. 174, 504 P.2d 1330 (Hawai'i 1973), aff'd on rehearing McBryde Sugar Co., Limited v. Hawaii, 417 U.S. 962, 94 S.Ct. 3164, 41 L.Ed.2d 1135 (1974), cert. denied McBryde Sugar Co., Ltd. v. Robinson, 55 Haw. 260, 517 P.2d 26 (Hawai'i 1973), *209, 210, 211, 212*

McLean, State ex rel. Erickson v., 62 N.M. 264, 308 P.2d 983 (N.M.1957), *119*

Meek, State ex rel. v. Hays, 246 Kan. 99, 785 P.2d 1356 (Kan. 1990), *228*

Metropolitan Denver Sewage Disposal Dist. No. 1 v. Farmers Reservoir & Irr. Co., 179 Colo. 36, 499 P.2d 1190 (Colo.1972), *171, 172*

Michels Pipeline Const., Inc., State v., 63 Wis.2d 278, 219 N.W.2d 308 (Wis.1974), *258*

Michels Pipeline Const., Inc., State v., 63 Wis.2d 278, 217 N.W.2d 339 (Wis.1974), *258*

Millis v. Board of County Com'rs of Larimer County, 626 P.2d 652 (Colo.1981), *433*

Milwaukee, City of v. Illinois, 451 U.S. 304, 101 S.Ct. 1784, 68 L.Ed.2d 114 (1981), *404*

Monongahela Nav. Co. v. United States, 148 U.S. 312, 13 S.Ct. 622, 37 L.Ed. 463 (1893), *354*

Montana v. United States, 450 U.S. 544, 101 S.Ct. 1245, 67 L.Ed.2d 493 (1981), *344*

Montana Coalition for Stream Access, Inc. v. Curran, 210 Mont. 38, 682 P.2d 163 (Mont.1984), *227*

Moore v. California Oregon Power Co., 22 Cal.2d 725, 140 P.2d 798 (Cal.1943), *38*

Mountain Meadow Ditch & Irr. Co. v. Park Ditch & Reservoir Co., 130 Colo. 537, 277 P.2d 527 (Colo.1954), *179*

Mowrer v. Ashland Oil & Refining Co., Inc., 518 F.2d 659 (7th Cir.1975), *290*

National Audubon Soc. v. Superior Court, 189 Cal.Rptr. 346, 658 P.2d 709 (Cal.1983), cert. denied Los Angeles Department of Water & Power, City of v. National Audubon Society, 464 U.S. 977, 104 S.Ct. 413, 78 L.Ed.2d 351 (1983), *148, 226*

National Wildlife Federation v. F.E.R.C., 801 F.2d 1505 (9th Cir.1986), *369, 370*

National Wildlife Federation v. Gorsuch, 693 F.2d 156, 224 U.S.App.D.C. 41 (D.C.Cir.1982), *382, 389*

Nebraska, State of v. State of Wyo., 325 U.S. 589, 65 S.Ct. 1332, 89 L.Ed. 1815 (1945), 345 U.S. 981, 73 S.Ct. 1041, 97 L.Ed. 1394 (1953), *406*

Nekoosa–Edwards Paper Co. v. Public Service Commission, 8 Wis.2d 582, 99 N.W.2d 821 (Wis.1959), *58*

Nevada v. United States, 463 U.S. 110, 103 S.Ct. 2906, 77 L.Ed.2d 509 (1983), *311, 333*

Nevius v. Smith, 86 Colo. 178, 279 P. 44 (Colo.1929), *306*

TABLE OF CASES

New Jersey, State of v. State of New York, 283 U.S. 336, 51 S.Ct. 478, 75 L.Ed. 1104 (1931), *405*

New Mexico, State of v. Aamodt, 537 F.2d 1102 (10th Cir.1976), cert. denied New Mexico v. United States, 429 U.S. 1121, 97 S.Ct. 1157, 51 L.Ed.2d 572 (1977), *216*

New Mexico, United States v., 438 U.S. 696, 98 S.Ct. 3012, 57 L.Ed.2d 1052 (1978), *116, 312, 320*

Nollan v. California Coastal Com'n, 483 U.S. 825, 107 S.Ct. 3141, 97 L.Ed.2d 677 (1987), *233*

North Carolina, State of v. Federal Power Commission, 533 F.2d 702, 174 U.S.App.D.C. 475 (D.C.Cir.1976), cert. granted, vacated and remanded 429 U.S. 891, 97 S.Ct. 250, 50 L.Ed.2d 174 (1976), *392*

North Carolina, State of v. Hudson, 731 F.Supp. 1261 (E.D.N.C. 1990), *52*

Oklahoma v. New Mexico, 501 U.S. 221, 111 S.Ct. 2281, 115 L.Ed.2d 207 (1991), *411*

Oklahoma ex rel. Phillips, State of v. Guy F. Atkinson Co., 313 U.S. 508, 61 S.Ct. 1050, 85 L.Ed. 1487 (1941), *349*

Oklahoma Water Resources Bd. v. Texas County Irr. and Water Resources Ass'n, Inc., 711 P.2d 38 (Okla.1984), *286*

Oregon, State of, United States v., 44 F.3d 758 (9th Cir.1994), *140, 335*

Pabst v. Finmand, 190 Cal. 124, 211 P. 11 (Cal.1922), *70, 205*

Pacific Live Stock Co. v. Lewis, 241 U.S. 440, 36 S.Ct. 637, 60 L.Ed. 1084 (1916), *140*

Parker v. Wallentine, 103 Idaho 506, 650 P.2d 648 (Idaho 1982), *255*

Pasadena, City of v. City of Alhambra, 33 Cal.2d 908, 207 P.2d 17 (Cal.1949), cert. denied California Michigan Land and Water Company v. City of Pasadena, 339 U.S. 937, 70 S.Ct. 671, 94 L.Ed. 1354 (1950) *250, 251*

Peck v. Bailey, 8 Haw. 658 (Hawai'i 1867), *208*

People v. ____ (see opposing party)

People ex rel. v. ____ (see opposing party and relator)

Peterson v. United States Dept. of Interior, 899 F.2d 799 (9th Cir.1990), *376*

Phillips v. Gardner, 2 Or.App. 423, 469 P.2d 42 (Or.App.1970), *105*

TABLE OF CASES

Phillips Petroleum Co. v. Mississippi, 484 U.S. 469, 108 S.Ct. 791, 98 L.Ed.2d 877 (1988), *221*

Pollard v. Hagan, 44 U.S. 212, 3 How. 212, 11 L.Ed. 565 (1845), *220*

Portland General Elec. Co. v. Federal Power Commission, 328 F.2d 165 (9th Cir.1964), *367*

Powers, United States v., 307 U.S. 214, 59 S.Ct. 805, 83 L.Ed. 1245 (1939), *328*

Prather v. Eisenmann, 200 Neb. 1, 261 N.W.2d 766 (Neb.1978), *257*

Prather v. Hoberg, 24 Cal.2d 549, 150 P.2d 405 (Cal.1944), *34*

Propeller Genesee Chief v. Fitzhugh, 53 U.S. 443, 12 How. 443, 13 L.Ed. 1058 (1851), *219*

Public Access Shoreline Hawaii v. Hawai'i County Planning Com'n by Fujimoto, 903 P.2d 1246 (Hawai'i 1995), *231*

Publix Super Markets, Inc. v. Pearson, 315 So.2d 98 (Fla.App. 2 Dist.1975), *235*

PUD No. 1 of Jefferson County v. Washington Dept. of Ecology, 511 U.S. 700, 114 S.Ct. 1900, 128 L.Ed.2d 716 (1994), *367, 384*

Purcellville, Town of v. Potts, 179 Va. 514, 19 S.E.2d 700 (Va.1942), *37*

Pyle v. Gilbert, 245 Ga. 403, 265 S.E.2d 584 (Ga.1980), *48, 53*

Pyramid Lake Paiute Tribe of Indians v. Morton, 499 F.2d 1095, 163 U.S.App.D.C. 90 (D.C.Cir.1974), *338*

Pyramid Lake Paiute Tribe of Indians v. Morton, 360 F.Supp. 669 (D.C.D.C.1973), *310*

Pyramid Lake Paiute Tribe v. Morton, 354 F.Supp. 252 (D.C.D.C. 1972), Supplemented 360 F.Supp. 669 (D.C.D.C.1973), *310*

Pyramid Lake Paiute Tribe of Indians v. Washoe County, 112 Nev. 743, 918 P.2d 697 (Nev.1996), *147*

Rands, United States v., 389 U.S. 121, 88 S.Ct. 265, 19 L.Ed.2d 329 (1967), *359, 360*

Rencken v. Young, 300 Or. 352, 711 P.2d 954 (Or.1985), *178*

Reppun v. Board of Water Supply, 65 Haw. 531, 656 P.2d 57 (Hawai'i 1982), *209, 211, 212*

Reynolds, State ex rel. v. South Springs Co., 80 N.M. 144, 452 P.2d 478 (N.M.1969), *178*

Richlands Irr. Co. v. Westview Irr. Co., 96 Utah 403, 80 P.2d 458 (Utah 1938), *305*

TABLE OF CASES

Rights to use Water in Big Horn River System, In re, 835 P.2d 273 (Wyo.1992), *323*

Rights to Use Water in the Big Horn River System, In re, 753 P.2d 76 (Wyo.1988), affirmed sub nom. Wyoming v. United States, 492 U.S. 406, 109 S.Ct. 2994, 106 L.Ed.2d 342 (1989) *322*

Rio Grande Dam & Irrigation Co., United States v., 174 U.S. 690, 19 S.Ct. 770, 43 L.Ed. 1136 (1899), *313, 349, 362*

Riverside Bayview Homes, Inc., United States v., 474 U.S. 121, 106 S.Ct. 455, 88 L.Ed.2d 419 (1985), *386*

Riverside Irr. Dist. v. Andrews, 758 F.2d 508 (10th Cir.1985), *388, 389*

Riverside Land Co. v. Jarvis, 174 Cal. 316, 163 P. 54 (Cal.1917), *425*

R.J.A., Inc. v. Water Users Ass'n of Dist. No. 6, 690 P.2d 823 (Colo.1984), *132*

Roath v. Driscoll, 20 Conn. 533 (Conn.1850), *248*

Robinson v. Ariyoshi, 753 F.2d 1468 (9th Cir.1985), *210*

Robinson v. Ariyoshi, 65 Haw. 641, 658 P.2d 287 (Hawai'i 1982), *211*

Robinson v. Ariyoshi, 441 F.Supp. 559 (D.C.Hawai'i 1977), *210, 211*

Robinson v. Booth–Orchard Grove Ditch Co., 94 Colo. 515, 31 P.2d 487 (Colo.1934), *426*

Robinson v. City of Boulder, 190 Colo. 357, 547 P.2d 228 (Colo. 1976), *429*

Rocky Mountain Power Co. v. Colorado River Water Conservation Dist., 646 P.2d 383 (Colo.1982), *91*

Rocky Mountain Power Co. v. White River Elec. Ass'n, 151 Colo. 45, 376 P.2d 158 (Colo.1962), *163*

Rogers, People ex rel. v. Letford, 102 Colo. 284, 79 P.2d 274 (Colo.1938), *430*

Roswell, City of v. Reynolds, 86 N.M. 249, 522 P.2d 796 (N.M. 1974), *267*

Rylands v. Fletcher, L.R. 3 H.L. 330 (Eng.1868), *39, 295*

Safranek v. Limon, 123 Colo. 330, 228 P.2d 975 (Colo.1951), *274*

Salt River Val. Water Users' Ass'n v. Kovacovich, 3 Ariz.App. 28, 411 P.2d 201 (Ariz.App.1966), *133*

Salyer Land Co. v. Tulare Lake Basin Water Storage Dist., 410 U.S. 719, 93 S.Ct. 1224, 35 L.Ed.2d 659 (1973), *432, 433*

Sand Point Water & Light Co. v. Panhandle Development Co., 11 Idaho 405, 83 P. 347 (Idaho 1905), *90*

Sanitary Dist. of Chicago v. United States, 266 U.S. 405, 45 S.Ct. 176, 69 L.Ed. 352 (1925), *396*

San Joaquin & Kings River Canal & Irrigation Co. v. Worswick, 187 Cal. 674, 203 P. 999 (Cal.1922), cert. denied 258 U.S. 625, 42 S.Ct. 382, 66 L.Ed. 797 (1922), *195*

Scenic Hudson Preservation Conference v. Federal Power Commission, 453 F.2d 463 (2nd Cir.1971), cert. denied 407 U.S. 926, 92 S.Ct. 2453, 32 L.Ed.2d 813 (1972), *367*

Schodde v. Twin Falls Land & Water Co., 224 U.S. 107, 32 S.Ct. 470, 56 L.Ed. 686 (1912), *124, 258*

Sea Ranch Ass'n v. California Coastal Commission, 527 F.Supp. 390 (N.D.Cal.1981), *233*

Sea Ranch Ass'n v. California Coastal Com'n, 454 U.S. 1070, 102 S.Ct. 622, 70 L.Ed.2d 606 (1981), *233*

Shirokow, People v., 162 Cal.Rptr. 30, 605 P.2d 859 (Cal.1980), *179*

Shokal v. Dunn, 109 Idaho 330, 707 P.2d 441 (Idaho 1985), *147*

Shoshone–Bannock Tribes v. Reno, 56 F.3d 1476, 312 U.S.App. D.C. 406 (D.C.Cir.1995), *338*

Sierra Club v. Yeutter, 911 F.2d 1405 (10th Cir.1990), *313, 321, 338*

Silver Blue Lake Apartments, Inc. v. Silver Blue Lake Home Owners Ass'n, 245 So.2d 609 (Fla.1971), *235*

Sims, State ex rel. Dyer v., 341 U.S. 22, 71 S.Ct. 557, 95 L.Ed. 713, 44 O.O. 364 (1951), *407, 408, 410*

Ensenada Land & Water Ass'n v. Sleeper, 107 N.M. 494, 760 P.2d 787 (N.M.App.1988), *164*

Smith v. Brooklyn, 160 N.Y. 357, 54 N.E. 787 (N.Y.1899), *273*

Snively v. Jaber, 48 Wash.2d 815, 296 P.2d 1015 (Wash.1956), *234*

Snow v. Parsons, 28 Vt. 459 (Vt.1856), *42*

Southeastern Colorado Water Conservancy Dist. v. Shelton Farms, Inc., 187 Colo. 181, 529 P.2d 1321 (Colo.1974), *113, 132*

Southgate Water Dist. v. Denver, 862 P.2d 949 (Colo.App.1992), *429*

South Springs Co., State ex rel. Reynolds v., 80 N.M. 144, 452 P.2d 478 (N.M.1969), *178*

Sporhase v. Nebraska, ex rel. Douglas, 458 U.S. 941, 102 S.Ct. 3456, 73 L.Ed.2d 1254 (1982), *84, 416*

Springer v. Joseph Schlitz Brewing Co., 510 F.2d 468 (4th Cir.1975), *44*

State v. ___ (see opposing party)

State, Dept. of Natural Resources v. Southwestern Colorado Water Conservation Dist., 671 P.2d 1294 (Colo.1983), cert. denied Young v. Southwestern Colorado Water Conservation District, 466 U.S. 944, 104 S.Ct. 1929, 80 L.Ed.2d 474 (1984), *253*

State, Dept. of Parks v. Idaho Dept. of Water Administration, 96 Idaho 440, 530 P.2d 924 (Idaho 1974), *96*

State ex rel. v. ___ (see opposing party and relator)

State of (see name of state)

State Water Resources Control Bd., United States v., 182 Cal. App.3d 82, 227 Cal.Rptr. 161 (Cal.App. 1 Dist.1986), *148*

Steed (Paul), Estate of v. New Escalante Irr. Co., 846 P.2d 1223 (Utah 1992), *132*

Stempel v. Department of Water Resources, 82 Wash.2d 109, 508 P.2d 166 (Wash.1973), *146*

Stephens v. Burton, 546 P.2d 240 (Utah 1976), *155*

Sterling, Town of v. Pawnee Ditch Extension Co., 42 Colo. 421, 94 P. 339 (Colo.1908), *105*

Stevens v. Cannon Beach, 317 Or. 131, 854 P.2d 449 (Or.1993), cert. denied 510 U.S. 1207, 114 S.Ct. 1332, 127 L.Ed.2d 679 (1994), *231*

Stevens v. Oakdale Irr. Dist., 13 Cal.2d 343, 90 P.2d 58 (Cal. 1939), *129*

Still v. Palouse Irr. & Power Co., 64 Wash. 606, 117 P. 466 (Wash.1911), *195*

Stokes v. Morgan, 101 N.M. 195, 680 P.2d 335 (N.M.1984), *286*

Stratton v. Mt. Hermon Boys' School, 216 Mass. 83, 103 N.E. 87 (Mass.1913), *53, 65*

Strom v. Sheldon, 12 Wash.App. 66, 527 P.2d 1382 (Wash.App. 1974), *69*

Sturgeon v. Brooks, 73 Wyo. 436, 281 P.2d 675 (Wyo.1955), *179*

Sullivan v. Blakesley, 35 Wyo. 73, 246 P. 918 (Wyo.1926), *433*

Tacoma, City of v. Taxpayers, 357 U.S. 320, 78 S.Ct. 1209, 2 L.Ed.2d 1345 (1958), *368*

Tanner v. Bacon, 103 Utah 494, 136 P.2d 957 (Utah 1943), *146*

Templeton v. Pecos Val. Artesian Conservancy Dist., 65 N.M. 59, 332 P.2d 465 (N.M.1958), *275*

Tennessee Valley Authority v. Hill, 437 U.S. 153, 98 S.Ct. 2279, 57 L.Ed.2d 117 (1978), *388*

Territory v. Gay, 52 F.2d 356 (9th Cir.1931), cert. denied 284 U.S. 677, 52 S.Ct. 131, 76 L.Ed. 572 (1931), *209*

Texas v. New Mexico, 482 U.S. 124, 107 S.Ct. 2279, 96 L.Ed.2d 105 (1987), *409*

Texas v. New Mexico, 462 U.S. 554, 103 S.Ct. 2558, 77 L.Ed.2d 1 (1983), *411*

Thayer v. California Development Co., 164 Cal. 117, 128 P. 21 (Cal.1912), *424*

Thayer v. City of Rawlins, 594 P.2d 951 (Wyo.1979), *131*

Thompson v. Enz, 385 Mich. 103, 188 N.W.2d 579 (Mich.1971), *236*

Thompson v. Enz, 379 Mich. 667, 154 N.W.2d 473 (Mich.1967), *236*

Thorton v. Farmers Reservoir & Irr. Co., 194 Colo. 526, 575 P.2d 382 (Colo.1978), *427*

Thornton, City of v. City of Fort Collins, 830 P.2d 915 (Colo. 1992), *97*

Thornton, City of, People ex rel. Danielson v., 775 P.2d 11 (Colo.1989), *177*

Thornton, State ex rel. v. Hay, 254 Or. 584, 462 P.2d 671 (Or.1969), *231*

Town of (see name of town)

Tucker v. Badoian, 376 Mass. 907, 384 N.E.2d 1195 (Mass.1978), *297*

Tulare Irr. Dist. v. Lindsay–Strathmore Irr. Dist., 3 Cal.2d 489, 45 P.2d 972 (Cal.1935), *197*

Turner v. Big Lake Oil Co., 128 Tex. 155, 96 S.W.2d 221 (Tex.1936), *305*

Tweedy v. Texas Co., 286 F.Supp. 383 (D.C.Mont.1968), *326*

Twin City Power Co., United States v., 350 U.S. 222, 76 S.Ct. 259, 100 L.Ed. 240 (1956), *349, 358*

Tyler v. Wilkinson, 24 F.Cas. 472 (C.C.R.I.1827), *19, 20, 69*

Union Bridge Co. v. United States, 204 U.S. 364, 27 S.Ct. 367, 51 L.Ed. 523 (1907), *354*

United Plainsmen Ass'n v. North Dakota State Water Conservation Commission, 247 N.W.2d 457 (N.D.1976), *147*

United States v. ___ (see opposing party)

Utah v. Kennecott Corp., 801 F.Supp. 553 (D.Utah 1992), *289*

TABLE OF CASES

Utah v. United States, 403 U.S. 9, 91 S.Ct. 1775, 29 L.Ed.2d 279 (1971), *221*

Vaughn v. Vermilion Corp., 444 U.S. 206, 100 S.Ct. 399, 62 L.Ed.2d 365 (1979), *357*

Vernon Irr. Co. v. City of Los Angeles, 106 Cal. 237, 39 P. 762 (Cal.1895), *214*

Virginia, Commonwealth of v. Tennessee, 148 U.S. 503, 13 S.Ct. 728, 37 L.Ed. 537 (1893), *408*

Virginia Elec. & Power Co., United States v., 365 U.S. 624, 81 S.Ct. 784, 5 L.Ed.2d 838 (1961), *360*

Vogel v. Minnesota Canal & Reservoir Co., 47 Colo. 534, 107 P. 1108 (Colo.1910), *165*

Wadsworth Ditch Co. v. Brown, 39 Colo. 57, 88 P. 1060 (Colo. 1907), *425*

Washington Dept. of Ecology v. Grimes, 121 Wash.2d 459, 852 P.2d 1044 (Wash.1993), *122*

Wasserburger v. Coffee, 180 Neb. 149, 141 N.W.2d 738 (Neb. 1966), modified on other grounds 180 Neb. 569, 144 N.W.2d 209 (Neb.1966), *200, 203*

Waters of Long Valley Creek Stream System, In re, 158 Cal.Rptr. 350, 599 P.2d 656 (Cal.1979), *87, 200, 203*

Water Supply and Storage Co. v. Curtis, 733 P.2d 680 (Colo. 1987), *111, 129*

Wayman v. Murray City Corp., 23 Utah 2d 97, 458 P.2d 861 (Utah 1969), *259*

Westminster, City of v. Church, 167 Colo. 1, 445 P.2d 52 (Colo. 1968), *170*

Westville, Borough of v. Whitney Home Builders, Inc., 40 N.J.Super. 62, 122 A.2d 233 (N.J.Super.A.D.1956), *42*

Wilbour v. Gallagher, 77 Wash.2d 306, 462 P.2d 232 (Wash. 1969), *236*

Willow Creek, In re, 74 Or. 592, 144 P. 505 (Or.1914), modified on other grounds 74 Or. 592, 146 P. 475 (Or.1915), *125, 140*

Willow River Power Co., United States v., 324 U.S. 499, 65 S.Ct. 761, 89 L.Ed. 1101 (1945), *356*

Windsor Reservoir & Canal Co. v. Lake Supply Ditch Co., 44 Colo. 214, 98 P. 729 (Colo.1908), *188*

Winters v. United States, 207 U.S. 564, 28 S.Ct. 207, 52 L.Ed. 340 (1908), *308, 310, 311, 323*

TABLE OF CASES

Wright v. Howard, 57 Eng.Rep. 76 (Eng.1823), *18*

Wyoming v. United States (Big Horn), 492 U.S. 406, 109 S.Ct. 2994, 106 L.Ed.2d 342 (1989), *322, 322, 323, 326, 337*

Wyoming Hereford Ranch v. Hammond Packing Co., 33 Wyo. 14, 236 P. 764 (Wyo.1925), *138*

Wyoming, State of v. State of Colo., 259 U.S. 419, 42 S.Ct. 552, 66 L.Ed. 999 (1922), *405*

Young & Norton v. Hinderlider, 15 N.M. 666, 110 P. 1045 (N.M.1910), *146*

Yucaipa Water Co. No. 1 v. Public Utilities Commission, 54 Cal.2d 823, 9 Cal.Rptr. 239, 357 P.2d 295 (Cal.1960), *426*

WATER LAW
IN A NUTSHELL
THIRD EDITION

*

CHAPTER ONE

OVERVIEW AND INTRODUC-
TION TO WATER LAW

I. THE STUDY OF WATER LAW

It is unusual for an area of law to be defined by a particular resource. But water is unique in the diversity and importance of needs it fills. Water quenches our thirst, gives life to essential food crops, furnishes habitat to fish resources, satisfies recreational and aesthetic needs, and purifies the air. It is one of the most plentiful substances, yet it is often considered precious because there is not always enough water of the right quality in the right place at the right time.

There is keen competition among water users. The same stream may be sought by a farmer for irrigation, a municipality for domestic use, a factory for carrying away waste, a power plant for cooling, a coal company for mixing with coal dust to be transported as slurry, boaters and fishers for recreation, and ecologists for preservation of the stream in its natural state. Single choices from among the array of possible uses can have far-reaching impacts. For instance, a decision to transport water from a rural area across a mountain range to a city may: force a decline in agricultural productivity

1

and the farming community built on it, facilitate more rapid growth in the importing area, prevent future development of the exporting area, curtail recreational opportunities, make sewage treatment more difficult as diluting streamflows are diminished, deprive the exporting area of groundwater recharge, and cause ecological changes in both areas.

The role of law is particularly important when so many varied needs must be recognized. An absence of order—of clearly defined rights and rules of liability—can be dangerous. Lives have literally been lost over water disputes in the western states.

The study of water law is, at one level, the study of property concepts, though rights to use water are peculiar. The fact that water is a moving resource necessarily limits the appropriateness of traditional concepts of ownership. Although water laws differ widely, notions of substantial public rights in the resource is a major theme across allocation regimes and through history. One result is that lawmakers have superimposed administrative systems in an attempt to enforce and regulate private water rights based on perceptions of a broader public interest.

The field of water law is implicitly a study of the legal process. In many areas, the law is well-developed and it changes only slowly and at the periphery, but water law is a comparatively young and dynamic field. It illustrates how courts and legislatures create and alter law according to societal stimuli: one set of historical conditions drove the initial development of water law but different modern circumstances provoke changes.

Three central tasks of legal study are: the comparison of established legal systems, the critical evaluation of the law's performance, and the search for solutions to unresolved problems. The law's success—in any field, but especially in water law— has to be evaluated in terms of what society needs from it.

We ask a lot of water law. Since we depend on water for so much, it touches our deepest values. Besides its pervasive commercial importance, it is at the core of things we care the most about: health, sustenance, ecological integrity, and aesthetics. It even provides community identity and spiritual satisfaction. Is it possible to satisfy all these values? To design a legal system that provides stability and fairness? With so much at stake, water law presents unparalleled opportunities for analysis and creativity. It is an evolving field bristling with conflicts among people's most cherished values.

II. LEGAL SYSTEMS FOR
WATER ALLOCATION

American jurisdictions can be grouped roughly into three systems of water law: riparian, prior appropriation, and hybrid states. This book treats the systems separately, so that readers may concentrate attention on issues within the system of particular interest. The systems, however, overlap and borrow from one another so that it is useful to compare them.

A.   Riparian Rights

Landowners bordering a waterway are considered riparians.   Their location gives them certain appurtenant rights under the laws of most states.   Historically, a riparian location had special advantages because it enabled the owner to operate water-driven mills and to have access to the water surface for boating, hunting, and fishing, and to consume reasonable quantities of water.

Theoretically, American jurisdictions subscribed to a "natural flow" rule that gave every riparian owner the right to have water flow past the land undiminished in quantity or quality.   In fact, the law as it was developed and enforced overcame the obvious objections to a rule that appeared so impractical as to bar all consumption.   Besides making exceptions for domestic uses, the early courts showed concern for existing users.   From some of the earliest cases, the courts tempered the doctrine with "reasonable use" principles.   Today, all riparian doctrine states (mostly located in the eastern United States) permit riparians to use water in a way that is "reasonable" relative to all other users. If there is insufficient water to satisfy the reasonable needs of all riparians, all must reduce usage of water in proportion to their rights, sometimes based on the amount of land they own.   There is generally no right to use water on non-riparian land, but the price of doing so is to pay for the harm to riparians. Because riparian rights inhere in land ownership, they need not be exercised to be kept alive. Thus, a landowner may initiate new uses at any time and other users must adjust in response.

Riparian rules have been altered by statute and case law so that today there are no riparian doctrine states governed simply by common law. Typically, riparians must obtain permits from a state agency in order to use water. Permits may also be available to non-riparians.

The riparian doctrine, which is covered in Chapter Two, still applies to some extent in twenty-nine states:

Alabama	Missouri
Arkansas	New Hampshire
Connecticut	New Jersey
Delaware	New York
Florida	North Carolina
Georgia	Ohio
Illinois	Pennsylvania
Indiana	Rhode Island
Iowa	South Carolina
Kentucky	Tennessee
Maine	Vermont
Maryland	Virginia
Massachusetts	West Virginia
Michigan	Wisconsin
Minnesota	

The doctrine also has some viability in the hybrid states listed in Section C.

In all states, regardless of the system they adopt for allocating rights to use water, riparian landowners have special rights to make use of the surface of waters adjoining their property. If the waterway is considered navigable, certain surface uses by members of the public also must be tolerated by riparians.

B. Prior Appropriation

The West was settled on lands owned by the federal government. The early miners, notably in California, sought water for their placer operations on the public lands. It was scarce, as it is throughout the arid lands west of the one-hundredth meridian. They could not assert riparian rights because they did not own land. So the miners simply followed the same rule they used in resolving disputes over the minerals they competed for on the public domain: "first in time, first in right." The earliest miner to put the water to work had a right to continue using it to the exclusion of others.

Early court decisions in the West recognized these water rights based on the miners' customs. The system worked satisfactorily for farmers, too, and became entrenched in the laws of virtually every western state. Rights, then, belong to anyone who puts water to a "beneficial use" anywhere (on riparian or non-riparian land), with superiority over anyone who later begins using water. Unlike riparian law, it depends on usage and not on land ownership. Once a person puts water to a beneficial use and complies with any statutory requirements, a water right is perfected and remains valid so long as it continues to be used.

Given a choice between riparian and appropriation law, states realized that riparian law, at least in its theoretical rigidity, did not fit local needs. Mines and farms needing water could not always be located on riparian lands in a region where waterways are few and far between. Further, development would have been frustrated if the fortunate landowners along streams could monopolize scarce water and keep it unused until they felt like putting it to some use. Appropriative water rights can be transferred if it is shown that the ability of others to exercise vested rights is not impaired.

The prior appropriation doctrine governs water rights in nine states:

Alaska	Nevada
Arizona	New Mexico
Colorado	Utah
Idaho	Wyoming
Montana	

All "pure" appropriation states (except Colorado) require permits to appropriate water. An administrative agency issues permits based on requirements designed to protect other water users. Most state agencies also consider public interest concerns. Prior appropriation is the subject of Chapter Three.

C. Hybrid Systems

Several states originally recognized riparian rights, but later converted to a system of appropriation while preserving existing riparian rights. These states that follow this hybrid approach are:

California	Oklahoma
Kansas	Oregon
Mississippi	South Dakota
Nebraska	Texas
North Dakota	Washington

Hawaii's system is a combination of rights established under laws of the ancient Hawaiian Kingdom and recent statutes. Louisiana's water law is adapted from the French Civil Code. Water laws of Hawaii and Louisiana are discussed along with hybrid systems in Chapter Four.

III. SPECIAL TYPES OF WATER

Most water available for use is subject to one of the three water allocation schemes listed above, but certain waters fall outside those systems.

A. Groundwater

There are two dominant concerns in water law: depletion of essentially nonrenewable stores of underground water and conflicts among competing well-owners. Contamination problems are an increasingly troubling area as well.

Vast underground resources supply much of the nation's needs. The law has been slow to deal with these problems. Until recently, the dynamics of groundwater occurrence and movement were considered too uncertain, even mysterious, to try to regulate. The failure of states to deal comprehensively with groundwater left overlying owners free to extract water from under their lands as they pleased.

Even when water beneath the surface of land was connected with a stream or lake, the law treated groundwater under a separate set of rules or no rules at all. More enlightened legal approaches now integrate groundwater and surface water management. For example, when pumping from a well would affect the rights of a person using stream water (or vice-versa) most states now administer it as a part of the stream system. Other laws deal with aquifers that are non-renewable from which water is "mined" and so groundwater must be allocated carefully over time.

Special rules are needed for groundwater management because waters may be withdrawn at a faster rate than they are replenished. Another problem is that a new well may endanger existing wells. Some theories for allocating rights in groundwater are analogous to riparian rights (absolute ownership of water underlying land) and prior appropriation (groundwater is subject to appropriation, with older wells protected against harm from newer pumpers).

Surface water allocation schemes, however, do not fit the physical realities of groundwater. Ownership theories do not prevent rapid draining of an aquifer or protect the interests of neighboring pumpers. Appropriation concepts, if strictly applied, would give such complete protection to the first pumper that almost any new use would cause harm and be subject to legal objections.

Consequently, special rules have been developed to balance competing interests of new and old well users and overlying owners, and to fulfill the state's obligation to prolong the life of the resource while allowing efficient usage. Many jurisdictions base rules of liability between pumpers and criteria for granting permits for new wells on a reasonable use standard, requiring that the relative utility of uses and equities of the parties be weighed. Groundwater laws are discussed in Chapter Six.

B. Diffused Surface Water

Ordinarily, only waters in natural streams are considered subject to state control. Obviously, not all water on earth is capable of management by governments. Thus, water rights systems exclude from their coverage water in the oceans, water in the process of evaporation or transpiration, and precipitation. For some time groundwater was not under any legal system because of the technical difficulty in tracing its movement and understanding where and how much was available.

Water that is on the surface of land because of rain, melting snow, or floods is called diffused surface water and generally is not subject to water allocation rules. Nearly all states allow diffused surface waters to be captured and used by a landowner without regulation or limitation. Such waters are simply outside the realm of state control.

The special rules concerning diffused surface waters were developed primarily to determine liability between landowners when one attempts to avoid such waters and causes problems for another. A majority of states allow landowners to divert or channel floodwaters away from their lands if it is reasonable under the circumstances. These matters are treated in Chapter Seven.

IV. PUBLIC RIGHTS

Water is legally and historically a public resource. Although private property rights can be perfected in the use of water, it remains essentially public; private rights are always incomplete and subject to the public's common needs. The earliest expression of these needs, still viable, was navigation. Navigable waters remain subject to public use and access for uses such as boating, bathing, fishing, hunting, and, more recently, recreational and aesthetic interests. Throughout the study of water law it is evident that private activity affecting the quantity and quality of water cannot lawfully interfere with the overriding public interest.

Chapter Five deals with the special public rights that exist in the use of the surface of waterways. These rights may turn on the definition of navigability, which is also the point of reference for ownership of the beds of waterways. Public rights to use the surface of non-navigable waters have also been recognized based on their capacity to support recreational uses, the public trust doctrine, and various state statutes. Access rights to and from the shores of waterbodies where public surface rights exist, including beaches, have been established based on several theories.

V.   INTERGOVERNMENTAL PROBLEMS

Although creation and regulation of rights to use water are primarily state affairs, there are important spheres of federal ownership and control. Chapter Eight is concerned with waters that the federal government holds for use on public lands that are reserved for special purposes like parks, forests, and military bases and lands Indian tribes hold for their reservations.

Chapter Nine deals with exercises of congressional power—from water projects to environmental laws—that may affect the way state water laws operate.

The difficult interjurisdictional problems of adjusting rights of states whose inhabitants are competing for use of water from a common source are treated in Chapter Ten.

A. Reserved Rights

The doctrine of reserved rights traces to early litigation to protect Indian reservations where tribes were confined to facilitate the settlement of the West and to convert Indians to farmers. The Supreme Court held that they could not be deprived of sufficient water to make the reservation a viable place to live and farm. That would defeat the purposes the government and the tribes had in mind in agreeing to move the Indians onto the reservation. The reserved rights doctrine recognized in the tribes a right to sufficient water to fulfill the purposes of the reservation. The same principle was later applied to federal reservations of public lands.

Reserved water rights have a priority as of the date the reservation was established, whether or not water has ever been used. In a system in which water rights are based on prior use, assertions of reserved water rights can cause dislocations among those whose water rights have a priority date later than the establishment of the reservation. To ease the effects of the reserved rights doctrine, the courts have narrowly construed the extent of rights reserved and Congress has allowed reserved rights to be quantified in state courts in general stream adjudications. There are adjudications proceeding in states throughout the West where federal and Indian lands are concentrated.

B. Federal Actions Affecting State Water Rights

The United States is involved in activities that sometimes affect, and because of federal supremacy, may preempt state water law. In the first half of the century the federal role in water resources was mostly in providing financial support and management of large water development projects for navigation, flood control, agriculture, power generation, and other uses. The last twenty-five years has seen intense federal involvement in environmental regulation. Today, federal laws that protect endangered species, wetlands, and water quality are at least as important as state water laws in shaping water development and use.

All of these federal functions are important to a significant part of the public. But when federal activities conflict with state water rights, serious federalism issues arise and courts must resolve close questions of whether Congress intended to override state law.

C. Interstate Problems

Tensions frequently exist among states that share access to rivers, lakes, and groundwater sources. Allocations among states can be made by compact— a negotiated interstate agreement made with the consent of Congress—or by adjudication in a judicial proceeding. In one instance, Congress passed legislation effectively allocating waters of the Colorado River among the abutting states, demonstrating a third means for interstate allocation.

In attempting to protect their water resources, states may not improperly inhibit interstate commerce by placing limits on exports. Water is considered an article of commerce and, as such, trade in it must not be restricted by regulations that discriminate against interstate commerce.

VI. WATER INSTITUTIONS

The final chapter describes a number of types of organizations formed to develop and distribute water. They are the operating entities that deliver most of the water in the country.

CHAPTER TWO

RIPARIAN RIGHTS

Twenty-nine states have systems rooted in the riparian doctrine. Ten others have a system based on some combination of riparian and prior appropriation doctrines. See Chapter Four. The states that fall into each classification of water law are listed on pages 5–8.

The fundamental principle of the riparian doctrine is that the owner of land bordering a waterbody acquires certain rights to use the water. Each landowner bordering on a waterbody may make reasonable use of the water on riparian land if the use does not interfere with reasonable uses of other riparians. Today statutory systems have largely replaced pure riparianism in virtually all jurisdictions, though courts and agencies apply elements of the doctrine in allocating and enforcing rights.

I. HISTORY OF THE RIPARIAN DOCTRINE

A. European Precedents

Scholars differ on the origin of the riparian doctrine. Some believe it is a product of the civil law; others maintain it has its roots in the English common law. Elements of the doctrine can be traced to precedents from both France and England but it is essentially an American doctrine.

Prior to the eighteenth century, most water cases involved rights of navigation and fishing. The dawn of the Industrial Revolution and the consequent increase in water-driven mills created a need for uniform principles of law that could be applied in the growing number of water disputes concerned with access to the flow of the stream. The law's response was the development of the riparian doctrine.

1. *France*

The Institutes of Justinian, published in 533–34 A.D., held that running water was a part of the "negative community" of things that could not be owned, along with air, seas, and wildlife. At the same time, it was recognized that things in the negative community could be used and that the "usufruct," or right to use the advantages of the resource, must be regulated to provide order and prevent over-exploitation. The Institutes declared that the right to use water belonged only to those who had access to the water by virtue of their ownership of riparian land. Others could not gain access without committing a trespass, unless the stream was on the public domain.

Doctrine was formalized in 1804 with the promulgation of the French Civil Code. The Code allowed a riparian landowner to use water from an abutting stream for irrigation if the water was returned to its ordinary course before it left the land. The antecedents of two riparian "rules" are found in the Code: the limitation confining water rights to riparian landowners, and the requirement that the water be restored to its ordinary course. The Code also provided that in disputes between riparian landowners the courts should reconcile the interests of agriculture with riparian property rights (for example, the right of a nonagricultural riparian to have a continued flow of water past the property). This provision is a forerunner of the reasonable use theory that was eventually incorporated into the American riparian law.

2. *England*

England developed a regular system of courts and lawyers only after the Norman Conquest. Prior to 1066, English society was largely decentralized, and disputes concerning water were apparently settled locally.

The early English law of water rights resembled the modern prior appropriation system. One who had made use of a stream from time immemorial was entitled to continue even if the use deprived others of the natural flow of the stream. In the eighteenth century, the English courts modified this doctrine of "ancient use" and substituted a test of "prior use." Under this test, one could not use or divert water if the effect would be to deprive a prior user of water. The principle protected earlier mills from interference with their water supplies by newer mills. E.g., Bealey v. Shaw (Eng.1805).

The prior use test was short-lived. In the 1820s the English courts began to accept a "natural flow" theory under which every riparian landowner, including important new industrial users, had an equal right to use water in the stream and a duty not to diminish the quantity of water otherwise flowing to proprietors lower on the stream. Wright v. Howard (Eng.1823). This remained the law in England for a few decades until the English judges, borrowing from the American opinions of Story and Kent, incorporated the "reasonable use" theory into English riparian doctrine. Mason v. Hill (Eng. 1833). Application of reasonable use principles modified the natural flow theory by allowing each riparian the right to make all reasonable uses of the waters so long as those uses did not interfere with the reasonable uses of other riparians.

B. Early Development in the Eastern United States

After the Revolutionary War each state began developing its own case law. The sparse population of the United States lived mostly on the eastern seaboard, a rainy area with abundant brooks, streams, and rivers. Some states, including Connecticut and Massachusetts, had few restrictions on the use of streams, and allowed diversions of water if the surplus was returned to the stream. Other states, such as New Jersey, adopted a type of natural flow rule that allowed a riparian landowner to make use of the stream in its natural state but prohibited any diversion that might materially reduce the flow to another. Farrell v. Richards (N.J.Ch.1879) (the court also stressed plaintiffs' long-established use).

With the industrial growth of nineteenth century America, large mills required reservoirs for storage, and irrigation and industry spread away from the stream banks. The notion of preserving the natural flow of the stream was rendered obsolete by the need to alter the stream to maximize water uses. Against this backdrop the famous case of Tyler v. Wilkinson (C.C.R.I.1827) was decided. The plaintiffs in *Tyler* were riparian proprietors with mills near a small dam used to impound water so that it would flow faster past their mills once it was released. The defendants constructed an upstream dam and diverted water into a trench that began above plaintiffs' mills. The defendants' water use thus deprived plaintiffs of the flow of water they otherwise would have stored behind the lower dam. Justice Story held that while the riparian plaintiffs had a right to the natural flow of the river, any rights to water for the dam and mills would have to be based on "actual appropriation and use." He went on to hold that the defendants were entitled to the quantity of water that was accustomed to flow in the trench during the twenty years before the initiation of the suit (the passage of time giving rise to a conclusive presumption that they had a right to water). In setting forth the principles of law applicable to watercourses in general, Justice Story stated that all riparians had an equal right to the use of the balance of the water naturally flowing in the stream and, departing from the natural flow doctrine, held that each riparian was entitled to make a reasonable use of the waters. That use could not interfere with the reasonable use of any other riparian landowner.

In 1828, less than one year after Story's decision in Tyler v. Wilkinson, Chancellor Kent discussed the law of water rights in his *Commentaries*. He embraced the reasonable use doctrine and specifically cited Story's opinion along with numerous civil law authorities (mostly dealing with diffused surface waters). Many courts in the United States and England relied on Kent's *Commentaries* and Story's decision in Tyler v. Wilkinson. The importance of the natural flow theory was always largely theoretical.

Today all riparian states have adopted some form of the reasonable use doctrine; nearly all of them have statutory permit schemes, further departing from early riparian doctrine. Though some courts continue to use "natural flow" language, most actually apply some variant of the reasonable use doctrine.

C. Repudiation and Recognition in the American West

The westward expansion of the United States was the product of a variety of factors. Acquisition of lands from foreign powers and the subjugation of American Indians paved the way for large numbers of people to settle in the West. The discovery of areas rich in timber, furs, and minerals, and vast land areas thought suitable for farming provided powerful incentives for westward movement.

The riparian doctrine was thought to be impractical for the arid region beyond the one-hundredth meridian (a line running south through the middle of North Dakota into Texas). A system that limited rights to owners of land bordering a stream and water use to the watershed of origin would have stifled development. Almost all western land was owned by the federal government, yet homesteaders and miners were encouraged to settle there. The early miners and homesteaders were essentially trespassers on the public domain; thus they could have no riparian rights. The most promising mineral deposits were often far from any stream; without water many mines, particularly placer mines, could not operate. Besides denying waters to any but property owners, the doctrine required water to be used only on lands abutting a stream. Often the dry lands settled by farmers were far from any stream, making importation of water necessary.

By its silence the federal government acquiesced in the settlers' trespasses and use of water. The miners developed their own customary "law." They rejected the riparian doctrine and simply allowed people to divert quantities of water from a stream, transport it many miles—usually via ditch, and put it to use for mining or irrigation. This right to "appropriate" a quantity of water was available on a first come-first served basis. Anyone could make a diversion that did not deprive "prior appropriators" of the quantity of water already being diverted by them. Prior appropriation was gradually adopted by state courts and incorporated into state statutes. The federal government also recognized the validity of the doctrine in early mining acts and in the Desert Land Act of 1877. See Chapter Three.

Some western states adopted riparian rights at first for their more humid regions. Eventually all of them legislatively phased out riparian rights but many preserved existing riparian rights. These "hybrid" states consequently still refer to riparian law in cases arising there. See Chapter Four.

D. Riparian Law Today

Increased population and development of the United States caused most eastern riparian states to adopt statutory permit systems for some or all water uses. See Section V of this chapter. Early statutory and case law defining reasonable use is reflected in the permit systems. In addition, common law disputes between individuals may be resolved by reference to riparian principles.

Besides securing a right to make reasonable use of water flowing past one's land, riparian ownership includes a right to have water remain unpolluted (the right of purity), and rights to fish, to have access to the stream, and to protect the banks of a stream from erosion. These rights all have been upheld to some extent in the appropriation states as well as in riparian states.

II. RIPARIAN LANDS

Only the owner of riparian land acquires any rights to make use of the adjacent watercourse. This section defines what constitutes riparian land and the types of waterbodies in which the owner of adjacent land may hold rights. The status of riparian rights if riparian land is divided into smaller parcels is then discussed.

A. Contiguity to Source

All land masses are surrounded by bodies of water and in that sense all land could be called riparian. The law, however, distinguishes between riparian land and non-riparian land through the somewhat artificial concept of ownership. Only the owner of a parcel of land touching the watercourse has riparian rights, but it is no longer required that the landowner own a portion of the bed of a watercourse. See Restatement (Second) of Torts § 843. Riparian rights to use water attach only to riparian land and do not extend to any portion of the tract that is outside the immediate watershed of the waterbody.

B. Types of Watercourses

To have riparian rights a landowner must own property adjacent to a waterbody that fits the definition of a "watercourse." No rights attach, for instance, to diffused surface waters.

1. Streams

The term "watercourse" means a natural stream flowing constantly or recurrently on the surface of the earth in a reasonably definite natural channel. The term may also include springs, lakes, or marshes in which a stream originates or through which it flows.

In the eastern states the courts generally require that a stream flow all year to constitute a watercourse. In the arid West natural streams may be dry for much of the year, coming to life only during the rainy season, and may still be included within the definition of a watercourse.

In contrast to a watercourse, diffused surface water usually comes from the runoff of rains or melting snow, and generally flows intermittently without a defined channel. It is not subject to riparian rights until it enters a watercourse. The special rules applicable to diffused surface water are covered in Chapter Seven.

2. Lakes and Ponds

A lake also is a watercourse subject to riparian rights. A lake is defined as a reasonably permanent body of water substantially at rest in a depression in the surface of the earth, if both the depression and the body of water are of natural origin or part of a watercourse. Smaller bodies of water, particularly ones with an abundance of aquatic life, are sometimes called ponds, but no legal distinction exists. In some eastern states bodies of water known as "great ponds" are considerably larger than many lakes.

A person who owns land bordering on a lake or pond is technically referred to as a "littoral" landowner, but it is also common to call such owners riparians. Some argue that littoral landowners actually own the water in the lake rather than simply possessing certain rights to make use of it, since water in a lake is stationary rather than flowing. This ignores a reality of the hydrologic cycle: water is constantly evaporating from lakes and being replaced with water from other sources such as streams, springs, surface runoff, and rainfall. It is now settled that the same riparian rights to use water attach to land abutting on a natural lake or pond as attach to land bordering on a flowing stream.

The rights of littoral landowners to use the surface of a lake for such purposes as fishing and boating usually depend on whether the lake is "navigable" or "non-navigable." Those rights are discussed in Section III B of this chapter. Generally, any person, whether or not a littoral owner, may make use of the surface of a navigable lake. Each state may adopt its own definition of navigability for this purpose. If the lake is non-navigable the majority rule is that all littoral landowners own the surface rights in common and each may use the entire surface provided the use does not unreasonably interfere with the exercise of similar rights by other littoral landowners. Some states follow this rule even if one littoral owner owns the bed of the entire lake. Other states hold that use of the surface of a non-navigable lake above that portion of the bed owned by another constitutes a trespass.

3. Springs and Other Natural Water Bodies

A spring is a concentrated flow of water coming to the surface from under the ground. Whether the owner of land with a spring on it has riparian rights depends upon the source of the spring. The riparian doctrine usually applies to springs emanating from definite underground watercourses, landowners being entitled only to make reasonable use of the waters from such springs. In the absence of evidence to the contrary, it is presumed that the spring was formed and fed by percolating groundwater and the law of groundwater treated in Chapter Six applies.

A spring will be treated as diffused surface water if its flow dissipates before reaching a watercourse or before leaving the boundary of the land on which it is located. See Chapter Seven. The owner of the land owns the spring and may use all the water from it. Sometimes courts treat springs as watercourses, however, even if the water from them does not flow off the owner's land in a regular, well-defined channel.

4. Underground Watercourses

The owner of land above a stream flowing underground has all rights of a riparian landowner. The course and the channel of the stream, however, must be definitely ascertained. An underground watercourse connecting two aquifers is usually treated as part of the groundwater system and not as an underground stream. (See Chapter 6, Section I A 4). Evidence of an underground stream is provided by soil composition, growth of vegetation in dry seasons, and by comparing amounts withdrawn from wells during certain periods with measurements of nearby surface water levels during the same periods.

A riparian landowner who believes that a neighbor's wells are affecting the use of the surface waterbody must prove that the waters are interconnected to establish liability. This may require the testimony of engineers. In most states there is a presumption that underground water is groundwater and not subject to surface water (riparian) principles. Courts may not apply the presumption, though, if wells are very close to surface watercourses.

5. *Foreign Waters*

Foreign waters are waters transported from one watershed into another by human effort. Use of water outside its watershed is often held to be unreasonable per se. But once water is exported, the exporter may obtain rights to it by prescription. Ownership of land bordering on a stream or ditch carrying foreign waters does not usually give the landowner riparian rights to the water.

6. *Artificially Created Watercourses*

Sometimes a canal is built, a stream re-channelled, or a lake created through human effort.

The new waterbody may be an important source of water for those adjoining it. Yet the general rule is that riparian rights attach only to natural watercourses and lakes. Thus, the rights of owners of land riparian to an artificial stream or lake are not controlled by riparian doctrine. Artificial watercourses that are maintained long enough, however, may be treated by courts as natural watercourses. In Bollinger v. Henry (Mo.1964) the court treated a century-old millrace as if it were a watercourse.

If an artificial lake is created by building a dam and the lake borders on the property of others, they may acquire certain rights in the lake based on theories of estoppel, reliance, or reciprocal easements. In the leading case of Kray v. Muggli (Minn.1901) a dam impounded water to form a lake. After forty years the defendants wanted to remove the dam. The court enjoined the defendants because the plaintiff had made improvements such as docks relying on the level of the lake. The court noted that defendants had acquired a prescriptive right (flowage easement) to flood plaintiff's uplands, and therefore plaintiff acquired a reciprocal prescriptive right to maintenance of the artificial water level.

A case more typical of modern trends is Kiwanis Club Found. Inc. v. Yost (Neb.1966). That case held that construction of a dam put the upper landowner, who had built a boys camp on the shore, on notice that the water level was artificial. No rights were created to maintain the lake, and the lower landowner was allowed to alter the level at will. A different result was reached in Greisinger v. Klinhardt (Mo.1928), in which a country club sold lakefront lots on an artificial lake to the plaintiffs thereby inducing them to make substantial improvements based on the understanding that the lake was to be permanent.

In upholding rights of plaintiffs in artificial watercourses the courts in *Kray* and *Greisinger* did not say that riparian rights existed in artificial waters. Instead, they held that the defendants were estopped from denying plaintiffs' rights or found that the waterway had become effectively a natural watercourse.

C. Extent

Riparian rights do not attach to certain lands. First, no rights attach to lands outside the watershed. Second, rights may be extinguished to the extent that a portion of the land without any frontage on the waterway is severed and conveyed separately.

1. Watershed Limitation

Riparian rights attach only to an owner's land within the watershed. This is true whether a parcel is a separate parcel of non-contiguous land or is part of a tract that fronts on a stream but is in another watershed. Although riparian rights do not attach, a riparian landowner still may be able to use water for land owned outside the watershed. Some jurisdictions do bar all use of water outside the watershed, but others permit it subject to the reasonable use restriction. Most jurisdictions consider use outside the watershed of origin to be unreasonable per se, although many will not prevent it unless another riparian is actually harmed. Long-standing non-watershed use may ripen into a prescriptive right. Several exceptions to the watershed limitation have developed. See Section IV B 3 of this chapter.

2. *Divisions of Riparian Land*

A conveyance of riparian land carries with it all of the appurtenant riparian rights unless there has been a severance of those rights. The extent to which rights can be reserved by a grantor or conveyed to a grantee are discussed in Section VI of this chapter. Riparian rights attach only to waterfront land; consequently, when a riparian owner conveys a parcel of land that is not on the water riparian rights no longer attach to the conveyed parcel. If the parcels are reunited under common ownership, the parcel of land that is not on the water may remain without riparian rights, depending on which of the following rules prevails in the jurisdiction.

a. *Unity of Title Rule*

Under the unity of title rule an entire tract of land fronting on a waterway held by a single owner is entitled to riparian rights. It does not matter that the land earlier had been divided into several parcels some of which did not front on the waterway. Thus all land contiguous to a riparian parcel that is held by the same riparian landowner has riparian rights regardless of when or from whom the contiguous lands were conveyed. Most riparian states follow this rule.

Example: In Figure 1 Jones severs riparian land and conveys the north plot to Smith. Only Smith has the riparian rights. Under the unity of title rule, if Smith later reconveys the north plot back to Jones, the entire tract (both plots) would again have riparian rights. Similarly, if Smith conveyed the south plot, kept the north plot, then later reacquired the south plot, riparian rights would attach to the entire tract.

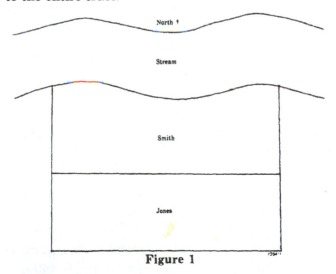

North ↑

Stream

Smith

Jones

Figure 1

b. *Source of Title Rule*

Under the source of title rule (also called the smallest tract rule), riparian rights attach only to the smallest subdivision of waterfront land in the chain of title leading to the present owner. Thus, even if the original riparian owner later reacquires the tract, only the smallest parcel with frontage on the waterway has riparian rights; any land ever severed from contact with the waterway by conveyance can never regain riparian rights. Under this rule the amount of riparian land shrinks as conveyances sever waterfront lands from uplands. An exception to the rule is that partition of riparian lands among tenants in common does not deprive non-waterfront parcels of riparian rights.

The source of title rule is applied in western states with a hybrid system of water law. The apparent harshness of reducing the amount of land subject to riparian rights is tempered by the fact that water rights may be acquired by appropriation for the severed parcels. The rule furthers the policy, typical in hybrid jurisdictions, of minimizing the reach of riparian rights and building a reliable system based on prior appropriation. Hybrid systems are discussed in Chapter Four.

Example: In Figure 1 Jones conveys the north portion of a tract of riparian land—the part bordering the stream—to Smith. No riparian rights remain with the south plot. If Smith later reconveys the north plot back to Jones riparian rights will not reattach to the south plot.

III. NATURE OF RIPARIAN RIGHTS

Under the riparian doctrine rights attach to riparian land, i.e., land bordering on a natural stream or lake, by virtue of its location. The riparian landowner does not actually own the waterbody, but does "own" numerous rights in it. In this sense the owner of riparian land has a significant property interest in the waterbody. The owner's rights include:

- The right to the flow of the stream;
- The right to make a reasonable use of the waterbody provided reasonable uses of other riparians are not injured;
- The right of access to the waterbody;
- The right to fish;
- The right to wharf out;
- The right to prevent erosion of the banks;
- The right to purity of the water;
- The right to claim title to the beds of non-navigable lakes and streams.

The ownership of riparian land not only creates rights, it also creates duties. Each riparian landowner has a duty to refrain from interfering with the rights of fellow riparians. Riparian rights are further limited by "public rights" to use the surface of certain waterways. At common law all persons had the right to travel any navigable river and the associated rights to hunt and fish along the river. Today public uses include not only navigation but recreation, and public rights have been extended to non-navigable waters in many states. Public surface use rights are covered in Chapter Five.

Use of water in place—instream uses—by the general public for navigation, recreation, and even aesthetics have substantial modern importance and may be recognized by statute or court decision in non-riparian jurisdictions.

A. Rights of Riparian Proprietors

1. *Preference for "Natural" Uses*

Riparian law distinguishes between "natural" uses and "artificial" uses. Natural uses include those that meet the domestic needs of the riparian landowner, such as drinking, washing, and watering small gardens or a few livestock. Under the natural flow rule a riparian could use water for natural (i.e., domestic) purposes even if it diminished the flow to the harm of lower riparians. Natural uses were the only consumptive uses allowed.

The reasonable use doctrine also reflects a preference for natural uses. E.g., Prather v. Hoberg (Cal.1944). In most jurisdictions today any riparian can make natural uses of the water in the adjacent stream regardless of consequences to lower riparians, while artificial uses such as for irrigation and industrial purposes are subject to reasonableness restrictions.

There are practical reasons for the preference for natural or domestic uses. First, such uses are unlikely to consume enough water to injure lower riparians. Second, enforcement of any restriction on domestic uses is difficult. Finally, such uses as are necessary to sustain life are bound to be "reasonable."

2. *Irrigation, Industrial, and Mining Uses*

At common law any significant irrigation was an "artificial" use of water. Theoretically, no irrigation was allowed except for small household gardens, but the reasonable use rule permits "reasonable" irrigation under the rules discussed in Section IV. Some riparian states have expressed their public policy by enacting laws that prefer agricultural uses. For example, in Kentucky permits required for other riparian uses are not required for agricultural uses. Other states single out specific crops for preferential treatment (e.g., Wisconsin allows cranberry growers to divert water to irrigate their crops). Agriculture also may get preferential treatment through statutes exempting farm ponds from regulations governing construction of dams.

Manufacturing and industrial uses of water are, like agricultural uses, artificial uses. Today those uses are subject to the reasonable use rule.

Mining often requires substantial amounts of water and is also considered an artificial use. Several riparian states (e.g., Michigan and Wisconsin), however, have declared mining to be in the public interest, thus giving the courts another factor to consider when determining reasonableness of a mining use. Some permit states (e.g., Minnesota) require a finding that a particular mining operation is in the public interest before a permit will be issued. Other states have statutes giving miners a right of access to waterways, implying that they have a right to use those waters (e.g., Georgia, Maine, North Carolina).

Industrial and mining uses may come into conflict with the rights of downstream riparians to pure water. The reasonable use rule requires a balancing test that may allow some pollution, similar to the approach used in actions for private nuisance or public nuisance brought by private litigants. Reasonableness may be measured by standards in state and federal legislation enacted to deal with water pollution (e.g., federal Clean Water Act). In riparian permit states, pollution is a factor to be weighed in issuing permits to take water.

3. *Municipal Uses*

When the United States was predominantly rural, local streams or individual wells provided most of the water needed for domestic uses. With urbanization came the growth of municipal water systems to supply domestic needs, fight fires and to water public parks. Since neither the cities themselves nor the residents served by these systems are riparian landowners, riparian doctrine had to be modified with exceptions allowing municipal uses.

a. *Common Law*

Generally, a city whose boundaries include or abut a stream or lake on the watercourse is not a riparian except to the extent it owns waterfront land. Therefore it may have no right to use water. If a city does own a tract of riparian land, then it is a riparian landowner entitled to make reasonable use of the waters on that land from the adjacent water body just like any other riparian landowner. E.g., Botton v. State (Wash.1966). But the city would have to own substantial riparian land to justify as "reasonable" the heavy burdens imposed on the stream by drawing enough water to supply its inhabitants.

The power of eminent domain allows municipalities to condemn private riparian water rights for a public purpose if just compensation is paid. Dimmock v. New London (Conn.1968); Town of Purcellville v. Potts (Va.1942). Eminent domain can be very expensive, particularly under the natural flow rule, which requires compensation even in the absence of present harm. The usual measure of compensation for condemnation of riparian rights is the diminution in the value of affected riparian land. If a city takes water without condemning the riparian right, injured riparians may bring an action for inverse condemnation, in effect forcing the city to condemn the riparian rights and compensate for the loss.

b. *Statutory and Charter Provisions*

The charters incorporating most cities gave them powers to procure water supplies for such purposes as firefighting, watering public parks, supplying public buildings, and for meeting the domestic needs of their residents. States have also passed special legislative acts giving such powers to particular cities. The trend today is to grant such powers in general statutes applicable to all municipalities.

In some cases, state laws empower private companies to supply water for domestic needs and grant the power to condemn land and water rights. Adams v. Greenwich Water Co. (Conn.1951). Often these companies are regulated as public utilities.

4. Storage Rights

A riparian owner may desire to build a dam to impound water during wet seasons and store it for use during dry seasons. A few courts have held storage to be unreasonable per se. See Evans v. Merriweather (Ill.1842). But with the demise of natural flow notions most courts have been convinced that storage ought to be governed by the general rule of reasonableness. Modern statutes give environmental agencies discretion to issue permits for water diversion and storage facilities. E.g., Hudson River Fisherman's Ass'n v. Williams (N.Y.A.D.1988)(allowing trout stream to be dried up).

Under the reasonable use rule a riparian can impound water so long as the reasonable uses of others are not impaired. Heise v. Schulz (Kan. 1949). Accordingly, it has been held that a riparian may not unreasonably alter the flow when releasing water from the storage facility. In Moore v. California Oregon Power Co. (Cal.1943), plaintiffs owned land riparian to the Klamath River. The defendant operated a dam above the plaintiffs' lands that generated electricity for a power plant and released water from the dam at intervals to satisfy peak demands for electricity. This caused the flow in the stream below the dam to fluctuate greatly, repeatedly washing away the plaintiffs' diversion works. The Supreme Court of California held for the plaintiffs on the ground that defendant's use deprived the lower riparians of the natural flow of the stream. Under a theory of reasonable use the outcome probably would have been the same because of the unreasonable nature of the defendant's storage and release methods.

The majority of states follow the rule of Rylands v. Fletcher (Eng.1868) that storage of water behind a dam can constitute an ultrahazardous activity and therefore the dam owner may be absolutely liable for any damage caused to another's property by escaping water. Liability can also be based on negligent construction or maintenance of storage dams.

5. *Water Power*

Harnessing the flow of a stream to generate power is one of the oldest uses of water. Water power uses range from the earliest waterwheels to large hydroelectric dams.

a. *Waterwheels, Mills, etc.*

Early in the nation's history, small waterwheels and mills adorned numerous streams, providing a cheap and accessible source of power. Eventually larger mills were needed for manufacturing. As bigger waterwheels were needed dams were often constructed upstream from the mills to create storage pools from which releases could be made to provide a stronger current. This could cause deepening and slowing of the flow that interfered with other uses. Thus, some state legislatures enacted mill dam acts to allow storage dams provided they did not injure existing mills. This built an element of priority into the riparian system by assuring protection to the earliest uses that relied on the flow of the stream.

b. *Hydroelectric Generation*

Generation of electrical power is an important riparian use. Under the reasonable use rule operators of a hydroelectric dam may not unreasonably store or release water to the detriment of other riparians. Factors weighed in determining the reasonableness of dam operators' storage and release methods include the stream size, the state of technology, and uses of the stream by other riparians. Hazard Powder Co. v. Somersville Mfg. Co. (Conn. 1905). Although riparian doctrine generally limits water use to riparian land, electricity generated from hydroelectric dams may be transmitted to and used by owners of non-riparian land.

The public also may be concerned with hydroelectric dams since such structures can interfere with use of the surface of navigable rivers. Exercising its power under the commerce clause, Congress has dictated in the Federal Power Act that no hydroelectric dam may be built on any navigable river unless first licensed by the Federal Energy Regulatory Commission (formerly the Federal Power Commission). Before it issues a license, the Commission must find that the proposed "project be best adapted to a comprehensive plan for improving or developing the waterway." See Chapter Nine, Section III.

6. *Recovery of Gravel*

The natural flow rule, giving each riparian the right to have the stream flow undiminished in quantity or quality, would incidentally protect a riparian owner's ability to take and sell gravel washed downstream. The reasonable use doctrine would balance the utility of using the waters to transport gravel against competing uses.

A riparian's right to recover sand and gravel was the issue in Joslin v. Marin Mun. Water Dist. (Cal. 1967). In that case the plaintiffs owned lands riparian to a stream that deposited sand and gravel on plaintiffs' lands enabling them to run a profitable sand and gravel business. The defendant water district built a dam upstream from the plaintiffs that caused the flow of suspended sand and gravel to cease, but still allowed water to flow past the plaintiffs' lands. The plaintiffs brought suit alleging that their land had diminished in value because they had been deprived of $25,000 worth of sand and gravel annually. Relief was denied. The court recognized that the public interest was served by the dam, but saw no comparable benefit to the public from operation of the sand and gravel business. It held that use of a stream to transport suspended sand and gravel was unreasonable as a matter of law. The result is odd in that both parties operated businesses that supplied products needed by the public. To hold that the plaintiffs' use was unreasonable as a matter of law forsakes the balancing approach applied under the reasonable use rule. Presumably the problem in *Joslin* could be solved by economic adjustments (payments) between the parties.

7. *Discharge of Waste*

Although the doctrine originally gave riparians the right, and reciprocal duty, to prevent any deterioration of water quality, this absolute prohibition has given way to reasonable use principles. Almost every use of water necessarily alters the chemistry or temperature of a stream or lake either because it discharges some waste back into the stream or because the removal of water makes the stream less capable of diluting other contaminants. Consequently, it has always been a question of fact whether or not the amount of change renders a water use unreasonable. Snow v. Parsons (Vt.1856)(remanded to determine if tannery discharging waste into stream was a reasonable use).

Even where the primary "use" of the waterway is to discharge waste, it is not necessarily unreasonable per se. Borough of Westville v. Whitney Home Builders, Inc. (N.J.Super.1956). The benefits of the discharger's use must be balanced against the detriment to other riparians according to the same criteria and standards that are applied when the dispute is over the quantity of water being taken by one riparian relative to another. Where a city discharging waste is a non-riparian the same issues arise as in the case of a city diverting water for use on non-riparian land.

A riparian also has a remedy in tort for pollution of a waterway by another. Causes of action exist in trespass (for negligent or intentional interference with the possession of land to which riparian rights are appurtenant), and in nuisance (for interference with the use and enjoyment of land). To find nuisance under Restatement (Second) of Torts § 826, a court uses a balancing test to decide if defendant's conduct was unreasonable by asking whether: "(a) the gravity of the harm outweighs the utility of the actor's conduct, or (b) the harm caused by the conduct is serious and the financial burden of compensating ... would not make continuation of the conduct not feasible."

Today most water pollution is regulated by statutes under which specific effluent limitations are applied to virtually every major discharger through a permitting system. See description of federal Clean Water Act, Chapter Nine, Section V A. Violation of such limitations may show that a use is unreasonable in an action for violation of riparian rights. Arguably, the satisfaction of statutory standards should not excuse the defendant's behavior in a nuisance suit. But courts have been reluctant to impose burdens that exceed statutory limitations on discharges.

There are many non-point sources of pollution, including from agricultural irrigation, that are exempt from the Clean Water Act's permit system. They could potentially be controlled through common law action but there is a dearth of cases. It is likely that the problems of proof and multiple parties have made it not worthwhile for riparians to pursue such cases.

One who discharges sewage into a municipal sewer is usually immune from civil liability. However, in Springer v. Joseph Schlitz Brewing Co. (4th Cir.1975) the court refused to give immunity to a discharger who used the sewer for waste disposal knowing that the city could not treat the sewage adequately and without giving the city accurate information. The court applied a negligence theory.

B. Rights in the Surface of Waterways

1. *Reciprocal Rights Among Riparians*

The property rights of riparians in waters overlying privately owned beds are qualified by the common right of other riparians to use all of the water surface for transportation, fishing and other purposes. Ownership of beds of navigable waterways is discussed in Chapter Five, Section I A.

Some courts have begun to recognize a riparian's right to make recreational uses of an adjoining waterway and to enjoy its scenic beauty. In Collens v. New Canaan Water Co. (Conn.1967), plaintiffs were awarded compensatory damages and injunctive relief because defendant's pumping of river water for municipal purposes had an adverse effect upon "the recreational and scenic advantages of the plaintiffs' [river-front] property." In an action to condemn the rights of riparian owners surrounding famous Mono Lake in northern California so that the lake could be drawn down for Los Angeles's water supply, the court awarded damages to owners based on scenic and recreational values. City of Los Angeles v. Aitken (Cal.App.1935).

2. *Rights of the Public*

a. *Navigable Waters*

The rights of riparians whose lands border navigable waters are limited to the extent that public rights exist in such waters. The English common law rule allowed any person to navigate on navigable waters and to make uses incident to navigation such as hunting and fishing. This rule has been universally accepted in the United States, although the definition of "navigable waters" has varied.

The public right to navigate on a navigable river or lake clearly includes the right to use it for transportation. To accommodate increased public demand for water-related recreational opportunities, some state legislatures and courts have broadened the scope of permissible uses of navigable waters. Court decisions and statutes qualify the property rights of riparians to the extent necessary to allow these public use rights. See Chapter 5, Section I B.

Riparian landowners on navigable waterways acquire certain rights that members of the public do not have. Most important is the right to "wharf out." This allows a riparian to build a wharf for private use if the structure does not impede navigation, although any obstruction which is a purpresture (an enclosure of what belongs to the public) is not allowed at common law. If the public right to navigation is injured, the obstruction can be removed as a nuisance. Courts ordinarily apply a balancing test. Most Eastern and Midwestern states recognize a right to wharf out; Pacific Coast states do not, except by statute. A Michigan law requires state permission for any private dock. The riparian landowner also usually has a right to erect structures to prevent bank erosion.

b. *Other Waterways*

State laws recognizing public rights in waterways over private lands also may qualify a riparian's rights in lakebeds and streambeds.

Wisconsin considers title to beds of non-navigable streams to have passed to riparians subject to public rights. A Minnesota statute declares certain defined waters that are managed or accessible for public purposes to be public waters. Since colonial times in the area now in the states of Maine, Massachusetts, and New Hampshire, large, freshwater lakes known as "great ponds" (having a surface area over ten acres), although non-navigable, have been considered open to public use with

limited right of public access across private lands to
reach the ponds.

State law, legislatures, and courts may dictate the
degree of public use allowed on waterways, whether
navigable or not.   Thus, public rights in waters
overlying private beds may limit riparian rights.
See Chapter Five for a fuller discussion of public
rights.

IV.   LIMITS ON RIPARIAN RIGHTS

A.   Reasonable Use Limitation

All riparian states follow some variant of the
reasonable use doctrine.   The reasonable use rule
allows riparian landowners to use adjacent waters if
the use does not interfere with the reasonable uses
of other riparians.   Reasonableness thus is determined in comparison with the uses of other riparians.   Some riparian states also have special rules to
deal with specific problems.   They include preferences for some types of uses over others and rules
governing municipal uses. See Section III of this
chapter.

Under the theoretical limits of the natural flow
rule each riparian had right to streamflow undiminished in quality or quantity and the right to make
only limited uses of the water as it flowed past.
The rule was impractical because a riparian landowner could obtain an injunction against any person who depleted the water flowing past the land,
even if the landowner was not injured.   Thus, reasonable use principles prevailed.   Some courts use

natural flow language, particularly in disputes between riparians and nonriparians, but they rarely enforce natural flow principles. E.g., Pyle v. Gilbert (Ga.1980)(rule of natural flow applies but is "modified by the right of the upper riparian to make a reasonable use of the water").

Most riparian states have adopted statutory schemes requiring permits for certain uses in a number of situations. See Section V of this chapter. Relative rights of riparians are determined by permit-granting authorities by reference to reasonable use criteria. Courts also apply the criteria in disputes between permittees over limited water. Unlike permit systems in most prior appropriation states, in the riparian states the holder of an earlier permit has no absolute preference over the holder of a later permit.

In disputes between riparians, courts determine the reasonableness of a riparian use by comparing it with the reasonableness of the uses of other riparians. The Restatement (Second) of Torts incorporates the common law notion that reasonableness is relative. It contains two sections applicable to riparian disputes that provide an analytical framework often used by the courts:

§ 850. Harm by One Riparian Proprietor to Another

A riparian proprietor is subject to liability for making an unreasonable use of the water of a watercourse or lake that causes harm to another riparian proprietor's reasonable use of the water or his land.

§ 850A. Reasonableness of the Use of Water

The determination of the reasonableness of a use of water depends upon a consideration of the interests of the riparian proprietor making the use, of any riparian proprietor harmed by it and of society as a whole. Factors that affect the determination include the following:

(a) the purpose of the use,

(b) the suitability of the use to the watercourse or lake,

(c) the economic value of the use,

(d) the social value of the use,

(e) the extent and amount of the harm it causes,

(f) the practicality of avoiding the harm by adjusting the use or method of use of one proprietor or the other,

(g) the practicality of adjusting the quantity of water used by each proprietor,

(h) the protection of existing values of water uses, land, investments and enterprises, and

(i) the justice of requiring the user causing harm to bear the loss.

In suits between riparian landowners the reasonableness of both uses is in issue. In proving that rights have been infringed, the plaintiff's own use of the water must be shown to be reasonable. This usually calls for application of factors (a)–(d). The same analysis is used to determine reasonableness of the defendant's use.

A dispute often involves riparians who are each putting the water to good use by suitable means, producing socially and economically desirable results. But the uses are inconsistent and the court must consider additional factors (e)–(i). Factor (e) requires in effect that insubstantial, or *de minimis*, harms be borne by the complaining party. Factors (f) and (g) require the court to determine if the dispute can be settled by making adjustments. In times of drought it is reasonable to require both the water and the harm to be shared.

Factors (h) and (i) generally are applied if the defendant's reasonable use causes serious harm that cannot be avoided by adjustments. For instance, a court might require that the parties use the stream at different times. E.g., Harris v. Harrison (Cal.1892). Factor (h) is a recognition that, other things being equal, it is usually unreasonable for a new use to destroy an existing use. Factor (i) allows courts to deal with situations in which the defendant's use is of greater utility but fairness requires that the defendant pay for the harm he has caused.

In Bollinger v. Henry (Mo.1964) the court applied the § 850A factors. The dispute involved a millrace that flowed through the defendant's land and then past the plaintiffs' land. Plaintiffs had a mill on their land and used the flow of the millrace to power a mill used once a week to grind corn. The defendant diverted water from the millrace during the summer months to irrigate land. The court denied plaintiffs' request for an injunction preventing the defendant from using the millrace. Although both uses appeared to be reasonable the harm suffered by the plaintiffs was minimal in that the defendant diverted water only a few months out of the year.

B. Non-Riparian Uses

Common law rules restricted use of water to "riparian land." As explained in Section II of this chapter, riparian lands are only the portions of parcels that abut a watercourse that are within the same watershed.

1. Use Limited to Riparian Land

Some early cases enjoined water use on parcels not touching the waterbody, even those owned by a riparian within the watershed, regardless of actual harm to the plaintiff. Reasonable use jurisdictions now generally require proof of actual harm from a riparian's use of water on non-riparian land within the watershed.

2. Use Limited to Watershed

At common law, any use of water on land outside the watershed (the area draining into the waterbody) of the source of supply was unreasonable per se and actionable even if it caused no injury. The philosophical premise of the rule is that watercourses and lakes exist primarily to benefit the lands through which they flow, rather than to benefit riparian landowners. Thus it applied even to portions of tracts that lay outside the watershed. Despite adoption of a reasonable use theory, the majority of states continue to apply the watershed limitation. Strict application of the watershed limitation has been the subject of much criticism and was rejected in the Restatement (Second) of Torts § 855. Several exceptions have evolved. Apart from the exceptions, large municipal diversions from one basin to another have proceeded unimpeded by riparian law. E.g., North Carolina v. Hudson (E.D.N.C.1990)(deferring to discretion of Corps of Engineers permit for large transbasin diversion).

3. *Limitations on Rules Preventing Non-Riparian Use*

a. *Restatement Rule*

The Restatement (Second) of Torts § 855 rejects the absolute prohibition of non-riparian uses. It says that reasonableness of a water use by a riparian proprietor is not controlled by classification of the use as riparian or non-riparian. Thus use on unconnected land or land outside the watershed may be reasonable.

The Restatement rule evaluates the reasonableness of non-riparian uses relative to riparian uses, but only if the user of the water on non-riparian land also owns riparian land. Expansion of the reasonable use approach to non-riparian uses recognizes that the best economic use of water may be for agriculture, mining, manufacturing, or other purposes on land apart from the waterbody. The Restatement rule retains the somewhat artificial requirement that one must own some riparian land to use water. The formality of owning a square foot of riparian land limits the right to use water on non-riparian land to people who are riparian landowners and also may provide an argument that the extent of riparian land owned should be a factor in determining reasonableness.

The Restatement approach has been generally followed in a number of states including Georgia, Kansas, Massachusetts, New Hampshire, New York, North Carolina, Oklahoma, Texas, and Vermont. See Pyle v. Gilbert (Ga.1980). The majority of riparian states continue to apply the common law rule limiting uses to riparian lands.

b. *Requirement of Actual Harm*

Some courts allow uses on non-riparian land or on land outside the watershed in the absence of harm to another riparian. In Stratton v. Mt. Hermon Boys' School (Mass.1913) the plaintiff was a riparian who owned a mill on a small stream. The defendant was a school that owned a tract of riparian land upstream from the plaintiff, but the actual campus was on a non-contiguous tract of land about one mile from the riparian land and in a different watershed. The school transported water from the stream to its campus. The diversion lowered the volume of water in the stream available to power the plaintiff's mill, causing substantial damages to the mill owner. Although the court held that riparian rights extended only to reasonable uses connected with riparian land and within the watershed, it said recovery depended on evidence of actual injury to the plaintiff's present or future reasonable use of water.

The rule requiring actual injury remains a minority rule; most states allow recovery against any person using water on unconnected land or outside the watershed even in the absence of actual harm to the complaining party.

New York has a "harmless use law" that allows a non-riparian to divert water if no riparian is harmed. The statute protects riparians by providing that the non-riparian cannot begin to acquire a prescriptive right until the use causes unreasonable harm to riparians.

c. *Permit and Hybrid States*

The harshness of the watershed limitation is tempered by permit systems and in hybrid states. Permits may be issued for water use outside the watershed of origin. The permittee need not be a riparian landowner. In hybrid states water rights for non-riparian lands may be established by appropriation if sufficient water is available.

d. *Prescription*

Because non-riparian uses are unreasonable per se, they are adverse to other riparians. Thus non-riparian uses can ripen into prescriptive rights if they continue for the statutory period. If the jurisdiction requires actual harm before a remedy will be granted, prescriptive rights arise only if the party against whom the right is asserted has been harmed. But in states where actual harm is not necessary, a non-riparian use can ripen into a prescriptive right because a riparian could have interrupted it by seeking a judicial remedy. Prescriptive rights are more fully discussed in Section VII C of this chapter.

e. *Economic Solutions*

A non-riparian use that is relatively more valuable to society than conflicting riparian uses presumably should be allowed. The requirement that one must show actual harm to get judicial relief from non-riparian uses reflects this policy. But courts generally do not balance relative harm in deciding whether to allow a remedy to a complaining riparian; any substantial harm will suffice. Balancing harm would amount to equal treatment of riparians and non-riparians.

Transfers of water rights are restricted in most riparian states. See Section VI of this chapter. But if state law allows non-riparians to purchase water rights from riparians, or allows non-riparian use with the consent of a riparian, the new uses must be reasonable in relation to riparian uses by others.

An alternative to transfer of riparian rights is to purchase riparian land. Purchasers acquire riparian rights, along with parcels bordering the stream. Where the Restatement rule applies, riparian land ownership allows the owner's use on non-riparian land if it is reasonable.

V. PERMIT SYSTEMS

For many years the common law of riparian rights was an acceptable way of allocating water in most of the eastern states. Increased demands from urban and industrial growth began to cause problems in dry years in the middle of this century. This led several states to adopt statutory permit systems. They were designed to protect the public's interest in sustaining a reliable supply of water. The legal requirement to obtain a permit before using water is a way to limit the number and size of rights inherent in riparian property ownership. Consequently, many permit requirements were challenged, although unsuccessfully.

Most riparian states now have permit statutes, at least for larger water uses (e.g., large diversions, hydropower, municipal use): Alabama, Arkansas, Delaware, Florida, Georgia, Illinois, Indiana, Iowa, Kentucky, Maryland, Massachusetts, Minnesota, New Jersey, New York, North Carolina, Pennsylvania, South Carolina, and Wisconsin. Several also require permits for use of groundwater.

A. Applicability of Permit Requirements

Permit statutes may require anyone wanting to divert or impound water to obtain a permit from a state administrative agency. Only a few states require permits of small domestic users. A number of states exempt springs, farm ponds, and other uses having minor effect on streamflows and supplies needed by others. Even agricultural irrigation is exempt from the permit requirement in Kentucky and Maryland (up to 10,000 gal./day). Permits are required only for water use in "critical areas" in Indiana, Vermont, and West Virginia.

B. Permit Criteria

Administrative officials charged with issuing permits must choose among competing users. They decide the quantity one may divert and set the terms and conditions. They may also determine how much water should remain in a stream at a particular point in order to sustain minimum stream flows needed for maintenance of fish and wildlife and other public purposes.

All permit legislation generally establishes criteria to be considered by the permitting agency. Criteria may relate to the type of watercourse, the probable impacts of the diversion and use (both negative and beneficial), and the effects on the public. Some states set forth detailed factors to be considered. E.g., Georgia lists factors quite similar to those contained in Restatement (Second) of Torts § 850A. See Section IV A of this chapter.

Arkansas, Illinois, Iowa, Kentucky, Maryland, and Minnesota have statutes setting priorities for allocation of water resources when there is not enough water for all applicants. Domestic uses rank highest.

No state awards priority to an applicant based solely on seniority of the applicant's use but most consider established use as a factor. In Wisconsin, unless waters are deemed "surplus," (in excess of existing beneficial uses) new uses depend on the consent of any riparians who will be injured. Nekoosa–Edwards Paper Co. v. Public Service Comm'n (Wis.1959).

C. Permit Provisions

About half the permit states grant perpetual permits. In the others, a permit is for a fixed term ranging from ten to fifty years. Renewal of fixed term permits is not automatic, but in Florida and Iowa renewal applications are favored.

A permit is specific as to the location, volume and rate of diversion and the location and nature of the permitted use. Some permit statutes allow use of water on non-riparian land and out of the watershed that ordinarily would be restricted by riparian doctrine. Generally permittees are required to monitor and report on their diversions.

Permits may be forfeited if their use does not commence soon after they are granted or if use is interrupted for a statutorily fixed time. See VII D 2 of this chapter.

Iowa and Kentucky provide that permits may be modified to deal with shortages or otherwise to accommodate the public interest or property rights of others.   Seniority gives no priority in times of shortage.

VI.   TRANSFERS OF RIPARIAN RIGHTS

A. Appurtenance

Riparian rights are property rights that may be held only by owners of riparian land.   Because parties generally intend to transfer water rights along with the land, the courts have held that a conveyance of riparian land carries with it all of the riparian rights appurtenant to that land even if not expressly conveyed by the deed.   The presumption that a conveyance of riparian land conveys the appurtenant riparian rights is rebuttable.   To avoid disputes, parties generally express their intent in the deed.

Riparian rights may be reserved from the conveyance of land and conveyed to others.   Riparian rights are interests in real property as opposed to personalty.   Consequently, any grant of riparian rights apart from land must be made in writing to satisfy the applicable statute of frauds.

B. Grants and Reservations

Although riparian rights attach only to riparian land, the right to use the water may be expressly reserved by a riparian landowner in conveying part of a riparian parcel to another.   Such grants are sometimes held to be binding only as between the parties.

Reservations typically arise in two settings. In the first, a landowner divides a riparian parcel, expressly reserving the water rights that had attached to the parcel. The grantor may later convey to some other person the retained portion of the riparian parcel, granting along with it the riparian rights expressly reserved from the first conveyance. As a practical matter, the grantor who reserves water rights in such a situation will usually allow the grantee at least sufficient water to satisfy the grantee's domestic needs.

In Figure 2 O owns a tract of riparian land. O conveys the eastern half of the tract to A, but expressly reserves all riparian rights. Subsequently O conveys the western half of the tract to B, granting B all riparian rights. B has a parcel of land with riparian rights and A has no riparian rights, although both border the stream. Note that O could have conveyed the western parcel to B and separately granted the previously reserved riparian rights to A in which case both A and B would have riparian rights.

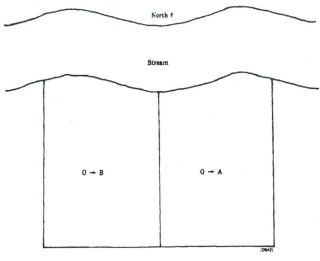

Figure 2

The second situation in which reservations are commonly used arises when a riparian landowner retains a portion of the original riparian tract that does not border on the waterbody and conveys the abutting riparian portion to another, reserving some or all riparian rights.

In Figure 3 O owns a tract of riparian land. O conveys the northern half to A, but retains the southern half reserving for the retained parcel all water rights from the entire tract. O has full riparian rights and A has none. If O subsequently conveys the southern half to B, B has full riparian rights. O could convey the southern half to B granting some riparian rights to B and some to A.

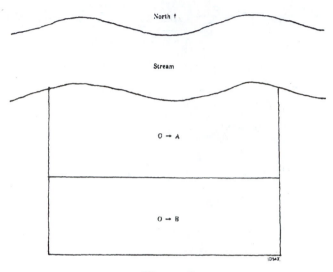

Figure 3

Conveyance of a portion of the riparian parcel not bordering on the waterbody transfers no riparian rights unless expressly granted. In states that follow the source of title rule discussed in Section II C 2 of this chapter, an express transfer of a portion of the riparian rights along with the nonriparian parcel may provide a way to circumvent the rule.

In Figure 3, assume that O conveys the southern half of the parcel to B, granting B a proportionate share of riparian rights, then the remainder of the land and water rights to A. Both A and B may have riparian rights even if the tract is in a source of title state.

The general rule is that a conveyance of riparian rights by a riparian landowner to a grantee is binding.　By making a grant the riparian owner gives up the right to divert or use any water to the detriment of the grantee.　In effect the grantor waives all claims based upon the doctrine of riparian rights and the waiver binds successors in interest.　Obviously, a riparian who grants away all riparian rights with a portion of the land cannot convey those rights with the remaining riparian land.

Although grants are valid as between the parties, a majority of states hold that grants of riparian rights separate from the grant of any portion of riparian land held by the grantor are invalid as to other riparians.　Duckworth v. Watsonville Water and Light Co. (Cal.1910).　Thus a non-riparian grantee of riparian water rights cannot object to a third party riparian's conduct even if the conduct would have been unreasonable as to the original riparian grantor.　However, a minority of jurisdictions allow the grantee any reasonable use that the grantor could have made.　In other words, if challenged by a riparian, the non-riparian grantee's use will be judged by the reasonable use rule just as if the riparian grantor were making a non-riparian use of water (See Section IV B of this chapter).　Lawrie v. Silsby (Vt.1904);　State v. Apfelbacher (Wis.1918).

The watershed limitation, discussed in Section IV B 2 of this chapter, limits a riparian's ability to grant riparian rights.　In states that hold use of water outside the watershed to be unreasonable per se, the riparian who owns a contiguous parcel (part of which is outside the watershed) and who transfers a non-abutting portion including the portion outside the watershed, cannot grant the purchaser any right to use water outside the watershed; however, many jurisdictions will not bar the non-riparian use unless others are harmed.

In Figure 4 O owns a riparian tract of land. O conveys the southern half, part of which is outside the watershed, to B, granting half the riparian rights. In states that allow water to be used outside the watershed so long as no riparian is actually harmed, O can grant B the right to use water outside the watershed and B can exercise the right so long as no other riparian is harmed.

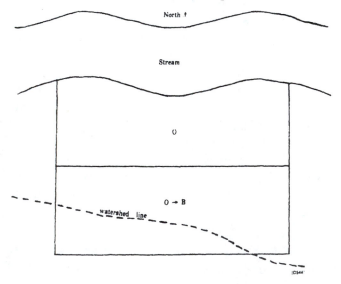

North ↑

Stream

O

O → B

watershed line

Figure 4

In Stratton v. Mt. Hermon Boys' School (discussed in Section IV B 3b of this chapter), the court said that the defendant, who owned separate riparian and non-riparian parcels, could use water on the tract outside the watershed subject to liability for any material injury to riparians. Presumably, a riparian who owns a non-contiguous tract outside the watershed may grant that tract to another with a proportionate share of riparian rights that the grantee could use in the absence of actual harm to another riparian.

In Figure 5, O owns a riparian tract of land and a non-contiguous tract outside the watershed. O grants the non-contiguous tract to A with some riparian rights. In states that allow use outside the watershed in the absence of actual harm to other riparians, A may be able to make a reasonable use of the water although the transfer of rights may technically fail.

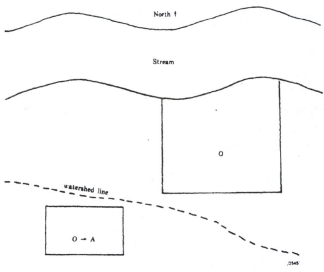

North ↑

Stream

O

watershed line

O → A

.0545'

Figure 5

VII. LOSS OF RIPARIAN RIGHTS

Riparian rights, like other property rights, can be terminated or "lost" in a number of ways. They may be extinguished by prescription, avulsion, and under permit systems. The general rule is that riparian rights cannot be lost by non-use. The rule, however, is not absolute. In most states with hybrid systems, statutes limit the right of a riparian to initiate new uses and may even declare vested riparian rights to be forfeited by non-use over a statutorily prescribed period. Statutory permit schemes that require a riparian to obtain a permit before initiating new uses effectively limit common law riparian rights. Riparian rights also may be lost by eminent domain, typically exercised by a city to secure a water supply.

A. Effect of Non–Use

Ordinarily, riparian rights are not lost by non-use. Because riparian rights attach only to riparian land, it follows that the owner of a riparian parcel also "owns" riparian rights in the adjacent waterbody whether those rights are exercised or not. As one court put it, "use did not create the right, and disuse cannot destroy or suspend it." Lux v. Haggin (Cal.1886). In prior appropriation states the rule is quite different; because the appropriative right is based on putting a certain quantity of water to a beneficial use, the failure to continue using it is evidence of intent to abandon it.

The rule that non-use (even for a long period of time) will not destroy riparian rights has often been criticized, particularly in the arid hybrid states where uses of appropriators are at risk of being disrupted by uses initiated by riparians. Hybrid states have typically adopted prior appropriation because the unmodified riparian system was inadequate to allocate water efficiently. Almost all hybrid states now have forfeiture statutes that limit the ability of riparian landowners to initiate new riparian uses after a certain date, although in most, vested riparian rights still cannot be lost simply by non-use.

B. Avulsion and Accretion

Avulsion occurs when a stream suddenly changes its channel. If avulsion moves a stream away from a landowner's property, the property boundary line remains where it was before the stream left its channel. Avulsion can effectively transform riparian land into non-riparian, thereby depriving the unfortunate owner of riparian rights. Conversely, a non-riparian landowner may suddenly gain riparian rights as a result of avulsion bringing the stream onto the owned land.

When a stream changes course over a period of many years, accretion and reliction may result. Accretion is the gradual addition of sediment to one bank along the waterline. Reliction occurs when water gradually withdraws from one side of the stream. If accretion and reliction occur, rather than avulsion, the rule is that the property boundary line shifts with the waterline so that a riparian adjacent to added land will gain title to the new land, keeping riparian rights. See Burkart v. City of Fort Lauderdale (Fla.1964). A riparian whose land is carried away loses title to that land but retains appurtenant riparian rights so long as the stream remains adjacent to the land.

Although the distinction between avulsion and accretion is not clear, most courts have held that a change in stream course constitutes avulsion if it is considerable, violent, and abrupt. Courts will consider the circumstances of the shift in channel and the consequences to the parties in deciding which rule to apply. Thus, in one case a court applied the accretion rule to a sudden shift in channel caused by the defendant's dredging and would have cut off the plaintiff entirely from stream access if the avulsion rule were applied. Strom v. Sheldon (Wash. App.1974).

C. Prescription

Typical adverse possession laws provide that the open and notorious, hostile, exclusive, actual, and continuous possession of property for a prescribed number of years vests title in the adverse possessor. Like other property rights, riparian rights can be lost by adverse possession. Obtaining a prescriptive right in riparian law turns on two factors: whether the person against whom the prescriptive right is sought is: (1) a riparian or a non-riparian; and (2) upstream or downstream from the riparian plaintiff.

Prescription has always been an important way to obtain exclusive rights to use water in riparian jurisdictions. Tyler v. Wilkinson (C.C.R.I.1827), considered the foundation case in American riparian law, stated that while "mere priority of appropriation of running water . . . confers no exclusive right . . . by our law, upon principles of public convenience, the term of twenty years of exclusive uninterrupted enjoyment has been held a conclusive presumption of a grant or right." The equities of longstanding users are thus protected in a system where prior use as such does not give rise to any rights. Of course water use for less than the full prescriptive period gives rise to no rights. Martin v. Bigelow (Vt.1827).

The natural flow theory gave each riparian the right to have the stream flow past the land undiminished in quantity or quality, subject only to the right of other riparians to limited domestic use of the water. Under this theory the prescriptive period would start to run as soon as an upstream riparian began to take more water than needed for domestic purposes. This was true even if the downstream riparian plaintiff was not actually harmed.

All states now follow some form of the reasonable use rule. When a prescription conflict is between two riparians—an upstream defendant and a downstream plaintiff—the rule is that an upper riparian's use is not adverse unless it unreasonably interferes with the rights of lower riparians. Pabst v. Finmand (Cal.1922). This rule is sensible because all riparians are entitled to make reasonable use of the water.

If a prescription conflict is between an upstream non-riparian defendant and a downstream riparian plaintiff, the reasonable use states have followed two different rules. Some courts have held that, under the reasonable use theory, if the non-riparian use does not unreasonably interfere with reasonable uses of downstream riparians, the non-riparian use cannot ripen into a prescriptive right. Other courts have held that a non-riparian use by an upstream defendant that does not unreasonably interfere with uses of lower riparians is nevertheless unlawful and can become a prescriptive right. Consequently the downstream riparian must seek injunctive relief, even in the absence of harm.

The courts have long held that a downstream user (riparian or non-riparian) cannot acquire prescriptive rights against upstream riparians. The rule is sometimes stated as "prescription does not run upstream." Its rationale is that since a downstream use cannot adversely affect an upstream riparian use, the downstream use is not hostile and cannot be the basis of a prescriptive right. For an interesting exception see Dontanello v. Gust (Wash.1915)(lower riparian acquired prescriptive right by building diversion mechanism on upper riparian's land).

To the extent prescriptive rights have been perfected on a waterway, the rights of riparians are diminished. Typically, courts (e.g., California) have recognized the right of an adverse user to a specific quantity of water based on the amount used in acquiring the prescriptive right. The right so acquired is similar to an appropriative right in that it is not diminished in times of shortage. However, some courts (e.g., Washington) have measured the prescriptive right as the proportion of the adverse use to the total flow of the river. Under this rule the adverse user would be required to reduce usage pro rata with other riparians in times of shortage.

Generally, the rules governing prescription in riparian states also apply in the hybrid states, at least as between riparian landowners. As between a riparian and a non-riparian the rules may differ because, under most appropriation systems, new (non-riparian) uses must be acquired by making an appropriation pursuant to statutory requirements. Prescription in hybrid states is discussed in Chapter Four, Section III C.

D. Legislation

1. *Statutes Modifying Water Rights*

a. *Permit Systems*

As population increased and new cities grew up far from the great eastern rivers, riparian states began to enact statutory schemes designed to promote efficient allocation of water. The most common statutory modification was adoption of permit systems discussed in section V of this chapter. Some states required permits not only for new riparian uses but also for existing uses. A few required that unused riparian rights be claimed and recognized to be valid in the future.

b. *Hybrid Systems*

Some states recognized both the prior appropriation and riparian doctrines. Because California was the first to announce its recognition of both types of rights, the hybrid approach is sometimes called the "California Doctrine." It is not truly a "doctrine," however, since important differences exist between systems developed by different states. Chapter Four discusses the development of hybrid systems. Constitutional challenges to statutory modifications of riparian rights in favor of the appropriation doctrine have been unsuccessful; they are discussed in Chapter Four, Section II C.

2. *Forfeiture Statutes*

Forfeiture is a statutory concept dictating that non-use for a specified period automatically terminates property rights regardless of the owner's intent. Many permit statutes in riparian states and in most hybrid states have provisions requiring forfeiture of riparian rights in certain circumstances. Typically one must begin using a permit within a reasonable time or forfeit it. Forfeiture may also occur if water use under a permit is discontinued for two or three years.

Conversion to statutory permit systems or to hybrid systems was intended in part to remedy the uncertainty and insecurity of the riparian system. A riparian's ability to commence any reasonable uses in the future, as well as to continue existing uses, allows great and unanticipated increases in water use. Forfeiture statutes cutting off or limiting riparian rights not exercised within a certain period of time diminish the problem. In the hybrid states of Kansas and Washington, even vested riparian rights—those the riparian has historically exercised—can be lost by a period of non-use under statutory forfeiture provisions.

CHAPTER THREE

PRIOR APPROPRIATION

I. GENERAL DESCRIPTION

The prior appropriation doctrine was developed to serve the practical demands of nineteenth century water users in the western United States. It originated in the customs of miners on the federal public lands who accorded the best rights to those who first used water. It was later extended to farmers and other users, even on private lands. Where it applies, water rights are granted according to when a person applies a particular quantity of water to a beneficial use. Those rights continue so long as the beneficial use is maintained.

Most appropriation jurisdictions consider water to be a public resource owned by no one. The right of individuals to use water under the prior appropriation system is based on application of a quantity of water to beneficial use.

The traditional elements of a valid appropriation are:

- *Intent* to apply water to a beneficial use;

- An actual *diversion* of water from a natural source;

- Application of the water to a *beneficial use* within a reasonable time.

The date of the appropriation determines the user's priority to use water, with the earliest user having the superior right. If water is insufficient to meet all needs, those early in time of appropriation (senior appropriators) will obtain all of their allotted water; those who appropriated later (junior appropriators) may receive only some, or none, of the water to which they have rights. Thus, the "first in time, first in right" concept contrasts sharply with the riparian tradition of prorating the entitlement to water among all users during times of scarcity.

A beneficial use that will support an appropriation must have a specific, stated purpose. The property where water is applied to a beneficial use does not have to be adjacent to the source and usually does not even need to be within the source's watershed. Most states allow the transfer of water away from the property to which the rights first attached if the rights of other appropriators are not harmed.

In general, water may be appropriated for any use the state deems beneficial. More economically or socially useful purposes which are commenced later in time ordinarily will not be preferred over less useful ones. Priority depends on which use was commenced earlier in time. Some state statutes or constitutions express preferences for certain uses, but they do not alter the basic principle of priority based on first use. Preferences may be used administratively in determining which potential users will be granted appropriation permits; more commonly, they are applied to grant holders of rights for more preferred uses the power of eminent domain over less preferred uses so that they can condemn water rights upon payment of compensation.

The measure of an appropriative right is the quantity that can be put to a beneficial use within a reasonable time using reasonable diligence. The right to use water does not include the right to waste it. Diverting more water than is reasonably necessary is wasteful, deprives other users, and, theoretically, should not be considered a beneficial use.

Long term failure to use appropriated water can result in loss of the right. If disuse is intentional, it may be construed as abandonment; unintended disuse results in forfeiture in some states.

Although the reasons for creating private rights to use public waters based on priority of asserting claims were short-lived, and today's uses diverse, the doctrine remains. It has, however, been tempered and modified. Although the underlying rights to most water in the West were established by prior appropriation, in nineteen states their use is governed, and new rights must be established, according to complex statutory schemes. Most require water users to have permits. Ten of those states have "hybrid" systems that employ elements of the riparian doctrine as well as the appropriation doctrine. Hybrid systems and other doctrinal variants are discussed in Chapter Four. Several aspects of riparian rights, relating principally to use of the surface of waterways, apply in all prior appropriation states. See Chapter Two, Section III.

When all legal requirements are met (e.g., diversion, beneficial use) and any other procedures specified by state law (e.g., posting, filing) have been followed, the appropriation is complete. Once a permit or decree is obtained from an administrative agency or court, the right is fully perfected.

In most states, statutes charge administrative agencies in with assuring that the appropriation is in the public interest, necessitating choices among competing appropriators based on whether the public interest will be served and, in some cases, necessitating denials or conditioning of new appropriations or changes of use. Some state courts have held that states have a "public trust" obligation not to allow water to be used inconsistently with public purposes. The public trust doctrine may negate even existing appropriations that are contrary to the public interest.

II.   DEVELOPMENT OF PRIOR APPROPRIATION DOCTRINE

The doctrine of prior appropriation that evolved into modern statutory systems can be traced to local customs and regulations developed during the nation's rapid western expansion, particularly after the discovery of gold in California in 1848. Available water sources were limited, and mining (especially placer mining) demanded large quantities of water. Agriculture to support a growing population also required water to irrigate crops on arid lands.

The common law riparian system did not meet the miners' needs because it restricted rights to those owning land bordering often scarce streams and barred use of water on other lands or outside the watershed. Furthermore, most lands were owned by the United States and miners were, therefore, essentially trespassers who assumed that they could take minerals from the public land.

Rules were developed in the mining camps to allocate the available water peaceably. The rules were similar to those adopted for the establishment and protection of mining claims on public lands: first in time, first in right. Essentially, the first user of water from a specific source held a right that would be protected against the claims of others who came later. The same system was applied to agricultural lands as homesteaders moved west. It prevented the farmers who took up land along the streams from monopolizing water that could be productively used on lands not touching any water source. This made sense in an arid region where much land—and a majority of homesteads, if not the best parcels—were far from a stream.

The United States disposed of its lands through a variety of public land laws. The territory it had acquired from foreign nations and Indian nations included nearly all the West. The government could have decided to convey the land and (riparian) water rights together. Instead, it acquiesced in the establishment of private water rights on public lands under local customs, including rights to divert water across public land to distant mining claims and irrigated tracts. Lands were then conveyed separately from these water rights, but were subject to any that were previously established.

A. Federal Statutes

1. *1866 Mining Act*

Shortly after the Civil War, proposals were made in Congress to withdraw mines from the public domain and operate or sell them to pay war debts. Western legislators in whose states private mineral exploration was rampant opposed this suggestion, resulting in enactment of the 1866 Mining Act, codified as amended at 30 U.S.C.A. § 51 and 43 U.S.C.A. § 661. A portion of the Act is quoted in Chapter Four, Section I B. The Act expressly confirmed the rights of miners and appropriators of water. It formally sanctioned appropriations of water on the public lands made before or after passage of the Act as well as rights of way for carrying the water across public lands. The Act failed to define any method of acquiring water rights from the federal government, thus deferring to established local customs, state or territorial laws, or court rulings. The law recognized the government's obligation to respect rights established with its tacit approval.

2. *1870 Amendment to Mining Act*

Even after the 1866 Act, it was not clear whether riparian landowners who obtained grants of land from the United States held riparian water rights superior or subject to claims of prior appropriators. The 1870 amendment to the Mining Act clarified that issue in favor of prior appropriators. It stipulated that anyone who acquired title to public lands through federal patents, homestead rights, or rights of preemption took title subject to any water rights, easements for water rights, or rights of way acquired by others while lands were in public ownership. These rights were good against the United States and its grantees.

3. *1877 Desert Land Act*

The Desert Land Act, codified at 43 U.S.C.A. §§ 321–329, provided that water from non-navigable sources on the public lands was available for appropriation for irrigation, mining and manufacturing purposes subject to existing rights. It applied specifically to arid lands within Arizona, California, Idaho, Montana, Nevada, New Mexico, North Dakota, Oregon, South Dakota, Utah, Washington, and Wyoming. Colorado was added by amendment in 1891.

Until 1935, western states were divided concerning whether the Desert Land Act applied only to desert lands. In that year the Supreme Court decided that the Act's acceptance of the appropriation doctrine applied to all public domain in the named states and territories. California Oregon

Power Co. v. Beaver Portland Cement Co. (S.Ct. 1935). The decision also said that the Desert Land Act severed the water from public lands, so that only water rights established under local law passed with a patent. Thus, all unappropriated waters of non-navigable sources remained open to appropriation and use according to state law. The Act is excerpted in Chapter Four, Section I B.

B. Development of Modern Systems

The appropriation system was an expedient means to encourage development of the arid West, where much of the land is distant from streams and water is limited. It rewarded those who first risked their effort and money with security for their investments.

The eight most arid states (Arizona, Colorado, Idaho, Montana, Nevada, New Mexico, Utah, and Wyoming) constitutionally or statutorily repudiated riparian rights very early and adopted prior appropriation as the sole method of acquiring rights to the use of water for all beneficial purposes. In these states statutory systems have evolved to provide for initiation of appropriations, establishment and enforcement of priorities, and water distribution.

Early in Alaska's development some riparian uses for mining purposes were allowed, but in 1966 its legislature enacted the Water Use Act, converting all riparian rights into appropriative water rights. This conversion of existing riparian rights is more ambitious than the approach taken by several other western states in which existing riparian rights were preserved to some extent after adoption of the appropriation doctrine.

Some degree of riparian common law continues to exist side-by-side with the statutory provisions of prior appropriation in California, Kansas, Mississippi, Nebraska, North Dakota, Oklahoma, Oregon, South Dakota, Texas, and Washington. These hybrid states generally recognized riparian rights but limited their expansion and recognized new rights only by prior appropriation. Hybrid systems are discussed in Chapter Four.

III. APPROPRIATIVE WATER RIGHTS AS PROPERTY

A. No Individual Ownership of Flowing Water

As a general rule, private persons do not "own" water in its natural state. Water, like fish and wildlife, ordinarily is a public resource. Governments use their police power to regulate uses of water and to conserve and allocate the resource in the interest of the public.

The prior appropriation states have all constitutionally or statutorily asserted their prerogative to administer use of water for the benefit of their citizens. Most declare that water belongs to the public or the state. These provisions assert sovereign rather than proprietary interests; they establish a state's power and duty to regulate appropriation of water by individuals.

The nature of the private property interest created by appropriation of water varies from state to state. One who lawfully diverts water for some useful purpose becomes the lawful custodian of the water, and has certain rights and duties with respect to other users and the state. Water thus should not be considered personal property while it is in canals, conduits, reservoirs, and pipes. When put into containers or held in swimming pools after being delivered to consumers, however, water may properly be treated as personal property. Some states go farther and treat all water in the hands of a beneficial user as personal property that can be bought and sold, stolen, and in some circumstances subject to taxation.

In appropriation states the property interest in water is limited to a right to divert and use a certain quantity. The right to divert water and to use it beneficially is called a "usufructuary" right, as opposed to a "possessory" right. As property, the right to appropriate water has certain standard characteristics throughout the West. Generally, the appropriative right can be used for a particular purpose on a particular parcel of land. In most states the holder of the right can, without loss of priority, transfer it to be used for a different purpose on another parcel of land or may sell the right to another party who will do so if other appropriators will not be injured. See Section IX of this chapter.

Water rights usually can be assigned and mortgaged, and cannot be taken from an appropriator by the state or federal government without just compensation. The Supreme Court has ruled that a water right is an article of commerce; thus states are forbidden to restrict unreasonably interstate commerce in such rights and Congress may legislate concerning them. The fact that the state retains an interest in the water is relevant to the question of whether state restrictions are reasonable under the commerce clause. Sporhase v. Nebraska *ex rel*. Douglas (S.Ct.1982).

Generally, it is held that an appropriator has an easement for the flow of water in the bed of the stream from which water is diverted and in the tributaries above the point of diversion. The appropriator may have legal and equitable remedies for diminution of quantity or quality of the available water.

Restrictions and regulation of use further define the property interest in water rights. States require that appropriated water continue to be used for the purpose for which it was originally taken. This purpose is determined when the priority date is established, as are the quantity, rate of flow, point of diversion, and times when water may be taken from the stream. Other regulations may concern the degree of efficiency required and restrict the pollution of the water source.

Once water has been used for its stated beneficial purpose, a portion of the water remaining unconsumed often is returned to the source by seepage, drainage ditches, or sewer pipes. At the point it leaves the control of the holder of the water right and use ceases, any private property interest in the water ends.

B. State Constitutional and Statutory Provisions

The nineteen appropriation and hybrid states assume that water in its natural state belongs to no person or entity, but rather is a common resource to be administered for the benefit of society. State control of water resources may be expressed in a constitutional or statutory provision stating that water "belong[s] to the public" (Arizona, Nevada, New Mexico, Oregon), is "property of the state" (Idaho, Montana, North Dakota, Texas, Wyoming), is "property of the people of the state" (California, Colorado, South Dakota), is "property of the public" (Nebraska and Utah) or similar language. Although state authority is typically expressed in ownership terms, the effect is essentially to assert broad police power over the resource while allowing private rights to be created in its use.

C. Statutes Limiting Riparian Rights

Statutes and constitutional provisions in nearly all prior appropriation states abrogate or limit the scope of any formerly recognized riparian rights. Ten states have instituted prior appropriation systems to replace or modify riparian rights. Riparian rights to use the surface of waterways (e.g., right of access, right to wharf out) are usually not affected. See Chapter Two, Section III B. The states generally restrict or abolish riparian rights to the reasonable use of water that were unused at the time of enactment. Compliance with statutory provisions for appropriation then becomes the sole method of acquiring water rights. States in which some riparian rights continue to coexist with rights by appropriation have "hybrid systems." See Chapter Four.

In rejecting the riparian system a common pattern has been to declare riparian rights "vested," and to fit them into the prior appropriation system according to the date of original acquisition of the riparian land from the government. Because riparian uses can later arise or expand, uncertainty as to how much water has been allocated is built into the hybrid systems. Many states have responded by recognizing riparian rights to extend only to the amount of water applied to a beneficial purpose within a designated time and by barring subsequent exercise of unused riparian rights. Such declarations obviously diminish the property right of riparian proprietors.

Challenges to statutes limiting riparian rights as takings of property requiring compensation under the Constitution have failed in most states. Some statutes are read as not applying to vested rights. In Baeth v. Hoisveen (N.D.1968), the North Dakota Supreme Court treated riparian water rights as inchoate until exercised. Thus, the rights had not vested, and no taking occurred when the right to expand reasonable use in the future was statutorily destroyed. The Kansas Supreme Court upheld legislation reducing the scope of riparian rights in order to achieve the goals of preventing (1) under-development caused by common-law owners holding water in perpetuity without using it and (2) the resultant injury to established users. It grounded broad legislative authority in the state's police power. F. Arthur Stone & Sons v. Gibson (Kan.1981).

The South Dakota court upheld a legislative modification of a riparian owner's "vested right" that limited it to "water having been applied to any beneficial use on March 2, 1955 or within three years immediately prior thereto to the extent of the existing beneficial use made thereof." Belle Fourche Irrigation Dist. v. Smiley (S.D.1970).

California's statutory adjudication procedure empowering the Water Resources Control Board to determine water rights in an entire stream system has withstood constitutional challenge even though it empowers the Board to define and limit the riparian owner's future right to use water in a stream system adjudication. This forces riparians to participate in proceedings to assert rights to future use of water and effectively enables the Board to recognize currently used appropriative rights as superior to unused riparian rights. *In re* Waters of Long Valley Creek Stream System (Cal.1979).

Riparian rights in Texas have been limited to the maximum amount used in any year from 1963–1967 by the Water Rights Adjudication Act of 1967. The Texas Supreme Court upheld the constitutionality of the provision, rejecting claims that early land grants carried vested riparian rights that are property rights not to be taken without compensation. *In re* Adjudication of Water Rights of Upper Guadalupe Segment of the Guadalupe River Basin (Tex. 1982). In Oklahoma, however, the court found a state law extinguishing the right to initiate future riparian uses to be unconstitutional. Franco–American Charolaise, Ltd. v. Oklahoma Water Resources Board (Okl.1990).

IV. ELEMENTS OF APPROPRIATION

Although the definitions and details of water rights by appropriation vary from state to state, a valid appropriation generally depends on water being *diverted* with an *intent* to appropriate it for a *beneficial use.*

At first the appropriation system was encumbered by few procedures and legal requirements. One who needed water usually had only to begin using it. But in order to perfect a legal right in the water the user had to show that the use amounted to an appropriation. The three elements—diversion, intent, beneficial use—were designed to prevent fraud and to provide some order in an otherwise unstructured system. Additionally, states have a special interest in assuring that water, as a public resource, is devoted to purposes consistent with the public good. Hence a requirement that water be applied to a beneficial use.

Historically, it was necessary for an appropriator to be able to prove that all three elements were satisfied. Now their importance is largely theoretical, since they have become incorporated into modern state water allocation statutes. Permit systems and administrative agencies that review the sufficiency of applications for water rights include requirements and criteria that achieve the purposes of the common law elements of appropriation.

A. Intent

An appropriation is not valid unless the appropriator intends to divert water and apply it to a beneficial use. Thus, one who diverts water away from its normal flow pattern in order to prevent flood damage is not an appropriator. But such a diverter who later perceives a beneficial use for the water as channeled may become an appropriator as of the time intent is manifested.

The problem of proving intent arises most frequently when one seeks to secure a priority that predates the diversion. The doctrine of relation back allows an appropriator to perfect a water right with a priority date as of the time an intent to appropriate was first formed. Evidence must be presented to prove that one had such intent and that work was proceeding toward an actual diversion of water (not just speculation) as of the priority date.

In states where a permit is required for a valid appropriation, application for a permit is objective evidence of intent. However, one may not apply for a water right and then seek a place to use it as that would constitute speculation. Lemmon v. Hardy (Idaho 1974). Early statutory systems gave appropriators the option of diverting or applying for a permit. A person could choose to divert without a permit and still relate back the priority to the time work on the diversion facilities began. Sand Point Water & Light Co. v. Panhandle Dev. Co. (Idaho 1905).

Where permits are not required for a valid appropriation, primarily in Colorado, proof of intent retains some importance. To establish the priority of an appropriation, an applicant must make a clear decision to use water and make an "open, physical demonstration of that intent." This physical act requirement is a means of giving notice to others that one intends to appropriate water though the actual diversion will be in the future.

The Colorado courts examine other relevant evidence besides the first open physical act in setting a priority date to determine whether the requisite intent was present. A survey not accompanied by a clear decision to undertake the project may not be sufficient. Colorado River Water Conservation Dist. v. Rocky Mountain Power Co. (Colo.1971)(water right dates from 1961 when final decision to build project was made, not from 1954 when survey was made). The priority date of an appropriation can be no earlier than the time an intent to divert water to put it to a beneficial use was formulated. But as the *Rocky Mountain Power* case shows, it is possible for intent to be formed after the physical act, in which case priority is based on the later of the two events. See Harvey Land & Cattle Co. v. Southeastern   Colo.   Water   Conservancy   Dist.

(Colo.1981)(drilling wells with capacity greater than old right constituted "physical act" for new water right but appropriation related back only to time, years after wells were drilled, when intent to use for larger quantity was later formed).

Colorado law provides for conditional decrees to hold rights to a particular quantity of water for a specific future use. Thus, anyone seriously pursuing a project requiring water seeks a conditional decree early in the planning. In order to get a conditional decree one must demonstrate present intent to put the water to a beneficial use and proceed with due diligence to divert the water. The applicant must describe with particularity the amount of water to be appropriated and the construction plans. Those opposing the proposed conditional decree can file objections, and the application is adjudicated with respect to the rights of all parties in the stream system.

Plans, but no firm contracts, to sell water to growing cities are not sufficient to show an intent to appropriate, but constitute only speculation. Colorado River Water Conservation Dist. v. Vidler Tunnel Water Co. (Colo.1979); Rocky Mountain Power Co. v. Colorado River Water Conservation Dist. (Colo.1982). A statute implementing this rule requires the applicant to establish that there is a substantial probability that the facilities necessary for the appropriation "can and will" be completed within a reasonable time and the water put to a beneficial use. The court has interpreted this statute, however, to allow disregard of pre-existing but not yet diverted conditional rights. Board of County Commissioners of the County of Arapahoe v. United States (Colo.1995). The same case held that environmental factors need not be considered in issuing the conditional decree (and hence in granting water rights) in Colorado.

The physical act requirement in Colorado has become something of a formality to obtain a conditional decree, with little pretense that it puts others on notice. Although the court has said that the physical act must be on the land where water will be diverted and that engineering work done in the office is not adequate, a cursory survey on the ground (that almost certainly would give no indication of the nature of one's intent) will suffice. Elk–Rifle Water Co. v. Templeton (Colo.1971). The physical act and other evidence of events showing intent may be important where the applicant seeks a priority predating the conditional decree.

B. Diversion

Some jurisdictions require that water be physically diverted from a stream in order to effect a valid appropriation. Others consider various uses that do not depend on structures or human acts, and even some instream uses, to be appropriations.

The diversion requirement historically provided notice to present and prospective appropriators that water had been appropriated. The capacity of diversion works could be used to define the quantity of water appropriated. These functions of the requirement are not important where there is a permitting process. An appropriation cannot be complete without some use of water, however, and the diversion requirement is often the last ingredient necessary to perfect a water right. In some jurisdictions it need not be satisfied by removal of the water from the stream.

1. *Types of Diversions*

A diversion is an alteration of part or all of a stream's flow away from its natural course. A common method of diversion is to build a dam across a stream, directing water into a canal or ditch. Water may be channeled farther into smaller ditches, each with a "headgate" that controls when and how much water is used in each of several parcels of land, often by several appropriators. Other methods of diverting water include reservoirs, flumes, pipes, pumps, and even water wheels.

Traditionally, a diversion had to be human-made, but courts have forged numerous exceptions as discussed below. Even in states adhering to a strict physical diversion requirement (e.g., California, Montana, New Mexico) exceptions are allowed for various water uses.

2. *Due Diligence Requirement and Conditional Rights*

In states that require a permit to appropriate water, the priority date may relate back to the date the application was filed. In order to keep that priority date and to perfect a water right, the appropriator must complete construction with due diligence and actually use the water within the time specified in the permit or statute.

Some state statutes set maximum time periods for construction of facilities and application of water to beneficial use, often five years, subject to extension for good cause (e.g., Arizona, Idaho, Nevada, Oregon, Wyoming; New Mexico allows four additional years after construction to use the water). A few require actual construction to begin within a certain time, ranging from six months to two years after approval of the application (Arizona, two years; Nebraska, six months; Oklahoma, two years; Oregon, one year; Texas, two years). Some states allow time extensions readily upon a showing that the applicant has proceeded with due diligence; others grant extensions only in narrowly defined or extraordinary circumstances. Idaho, for example, allows extensions after its five year limit only if the applicant is prevented from continuing by delays in necessary federal approvals or the completion of litigation, or if the project is extremely large.

In Colorado, which does not have a permit system, an appropriator's priority date is generally the date of an application for a conditional right. But, priorities can relate back to the first open, physical act toward appropriating water such as the date construction of diversion facilities commenced. City and County of Denver v. Sheriff (Colo.1939).

An early priority date will be lost, however, unless the prospective appropriator completes construction with due diligence within a reasonable time. A finding of due diligence involves consideration of the difficulty and expense of the work required to complete construction.

Colorado's procedure for protecting unused rights by obtaining a conditional decree is discussed in the preceding subsection. If a conditional decree is granted, the prospective user must proceed with due diligence in constructing the waterworks or risk forfeiture of the conditional right. The decree holder must obtain a finding of due diligence by a water court referee every six years. Failure to do so will result in cancellation of the conditionally decreed water rights. Town of De Beque v. Enewold (Colo. 1980). Once the diversion takes place an absolute decree can be obtained that is senior to all appropriators who commenced their appropriations after the initiation of the conditional decree.

3. *Exceptions to the Diversion Requirement*

Several states no longer require an actual, physical diversion from the stream; exceptions have been fashioned to meet particular policy considerations. A physical diversion from a stream may not be required if intent to appropriate to a beneficial use, notice to others, and actual application to a beneficial use are clearly established. For example, courts in Montana and Oregon have held that farm land can be irrigated naturally, with the help of existing channels and depressions, if it would be a waste of money to require a system of artificial ditches. California, Colorado, Idaho, and Nevada consider it to be an appropriation when ranchers allow livestock to drink water from ponds, marshes or directly from a stream. One court even said that mist from a waterfall that nourished vegetation might constitute an appropriation. Empire Water & Power Co. v. Cascade Town Co. (8th Cir.1913).

Several states have embraced a trend allowing instream (*in situ*) appropriations of water. Even where the state constitution refers to water rights as "the right to divert" such state legislation has been upheld. Nebraska Game and Parks Comm'n v. 25 Corporation, Inc. (Neb.1990). They recognize that water can be put to beneficial use while flowing in the stream itself, for recreation, hydropower, aesthetics, navigation, or simply to protect the surrounding ecosystem. See State, Dept. of Parks v. Idaho Dept. of Water Administration (Idaho 1974)(upholding a statute declaring preservation of waters in Malad Canyon for scenic and recreational purpose to be a beneficial use). An instream appropriation right generally requires that an amount of water be allowed to flow through a stretch of stream in order to protect fish and wildlife, scenic beauty, or water-borne recreation.

The following states have legislation allowing instream uses of water: Alaska, California, Colorado, Hawaii, Idaho, Kansas, Montana, Nebraska, Okla-

homa, Oregon, Utah, Washington, and Wyoming.
Instream flows generally may be appropriated or
reserved only by a state agency, although the agency may be able to act upon requests of private
individuals, other state and local agencies, or the
federal government.   The Colorado statute allows
rights to instream flow to be appropriated only by
the state board, but others can obtain a water right
that effectively protects flowing water by constructing some kind of facilities to control the stream
without actually removing water (e.g., boat chute
and fish ladder).   City of Thornton v. City of Fort
Collins (Colo.1992).

C.   Beneficial Use

The last and most important step in perfecting an
appropriation is application of the water to beneficial use. All prior appropriation states consider
domestic, municipal, agricultural, and industrial
uses to be beneficial uses.   Recognized types of
beneficial uses may be defined more elaborately by
statute or case law (see Table A).   Just because a
use is among the types listed, however, does not
mean it will be deemed "beneficial" under the
circumstances or for all time.   Indeed, yesterday's
beneficial use may be unreasonable or wasteful, and
thus impermissible, today.   Besides being the basis
of every appropriation, the concept of beneficial use
can limit the amount and manner of use discussed
in Section VII of this chapter.

BENEFICIAL USES SPECIFIED BY STATE LAW

Use:	Domestic	Municipal	Irrigation or agricultural	Industrial	Stock-watering	Power	Mining	Recreation	Fish & wildlife	Other
Alaska	X	X	X	X		X	X	X	X	manufacturing, navigation, transportation, water quality
Arizona	X	X	X		X	X	X	X	X	groundwater recharge
California	X	X	X	X	X	X	X	X	X	water quality
Colorado	X	X	X	X				X	X	
Idaho*	X		X	X		X		X		
Kansas	X	X	X	X		X		X		
Montana	X	X	X	X		X	X	X		
Nebraska*					X	X			X	
Nevada*	X		X				X	X	X	state conservation purposes
New Mexico**									X	
North Dakota			X	X	X			X	X	
Oklahoma*	X	X	X	X			X	X	X	not limited to these
Oregon	X	X	X	X		X	X	X	X	pollution abatement
South Dakota***										
Texas	X	X	X	X	X	X	X	X	X	parks, aquifer recharge. "any other beneficial use"
Utah*			X		X					
Washington	X		X	X	X	X	X	X	X	frost protection
Wyoming*	X	X	X		X	X	X	X	X	

*   No comprehensive definition furnished by statute or case law.

‡   Case law defines beneficial use as "the use of such water as may be necessary for some useful and beneficial purpose in connection with the land from which it is taken." Erickson v. McLean, 62 N.M. 264, 308 P.2d 983 (1957).

***   Statute defines beneficial use as "any use of water within or outside of the state, that is reasonable and useful and beneficial to the appropriator, and at the same time is consistent with the interests of the public...." S.D.Cod.Laws § 46-1-6 (3).

Domestic use generally includes household uses such as eating, drinking, laundering, washing, and watering a small garden. In rural areas domestic use also includes water for raising animals on a small scale, such as keeping a few dairy cows or chickens. Municipal use includes domestic use by residents, water used in operation of public buildings, and even irrigation of city parks.

Initially the range of beneficial uses was very limited. In Empire Water & Power Co. v. Cascade Town Co. (8th Cir.1913), a federal appeals court refused to consider recreation a beneficial use. The court would not allow the resort town of Cascade, Colorado to assert the right to keep the town's major attraction, a waterfall, flowing merely to retain its scenic beauty. However, the court seemed willing to allow the waterfall to continue flowing if the town could assert an agricultural use, such as misting the vegetation growing on the banks of Cascade Falls. Most states now have accepted recreation as a beneficial use. Some even specify that scenic or aesthetic uses are beneficial.

Once an appropriator puts water to a use considered beneficial by state law, the right is perfected. The right becomes absolute and its priority in times of shortage will not be defeated even by more socially important, economically more valuable, or more efficient uses by a junior appropriator. Thus, a senior user applying vast quantities of water to the unprofitable production of rice in the desert might prevent a city with a junior right from receiving desperately needed water for domestic purposes, or a highly profitable industry from taking the water that it requires.

Some jurisdictions have preference statutes creating a hierarchy of rights that allows persons seeking certain uses, primarily municipalities, to condemn rights that are being put to a less beneficial use. See Section V D of this chapter. Furthermore, modern interpretations of beneficial use require that water not be wasted by inefficient diversion works and excessive applications (e.g., more water than the crops need). These limitations are embodied in statutes and administrative regulations on the manner and quantity of water that may be put to a particular beneficial use. Section VII B of this chapter. When a change in use or transfer of right is sought by an appropriator, courts and agencies have limited the quantity of one's water rights to the amount necessary for the former uses using reasonably efficient methods.

Some states permit municipal water agencies to perfect rights in water they do not yet need so that they may justify investments in diversion facilities to accommodate future growth. In City and County of Denver v. Sheriff (Colo.1939), the Court recognized the validity of an appropriation for municipal purposes although the city leased a large quantity of water to irrigators until it was needed for municipal uses, in compliance with Colorado statutes. Most states allow municipal users to appropriate excess water for anticipated future uses without requiring that the water be used until needed.

V. PRIORITY: LINCHPIN OF THE APPROPRIATIVE RIGHT

A. Priority

Priority is the essential feature of the doctrine of prior appropriation. A person whose appropriation is first in time (the prior appropriator) has the highest priority and hence a right to make beneficial use of water superior to all others. An appropriator with an earlier priority date is known as the senior when compared to a later appropriator, who is the junior. When there is not enough water for both senior and junior appropriators, the doctrine of priority allows the full senior right to be exercised before the junior can use any water. The first user to be limited is the most junior on the list of priorities; juniors must abate their use until everyone senior to them has been served. All water rights holders are ranked according to the dates of their appropriations.

As discussed in the preceding section, the priority date may relate back to an earlier date when one first formulated the intent to appropriate or received a permit or decree for a planned future use. Thus, the doctrine protects priorities of early appropriators, providing an incentive for water users to invest in expensive diversion works by assuring them of legal protection for their water supply as against juniors, in times of shortage. But the doctrine as applied may have adverse economic consequences in its application. First, appropriators may build diversion works prematurely or unnecessarily in order to protect their early priority. Second, the appropriation doctrine often frustrates transfers of water to higher economic uses. For example, a senior may hold a reliable water right to irrigate crops of comparatively low value. If a municipal or industrial user wishes to use that water in a higher-value use, it may "buy out" the senior's water right. In practice, however, the transfer of water rights may be legally prohibited or at least inhibited by transaction costs. Ordinarily transfers are permitted only if a transferee can show other appropriators will not be injured. Legal challenges may generate such high costs that the transfer is rendered impractical, and the water rights "frozen" into a low-value use.

B. Qualifications of the Senior's Right

A senior cannot change an established use to the detriment of a junior. The courts have said that a senior is obligated to ensure a junior the same stream conditions that existed at the time the junior began using water. Farmers Highline Canal & Reservoir Co. v. City of Golden (Colo.1954). That case held that the senior could not change the place water was taken out of the stream ("point of diversion") if it adversely affected a junior. The same rule applies to a change of place, purpose, or time of the use. If, for example, an appropriator has only used water during a specific growing season, a transferee's use of the right may be limited to that season. See Section IX D 3 of this chapter.

A senior cannot waste water. Water in a stream belongs to the public, and private rights are allowed only to the extent that appropriators can use water beneficially. As a practical matter, however, one who holds a right to a specific quantity of water is rarely restricted from diverting the full quantity so long as it is not applied to different lands or different uses. States are beginning to be more rigorous in imposing regulations that prevent polluting, wasteful, or inefficient uses. Many states also limit the amount of water that one can transfer to another to the quantity that is actually needed for the beneficial use, regardless of whether one has a permit or court decree for greater rights. See Section IX D 4 of this chapter.

C. Enforcement of Priorities

Juniors may not deprive seniors of water in quantities, at times, at places, or of a quality necessary to support the seniors' use. This does not mean a senior can force the junior to stop taking water out of turn under all circumstances. A senior cannot enforce a water right if a junior can prove that the water would not be put to a beneficial use by the senior or that water would not reach the senior in usable quantities.

A senior appropriator seeking to enforce rights as against a junior "calls the river." It is usually the job of the state engineer or some other official to ensure that appropriators do not take water out of priority. If shutting down the junior will not actually result in water being delivered to the senior, however, the senior is said to have made a "futile call" and it will not be enforced by the state engineer.

Strict enforcement of priorities can cause waste. This possibility is graphically illustrated by State *ex rel.* Cary v. Cochran (Neb.1940). In *Cary* senior appropriators downstream on the Platte River sued to compel the state engineer to prevent upstream junior appropriators from interfering with their rights. Because of seepage and evaporation losses along the lengthy stretch of river between the juniors and seniors the juniors had to let 700 c.f.s. of water go by in order for the 162 c.f.s. needed to satisfy the seniors' rights to reach them. The court enforced the seniors' right to shut off the juniors but only so long as any usable quantity would reach the seniors. Requiring some water to be deliverable before the seniors' call would be heeded prevented a futile call when little water was in the stream. Yet other times the juniors were prevented from taking a substantial amount of water to allow small usable quantities to pass to the seniors.

D. Preferences

Many states have statutes or constitutional provisions that express a preference for certain types of water use over others. Typically they rank uses according to the prevailing view of the relative importance of various uses at the time the preferences were established. Almost all reserve the highest use for domestic or municipal purposes.

Although there are many variations, most put agricultural use second and industrial and mining third.

Preference laws in most states appear to require that in times of shortage those with rights for the most preferred uses receive water before those with rights for less preferred uses, but they are rarely so applied because it would upset the system of priorities based on time. E.g., Phillips v. Gardner (Or.App.1970)(legislature intended statutory adoption of prior appropriation to supersede earlier enacted preference statute). Other courts have said that application of preferences over prior rights would be a taking of property requiring compensation.

Some statutes or constitutional provisions require condemnation and compensation as the means of effectuating preferred uses—more preferred users must condemn rights of less preferred users. E.g., Idaho, Kansas, Nebraska, Wyoming. In other states, courts have given the identical effect to preference laws that appear to require preference among users in times of shortage. E.g., Town of Sterling v. Pawnee Ditch Extension Co. (Colo.1908). A few state preference laws are stated or interpreted essentially as mandates for agencies to give preference to applicants for higher water uses over those whose applications for less preferred uses are simultaneously pending. E.g., Alaska, Arizona, California, Nebraska, North Dakota, Texas. See East Bay Municipal Utility Dist. v. Department of Public Works (Cal.1934)(upholding preference favoring ap-

plicant for future preferred use over applicant for
present lower uses).

VI. WATERS SUBJECT TO
APPROPRIATION

Private rights to use water cannot be acquired in
all types of water. A state's constitution or statutes
may define waters subject to state jurisdiction and
control in a way that excludes certain waters within
the state from allocation of water rights to private
parties. As discussed in Section III of this chapter,
such constitutional or statutory provisions may describe waters of a "natural stream" as being "public property" or subject to appropriation, or they
may exclude certain types of waters (such as runoff
or seasonal floods) from the reach of state water
law. State law may also recognize greater or lesser
private property rights in various types of water
(e.g., groundwater) and define the extent to which
waters are subject to public use. Private rights to
use water are subject to state regulation of and the
manner in which they are perfected and administered.

A. Watercourses

Once water joins a watercourse it becomes subject
to state control; in appropriation states it becomes
available for appropriation to private uses according
to state law.

As explained in Chapter Seven, Section I A, a
watercourse could be defined to include not only

rivers and lakes, but every tiny brook flowing into them, all the gullies through which water flows to the brooks, the snowpack and rainfall that feed them, and the evaporating or transpiring water in the process of forming clouds. But we need not require scientists to trace water to such remote sources because it would be beyond the ability of governments to regulate these sources. Legal definitions are intended to define a point beyond which a state does not regulate water use. Usually that point is when water is not in a "natural stream."

Diffused surface water ordinarily may be freely taken and used by landowners without state regulation. Alaska, Montana, Nevada, Oregon, Texas, and Utah specifically claim broader control of waters within their states. Only Utah and Colorado construe this authority to extend beyond natural watercourses to assert state control of virtually all surface water in the state.

A "watercourse" is often defined by courts as a body of water flowing in a defined channel with a bed and banks. Generally the waterbody must have some permanence. A variety of other tests are sometimes used. Disputes are often resolved by a rule of reason.

1. *Streams*

Although requirements of a definite bed, bank, and channel are universal, resort to them rarely resolves hard cases. For example, freshets (flows due to runoff from rainfall or melting snow) may appear to be streams at least part of the year, cutting draws or ravines as waters flow toward rivers and their tributaries, but a court may require in addition that it have a continuous flow to be a natural stream. It has been held that to be a "watercourse" a stream must do more than conduct seasonal runoffs of precipitation. Yet some indisputable "watercourses" flow only intermittently and are made up solely of snowmelt and rainwater. This is especially true in the high mountains of the West where streams dry up in summer months after snows have melted. Further, some genuine streams simply do not run in great enough volume or speed to carve out banks or scour a bed. In flat areas a river may spread out and avoid cutting a defined channel, or it may meander through different routes each season.

In addition to considering the geographic characteristics discussed above, some courts resort to a functional test. In Texas the courts have asked whether the volume and regularity make it practicable to use the stream for irrigation. Hoefs v. Short (Tex.1925).

Courts tend to rest their decisions on factual determinations that escape easy classification. In State v. Hiber (Wyo.1935) the state sought to enjoin the defendant from impounding waters that flowed down a swale or draw behind a small dam because it allegedly interfered with the flow of a natural stream. The court reviewed decisions in various states that distinguished between watercourses and diffused surface water. It found some attributes of a watercourse present, some lacking. Concluding that it was not a watercourse, the court leaned heavily on the peculiar characteristics of the water flow in question, stating "[j]udging from the testimony, no one would instantaneously perceive that it is a watercourse."

This perception test ("I know a stream when I see it") may seem unworkable, but in difficult cases determining the appropriate limits of state authority, the outcome may be dictated by the practicality and utility of state regulation of the water. Presumably, the more arid the area, the more important a small flow will be and the greater the likelihood it will be found to be a watercourse in a close case.

2. *Lakes and Ponds*

The water of natural lakes and ponds ordinarily is subject to appropriation by state law. The right to appropriate water from such sources may be qualified by rights to use the surface (as distinguished from rights to consume water) that are recognized in littoral (lakeshore) landowners appurtenant to riparian land, even in prior appropriation states. See Chapter Two, Section III. For instance, an appropriator may be precluded from drawing water from a lake if it would substantially lower water level. See *In re* Martha Lake Water Co. No. 1 (Wash.1929).

3. *Springs*

The treatment of spring water varies with the state in question and with the type of spring. The laws of some states (e.g., Oklahoma) consider a spring subject to appropriation only if its flow forms a stream. Others (e.g., Arizona and Utah) make spring water subject to appropriation even if the water would remain entirely on private property. A few states regulate springs as part of the groundwater system.

B. Waters Made Available by Human Effort

Sometimes water is in a natural stream at times and places and in quantities other than would occur in nature. This may be simply because irrigation return flows delay the seasonal decline in natural streamflow, or it may be the result of massive diversions from one watershed to another. The general rule is that water that would never be available in the stream except for human efforts can be used without restriction by the person responsible for its being there, and it is not subject to appropriation until that person abandons it.

1. *Foreign and Developed Water*

Foreign or developed water would not have been in a stream without human effort. It includes imported water brought to the stream from another watershed by tunnels, canals, pumps, and other facilities. It also includes groundwater pumped from an aquifer not hydrologically connected with the stream or trapped water recovered from a mine. If groundwater is hydrologically connected with the stream it is subject to appropriation as part of the stream in many states. The rainfall from artificially-induced precipitation, i.e., "rain-making" by seeding clouds, is considered developed water in some states but not others. It may be sound policy to reward such private efforts, although it is virtually impossible to differentiate natural precipitation from the results of cloud seeding.

Imported or foreign water, e.g., from transbasin diversions, is not part of the stream and thus not subject to appropriation. City and County of Denver v. Fulton Irrigating Ditch Co. (Colo.1972). Thus, foreign water, unlike water subject to appropriation, is not subject to restrictions on recapture and reuse. Water Supply and Storage Co. v. Curtis (Colo.1987); see Section VIII C of this chapter. Similarly, such water is not subject to the change of use restrictions discussed in Section IX D of this chapter. Western irrigation practices involve repeated diversion, applications, and return flow of waters as they move downstream. Thus, successive irrigators, often relying on return flows from upstream irrigators, depend upon waters being used in essentially the same manner year after year. The reliance factor is not present, however, if water is not naturally in the stream.

Thanks to importers, appropriators may have supplies available to them at times when they otherwise would have insufficient water. For instance, in a year of low natural flow juniors below the point where a large importer ceases using water may, in effect, be using almost entirely return flows of imported water. Although such water users may benefit incidentally, they can gain no appropriative right in the imported water.

An importer, of course, can stop importing water at any time. Similarly an importer can decide to reuse the water, remove it from the stream at a different location, or sell it to others, without legal restraint. Typically the water has been obtained from another watershed pursuant to a water right in that watershed. The right is, as to the original watershed, 100% consumptive. Streams in the new watershed are used only to transport the water; it never becomes a part of the "natural stream." An exception arises if both the importing and exporting watersheds are part of the same larger watershed. In that case the water remaining in the stream below the confluence of the two sub-watersheds would belong to the stream and again be subject to appropriation.

Once an importer ceases using imported waters, they are similar to abandoned personalty. See Elgin v. Weatherstone (Wash.1923). They can be taken and used by others. Still, no right in them can arise under the prior appropriation system because they are not technically subject to appropriation. In a heavily appropriated stream the "abandoned" waters will be consumed in relative priority by appropriators who otherwise would not have the water available to them.

2. *Salvaged Water Distinguished*

Foreign or developed water would not naturally be in a stream but for human effort. Salvaged water is recovered from existing uses or losses within the watershed. For instance, if seepage or evaporative losses are prevented by human effort, fuller use could be made of it. But it is not "new" to the stream in the same sense that imported water is. Thus, salvaged water is considered subject to appropriation. It can be recaptured and reused according to rules discussed in Section VII C of this chapter, but it is subject to the priority system. In Southeastern Colorado Water Conservancy Dist. v. Shelton Farms, Inc. (Colo.1974), the court denied water rights free of all calls to applicants who had cleared water consuming plants and therefore increased river flow. The flaw in the salvage scheme seems to have been exempting the applicants from the priority system by making rights to the salvaged water the best on the stream.

C.   Withdrawals From Appropriation

Water in natural watercourses can be removed from availability for some or all forms of appropriation by state action or federal law to preserve it for some future use or for instream flows.

1.   Maintenance of Instream Flows

Protection of streamflows or lake levels for fish and wildlife, recreation, water quality, and scenic beauty is accomplished in two ways. The waters can be "appropriated" for instream uses or can be considered withdrawn from appropriation so that the instream flows are preserved from depletion by private appropriators. The first approach initially encountered the fundamental requirements of the appropriation doctrine that water be diverted and put to a beneficial use. Now several states have expressly relaxed diversion requirements, and most now consider recreation and wildlife protection to be beneficial uses. See Section IV B 3 of this chapter.

Withdrawing water from appropriation was pursued as a way of avoiding the obstacles that prevented appropriations for instream flows. Laws were passed in Oregon and Idaho early in the century that removed certain rivers and lakes from appropriation and protected them from damage by state or private projects. More recent state laws identify rivers or lakes to be protected, for example, as "recreation rivers," "scenic river areas," "wild rivers," or "free-flowing rivers" (e.g., Alaska, Oklahoma, California). Utah allows its state engineer to deny appropriation rights if they would be inimical to recreation or the natural stream environment. Arizona has no specific provision but statute and case law have recognized state power to maintain water flows. The state engineer of North Dakota has power to reserve water for maintaining aquatic life, recreation, or other beneficial uses in the future.

Washington allows administrative withdrawal of certain amounts of water from important rivers or lakes. Montana enacted the most sweeping law of this type in 1973. State, municipal, and federal agencies were given the right to apply for the reservation of waters for instream flows for fish and wildlife, recreation, and water quality. Such reservations may not exceed 50% of the average annual flow. Montana law also allows for reservations of water for future uses, as discussed in the next subsection.

Instream flows can have some protection under the federal Wild and Scenic Rivers Act, 16 U.S.C.A. §§ 1271–87. See Chapter Nine, Section V D. Congress, or state legislatures with the Secretary of Interior's approval, may designate certain river segments that contain "remarkable scenic, recreational, geologic, fish and wildlife, historic, cultural or other similar values." Once a river is designated, projects that affect its flow are restricted. But if the United States wants to protect the flow from existing appropriations it must purchase rights or exercise its power of eminent domain to purchase the rights of existing appropriators.

Statutes that remove waters from appropriation usually preserve all appropriations existing on the date of enactment. Whether police power regulations could restrict the use of existing appropriations to preserve instream flows would depend on the degree of interference. Extinguishing private rights would amount to a taking of private property for a public use and would require just compensation.

The doctrine of federal reserved water rights (see Chapter Eight) may also be applied to preserve instream flows on federal public lands or Indian lands. If the federal government reserves the public land for particular uses that require maintenance of instream flows (e.g., enough water to sustain aquatic life in a wildlife refuge, natural conditions in a park, a fishery, or an Indian reservation), the courts have held that the government has impliedly reserved rights to sufficient water to fulfill that purpose. Each reservation must be examined to determine whether reserved instream flows were essential to its purposes. United States v. New Mexico (S.Ct.1978)(water was not reserved for instream flows in national forest because fish and wildlife maintenance was not among the original purposes of the national forest reservation).

2. *Reservations for Future Uses*

Many states provide by statute (Arizona, California, Nevada, Oklahoma, Oregon, Washington) or by judicial decision (Idaho, Wyoming), or both (Colorado), that municipalities can appropriate water for reasonably anticipated needs. In most states the water need not be put to a beneficial use in the meantime. Colorado and California require that a beneficial use be made, but this can be satisfied by leasing the water for other purposes.

The 1973 Montana Water Use Act, however, allowed all levels of government to apply for water to be reserved for any future beneficial use (including municipal or irrigation). To accommodate agency planning for these future uses the legislature declared a three-year moratorium on all new appropriations in the Yellowstone River basin where applications were being made for massive appropriations for energy-related developments. No other western state has so qualified the scope of the right to appropriate water for present needs in order to protect future public needs. Kansas provides for reservation of water storage rights in federal reservoirs by application to the responsible federal agency.

VII. EXTENT OF THE APPROPRIATIVE RIGHT

The quantity of water to which one is entitled under the prior appropriation doctrine is theoretically the amount of water continuously taken and beneficially used. The quantities stated in many old permits or decrees manifesting rights of appropriators, however, are much larger than the amounts actually diverted or needed for the appropriator's purposes. This is because old paper rights often were based only on declarations of the appropriators or the capacity of the diversion works. Overstating rights is less widespread today, largely because state appropriative water rights systems are administered by professional engineers who verify claims before rights are granted.

The right also extends to a sufficient quality of water to allow a continuation of beneficial uses, however, assertion of rights under the appropriation doctrine has not been used extensively to prevent water pollution. Early cases prevented upstream miners from polluting water to the detriment of downstream seniors.

All modern appropriation systems provide that persons may object to the granting or recognition of a new right by an administrative agency or court on the ground that the right is excessive for the purposes claimed. See Section VIII of this chapter. In addition, junior appropriators may challenge water rights of a senior, claiming that some portion of the rights has been abandoned by lengthy non-use. A state legislature or court presumably could declare that rights in excess of reasonable needs for beneficial uses were not properly granted since private rights depend on water being put to a beneficial use.

A. Measure of the Right: Beneficial Use

Beneficial use is said to be the basis, the measure, and the limit of the appropriator's right to use water. Before development of modern administrative systems, an appropriator claimed a right to use a certain quantity of water. Usually the only limit on the claim was the capacity of the diversion facilities. See Fort Morgan Land & Canal Co. v. South Platte Ditch Co. (Colo.1892). This was based on the reasonable assumption that one would not go to the expense of building ditches with a capacity far greater than was necessary. In fact, it sanctioned excessive claims because most appropriators built oversized ditches to be certain they had sufficient capacity. Further, they did not use the ditches continuously during every irrigation season although they sometimes claimed rights to do so. Challenges to an appropriator's claim were rare.

Most overclaimed and sometimes the claims on a stream amounted to many times its total flow. Only in extreme cases did a court find that an appropriator's right exceeded beneficial use. E.g., State *ex rel.* Erickson v. McLean (N.M.1957)(uncontrolled flooding of grazing lands for 24 hours a day is not a beneficial use).

Now the statutory systems of all states include administrative mechanisms for verifying amounts of water that are to be put to a beneficial use before rights are embodied in a permit or decree. Many systems provided for review of old rights and required persons claiming water rights to justify their claims before recognizing the rights in a new permit or decree. This usually was not a rigorous process demanding exacting proof, but it caught some flagrant abuses.

Adjudications of all existing rights throughout large watersheds are now underway in Arizona, Idaho, Montana, and Washington. They typically require holders of existing rights to prove their existing uses and they apply standards intended to check inefficient use. All competing users may participate before the responsible agency or court and object to appropriations of excessive quantities of water.

A water right once manifested in a permit or decree is rarely disturbed. Change of place or purpose of use or of point of diversion requires permission by an agency or court. No change in use may be made if it results in harm to other appropriators.

In assessing harm, the agency or court may deny the application if the change will result in an increase in the amount of water that has historically been put to a beneficial use. Thus, the quantity of the right may be reduced to less than the amount of the original appropriation. The same process is followed when one appropriator seeks to transfer a water right to another. Historical use may be limited to the amount of water actually required for optimum beneficial uses of the kind made. The historical use approach could be equally useful in showing that one has abandoned the unused portion of a water right. In fact there are few reported cases in which a court or administrative body has found partial abandonment on this basis.

B. Beneficial Use as a Limit

Appropriative rights extend only to beneficial use, and therefore there is no right to use water wastefully. State laws and court decisions interpret "beneficial use" as requiring that water use be "reasonable" or "reasonably efficient." Standards for reasonableness or efficiency change as the demand for scarce western water grows and conservation technology improves leading to stricter regulation.

Because there is no vested right to waste water state regulation of water use can restrict the amount of water used to amounts less than a permit or decree provides and to means of diversion and manner of application other than were used historically. When the California State Water Resources Control Board found that hundreds of thousands of acre-feet of water were being lost by inefficient delivery and distribution systems in the Imperial Irrigation District it required major conservation efforts, substantially changing the district's use of water. The district challenged the Board's order as an interference with vested property rights to continue long-standing uses. The court held that since the district's wasteful use was "unreasonable," it had no vested rights to continue its water use. Imperial Irrigation Dist. v. State Water Resources Control Board (Cal.App.1990).

Some state laws promote efficient use of water. Several impose absolute "duty of water" limits on the amount or rate of irrigation diversions for certain land areas. Others require that appropriators divert, transport, and use water reasonably. States are also beginning to require the use of water conserving devices such as low-flush toilets.

The basin-wide general stream adjudications of water rights occurring in states throughout the West provide opportunities for examining the quantity and manner of water use. Existing water users are typically required to prove their water rights by showing the amount of water they have historically put to beneficial use. Besides providing evidence that they have actually diverted a quantity of water, the use must be beneficial, i.e., consistent with actual necessities under the circumstances. Thus, the Washington court affirmed a determination that reduced the water rights of a user to half of the amount historically diverted because the delivery system was highly inefficient. Washington Department of Ecology v. Grimes (Wash.1993). The court found the limitation justified based on statutory definitions speaking in terms of "reasonable use" and "usual methods" of irrigation. Because a vested property right could exist only to the extent of beneficial use, the limitation was held not to constitute an unconstitutional taking.

1. *"Duty of Water" Limitations*

Irrigation uses account for 90% of all water withdrawals in the West. Water is sometimes applied to land far in excess of what crops can use; thus an early approach was to limit the volume or rate of water use on an acre of land based on a presumption of the maximum quantity or rate of flow required in the area. This limit is called the "duty of water." South Dakota, Wyoming, and Nebraska, for example, allow an appropriator to apply water at a rate of no more than one cubic foot per second (c.f.s.) for every seventy acres irrigated. Idaho allows appropriations of 1 c.f.s. for every fifty acres, and North Dakota allows 1 c.f.s. for eighty acres. In addition North Dakota, South Dakota, and Nebraska allow a volume of no more than three acre feet of water to be used each year for each acre of land. New Mexico requires the amount of water appropriated for irrigation to be consistent with good agricultural practices. Rates or volumes are determined according to informed judgments of the maximum amounts of water needed for agriculture in the area and the maximum rate at which it could be applied without waste considering soil conditions, climate, crops, and other relevant factors. State engineers and courts also consider the duty of water when they review applications for new appropriations or changes in use.

If a duty of water statute unreasonably limits the ability of the appropriator to make the beneficial use that is the basis of the right, the law may constitute an impermissible interference with vested water rights. In Enterprise Irrigation Dist. v. Willis (Neb.1939), the Nebraska Supreme Court enjoined enforcement of a state law limiting irrigation appropriations to 1 c.f.s. per 70 acres of land and 3 acre feet per acre per year against an appropriator who had perfected greater rights before passage of the act. Although the opinion broadly disapproved of applying a statute enacted after the water right was perfected to limit exercise of the right, it can be read as limited to the circumstances of the case. There was evidence that crops reasonably required more water than the duty of water allowed and enforcement of the limitation would result in crop losses.

2. *Reasonably Efficient Means of Diversion*

The earliest cases invoking the beneficial use doctrine to prevent wasteful uses involved inefficient diversion and conveyance facilities and stream pollution.

Many cases hold that facilities for diversion and transportation of water must be reasonably efficient. Easy cases concern facilities that are absolutely wasteful. For instance where ⅞ths of the water diverted by an appropriator was lost to evaporation, evapotranspiration, and seepage in a 2.5 mile open ditch the court said it was an unreasonable waste. Erickson v. Queen Valley Ranch Co. (Cal.App.1971). More difficult cases involve facilities and uses that are inefficient compared to those of other appropriators.

In an early case the Supreme Court refused relief to a party whose waterwheel, used to remove water from the Snake River to irrigate 429 acres, was inundated by the defendant's downstream dam which was part of a project to irrigate some 300,000 acres. Schodde v. Twin Falls Land & Water Co. (S.Ct.1912). One of the Court's alternate holdings was that an unreasonable and inefficient means of diversion could not interfere with the reasonable use of water by others. *Schodde* suggests a balancing of the utility of each appropriator's use.

State courts generally insist only that a senior have a reasonably efficient means of diversion, judged by standards applicable when the diversion works were built. Thus in State *ex rel.* Crowley v. District Court (Mont.1939), the court upheld the right of a downstream senior appropriator to insist that upstream juniors leave sufficient water in the stream to reach the senior's rudimentary, turn-of-the-century wing dam. Water in the stream was adequate but to divert it would have required modification of the senior's diversion dam. A few states, such as Oregon, take the approach that diversion facilities efficient enough to support a water right at the time they are built nevertheless may have to be made more efficient as conditions and technology change. E.g., *In re* Willow Creek (Or.1914).

Economic theory indicates that water use will become efficient whether the burden of efficiency is placed on the senior or junior. Under the *Crowley* rule, if greater efficiency by the senior would benefit the junior appropriators, the juniors would pay the senior to make the needed improvements or buy out the senior's rights. If the Oregon rule applied and the senior had to bear the burden of upgrading the diversion facilities to modern standards, the senior would either make the expenditure or buy out the juniors. If it was not to the senior's advantage to do so, the senior would sell to the juniors. In practice, transaction costs may be barriers to moving water to efficient use in these ways. Other factors may also impede market responses. Devotion to a lifestyle or a location, stubbornness, immobility, disparity in size of use, and other causes of resistance may prevent sound economic decisions. Thus legislatures and courts seek rules that maximize efficiency.

The statutes of some states (e.g., Alaska, Colorado, Idaho, Oregon, South Dakota) require water facilities to be reasonably efficient. Decisions of most courts confronting the issue also support the requirement of reasonable efficiency. For instance, the Idaho court refused to apply the rule applicable in some states (e.g., California) that the quantity one is entitled to appropriate is measured at the place of use. Instead, it held that one's entitlement should be measured at the point of diversion. Glenn Dale Ranches, Inc. v. Shaub (Idaho 1972). In this way losses from inefficient facilities are borne by the diverter. If the loss through diversion facilities (by evaporation, leaky ditches, weeds and trees, and so on) is great enough the appropriator will find it economical to repair and improve the ditches.

A novel case illustrates the modern thinking concerning the need for more efficient facilities and use. In A–B Cattle Co. v. United States (Colo. 1978), the Colorado Supreme Court refused to recognize the right of appropriators to insist on a certain silt content in their water. The presence of silt in the water served to seal unlined earthen canals and ditches and prevent seepage losses. When the federal government constructed a dam on the river, the silt settled out. The clear water released from the dam seeped from the ditches more readily, resulting in less water being delivered, and the appropriators sought damages. But the court found that they had no right to maintain earthen ditches; the right was solely to divert a quantity of water. Citing the principle of maximum utilization of water it suggested that at some time in the future, the maximum utilization principle may qualify the notion of beneficial use to require installation of pipes or lining of irrigation ditches.

The Colorado decision anticipates incorporation of economic considerations into the beneficial use doctrine. A later case indicated that the state engineer should require optimum utilization of water through the rules and regulations made upon a consideration of "all significant factors, including environmental and economic concerns." Alamosa–La Jara Water Users Protection Ass'n v. Gould (Colo.1983). The court held that rules could require seniors to construct wells to divert stream water for themselves rather than preventing juniors from taking water from the stream to protect the seniors' diversions.

It should be noted that there are legal rules in the appropriation system that inhibit efficient uses. For instance, reuse of salvaged water may be restricted as discussed in the next subsection of this chapter. The problem is compounded by the fact that changes in use of water are sometimes inhibited by the no harm rule and other restrictions that prohibit or increase transaction costs of transfers that could improve efficiency. See Section IX of this chapter.

Use of the beneficial use doctrine to force efficient water use is bound to be an area of increased activity. Junior water users will challenge wasteful (including relatively unproductive) senior uses. Recreationists may seek to invalidate excessive diversions to maintain more water for streamflows. And water administrators are already under greater public pressure to insist on efficient use through their regulations and administration of water laws. The issue is what degree of efficiency should be required for a water use to be "beneficial." This involves assessing available technology, economic analysis and, ultimately, comparing relative efficiencies of competing users.

3. *The Expanding Concept of Beneficial Use*

Water is a public resource but rights to use it may be appropriated by private parties so long as the use is "beneficial." This essential idea of beneficial use ensured that water was not wasted. Historically, this meant that private people could not have rights to water that they did not use productively, that they used excessively, or that they used in a way that harmed others. Modern cases emphasize the dynamic nature of beneficial use. Inefficient diversions and ditches that once were acceptable may no longer be acceptable.

The doctrine of beneficial use is also viewed by some modern courts as a relative concept. As water becomes scarcer the negative consequences of allowing less socially valuable uses of water come into question. In Environmental Defense Fund, Inc. v. East Bay Municipal Utilities Dist. (Cal.App.1975) it was argued that the state's constitutional provision requiring reasonable and beneficial use of water could be the basis of claims that the application for water rights would result in misuse because the applicant was not reclaiming its *existing* water supply, and because choosing an upstream diversion point would prevent multiple uses that could occur if they took water out downstream.

The beneficial use doctrine can provide a means to account for changing values. The public's greater understanding of the physical environment, and the resulting importance of protecting fish and wild-life and functioning ecosystems, influence decisions about water allocation and uses. In addition, there is a wider array of competing uses and the benefits produced by them—both non-economic (beauty, spiritual fulfillment) and economic (recreation).

C. Recapture and Reuse

Water is "reused" multiple times. Agricultural water is diverted, spread on fields, and then some is returned through tail ditches or by seepage to a stream. Municipal water is usually returned as treated (or untreated) sewage to a waterway, where others may divert and use it. These return flows become supplies for other water users to appropriate. Maximizing the number and extent of uses promotes efficiency and is an important conservation goal. A legal question arises, however, when an appropriator seeks to recapture and reuse water without initiating a new appropriation.

Waters originating within the watershed generally can be recaptured and reused by an appropriator if: (1) the total used does not exceed rights under a permit or decree; and (2) the recapture and reuse occur within the land for which the appropriation was made. No such limits are imposed on reuse of foreign waters imported by an appropriator. Stevens v. Oakdale Irrig. Dist. (Cal.1939); Water Supply and Storage Co. v. Curtis (Colo.1987).

Recapture and reuse of water encourages conservation and maximum utilization of water. Much of the water diverted for irrigation is not consumed by crops. It may be needed to saturate the soil sufficiently for the plants to benefit from irrigation. It is also used to transport water actually used through ditches subject to seepage and evaporation. This is called "carriage water." In addition to carriage water needs, more water is often applied than is necessary because irrigation practices are notoriously imprecise, farmers may not know exactly how much water the crops require and, if they did, their ability to measure it usually would be limited.

Most unconsumed water seeps into the ground or goes back to the stream as waste or return flow and is appropriated and put to use by others. Such water is not truly "wasted" in the sense that it cannot be used by anyone. Still, significant amounts of water used in irrigation become unusable by becoming "trapped" in marshy areas or as unrecoverable groundwater or by flowing away from the stream. Much is lost by evaporation from open canals or transpiration through unwanted (non-crop) plants that draw water out of the earth. Because millions of acre-feet of water are "lost" annually, states are seeking ways to encourage greater efficiency through reuse and other methods.

1. *Total Use Must Not Exceed Water Right*

Typically one uses only a portion of the total water diverted and returns the rest to the stream. Water rights are usually expressed as a maximum amount or rate of flow that may be diverted for a certain use on specific land. A right may also be limited by the amount that may be consumed. Within these limits, consumption may be increased by reuse so long as nothing occurs that would constitute a change of use—a change in the place, purpose, or time of use, or the means or point of diversion. Thus, an appropriator ordinarily may "recycle" irrigation return flows or capture seepage and use it within limits imposed by state law.

The upstream appropriator's increased efficiency or reuse of water on the original land can reduce the downstream appropriator's supply. Downstream appropriators often are dependent on the upstream appropriator's "waste" as a source of supply. If the increased consumption came about by a change in use it would not be allowed to harm other appropriators. But when it is the result of recapture and reuse or conservation measures on the same land it will be permitted without regard to harm caused to others so long as the amount diverted (and the amount consumed if it has been quantified) does not exceed one's "paper right" (i.e., the amount specified in a permit or court decree). The applicable principle is that a junior appropriator who depends on a senior's waste as a source of supply is subject to the waste being curtailed. See Thayer v. City of Rawlins (Wyo.1979). Indeed, the Arizona Supreme Court has ruled that cities may sell sewage effluent for reuse by others to the detriment of water users downstream of the former sewage return. Arizona Public Service Co. v. Long (Ariz.1989).

The Colorado Supreme Court has held that one may not enlarge a decreed right by means of a novel water salvage technique. In Southeastern Colorado Water Conservancy Dist. v. Shelton Farms, Inc. (Colo.1974), a landowner removed streamside phreatophytes (plants that consume large amounts of water) and filled in marshy areas. The court recognized that the increase in phreatophytes over the years had gradually deprived many junior users of the water to which they were entitled. Since the saved water was originally in the stream and had been appropriated by juniors, the court held that it was error to create a new and senior right in it. See also R.J.A., Inc. v. Water Users Ass'n of Dist. No. 6 (Colo.1984) denying an expansion of a senior water right to include water saved in draining a 3000 year old peat bog. Thus the water belonged to the stream and could not be used to enlarge an existing right. Presumably the court would have allowed the senior in each case to have rights to the water if its source had been the senior's diversion and the total amount of the senior's right was not enlarged beyond the decree. The senior also could have made a junior appropriation of the water added to the stream.

2. *Reuse Limited to Original Land*

The general rule is that one may recapture and reuse seepage and "waste-water" so long as it is within the original land and for the original purpose of the right. Cleaver v. Judd (Or.1964); Estate of Steed (Paul) v. New Escalante Irrig. Co. (Utah

1992). Such waters may be used on the same land
to increase yield. But one may not reuse on an
adjoining parcel water saved by lining irrigation
ditches. Salt River Valley Water Users' Ass'n v.
Kovacovich (Ariz.App.1966). Of course, if the diversion point, means of diversion, or place, time, or
purpose of use is changed a reuse will be allowed
only if no harm occurs to other appropriators. See
Section IX of this chapter. Once the water leaves
the appropriator's land and is in or destined for a
natural stream, it may be subject to appropriation
by others. Fuss v. Franks (Wyo.1980). Some
states qualify this rule, requiring that the appropriator must have intended to recapture the water
when it was appropriated and must actually recapture it within a reasonable time or else the water
will be considered abandoned to the stream. Jones
v. Warmsprings Irrig. Dist. (Or.1939). A minority
of jurisdictions hold that waters that enter a stream
or seep into the ground, even while on the original
land, are not subject to recapture and reuse. Fort
Morgan Reservoir & Irr. Co. v. McCune (Colo.1922)
(seepage from dam on owner's land was destined for
stream and could not be recaptured).

The rule allowing recapture and reuse of salvaged
water on the original land can result in more water
being consumed. For instance, if a water user is
consuming less than the permitted amount of water
and plants a more water-intensive crop or puts in a
more efficient irrigation system, most or all of the
water that had previously been returned to the
stream might be consumed. This can deprive other

appropriators of water on which they depend but it is allowed since it is technically within the terms of the original appropriation.

Water that is salvaged by using less water-intensive crops or more efficient irrigation systems may not be used on other than the original land or for new purposes (e.g., industrial instead of agricultural) without permission. This is true notwithstanding the fact that the salvager may not be using the full quantity of water allowed under the original appropriation. These types of salvage are considered changes of use and are subject to the no harm rule discussed in Section IX D 1 of this chapter. The rule disallows changes of use that deprive juniors of a senior's return flows which supply their appropriations. E.g., Comstock v. Ramsay (Colo. 1913).

The amount of water that may be put to a changed use is limited to the quantity of water one historically used, even if there was a paper right to use more. This protects other appropriators' expectations. Procedures for making such changes may be burdensome. To encourage more efficient water use some states (e.g., California and Oregon) have passed laws facilitating the use of salvaged water on other land or for new purposes.

The advantage to an appropriator of being able to recapture and reuse water on the land benefited by the original use is substantial when the principle is applied to irrigation districts or federal water projects having extensive geographic scope. See Department of Ecology v. U.S. Bureau of Reclamation (Wash.1992)(federal reclamation project irrigating lands in Columbia River basin retained right to recapture waste, seepage, and return flow throughout project area).

If any person, including the original appropriator, intercepts seepage water that has left the land, it is considered a junior appropriation subject to the rights of all prior appropriators. An appropriator of seepage water remains at the mercy of the person whose activity makes the seepage available. The original appropriator may cause the seepage to stop by making more efficient use of it, by lining, relocating, or abandoning a canal or reservoir, or by ceasing the appropriation without liability to the seepage appropriator. Bower v. Big Horn Canal Ass'n (Wyo.1957).

VIII. PROCEDURES FOR PERFECTING AND ADMINISTERING RIGHTS

A. Early Systems

1. *Prestatutory Period (1840–1870)*

Appropriation of water began several years before statehood in most western states. Miners developed customs and rules for water appropriation whose basic principles were relatively uniform throughout the mining camps. Rights and procedural customs of the prior appropriation doctrine were incorporated into the common law of water rights by the early territorial and state court systems. A miner's right to get water depended upon two acts: posting notice at the point of diversion and diverting the water to apply it to a beneficial use.

The quaint system of appropriation that spread throughout the West reflected the independent-minded miners who conceived it. There was no administration required, no central authority, not even records. But there were conflicts. Courts were called upon to resolve disputes between appropriators competing for the right and priority to water. Litigation, however, was determinative only of the rights of the parties, not of all users of the same water sources. In several states the courts allowed a plaintiff to join all persons claiming rights in a stream in a lawsuit to determine water rights of them all. This approach was unsatisfactory because of its expense, slowness, and difficulty. Further, the resulting decrees were not compiled or easily available to prospective appropriators in search of unappropriated water.

2. Early Statutes

The first state to enact a statutory appropriation procedure was California in 1873. The California statute simply gave legislative sanction to the methods of appropriation previously developed by local custom. It required: (a) posting notice of quantity, purpose, and place of use of water at the diversion point; (b) recording with the county within ten days; and (c) completing the appropriation and applying it to a beneficial use with due diligence. A diligent appropriator was given a priority date relating back to the time of posting notice.

Statutory systems discouraged applications for permits in streams the administrator found to be overappropriated, and served to warn developers of the risks involved. In some states such as Oregon the legislation resolved conflicts between appropriative and superior riparian rights.

Many early statutes anticipated that water users would later have their rights acknowledged by a court. Adjudication of rights could occur many years after rights were established or, under some statutes, not at all.

3. *Problems With Early Statutes*

The early statutes had several critical weaknesses. Statutory procedures were not exclusive; a water right held under the common law appropriation doctrine was just as valid. This left many water rights unrecorded, and those that were recorded were not filed centrally. On a stream that ran through several counties anyone searching the records had to go to all the county courthouses in the stream basin. This lack of centralized record-keeping made day to day administration difficult. Existing records were unreliable, even as to those who did file. People tended to file for excessive amounts of water, and there was no reasonable way to determine if they had actually applied that quantity to a beneficial use. The posting and filing method caused insecurity for investors. Not only were there evidentiary problems in proving the extent of a water right, but the uncertainties in the court-administered relation back doctrine meant a developer could not be sure of the priority date of a project. Adjudication procedures were slow and left uncertainty about the availability of water for appropriation, sometimes for many years.

B. Current Permit Systems

1. *Purpose*

All western states have statutory systems to allocate and administer rights to use water. Every state but Colorado has vested authority in an administrative agency. Colorado has a judicial system whose function is similar to agencies in other states.

The chief purpose of administrative procedures is to provide an orderly method for appropriating water and regulating established water rights. Some states allow appropriators the options of applying for a permit or perfecting a common law appropriation by posting notice and diverting water. More typically, state law requires a permit as the exclusive means of making a valid appropriation. Wyoming Hereford Ranch v. Hammond Packing Co. (Wyo.1925).

2. *Constitutionality*

a.   *Source of Authority*

The authority to enact and enforce permit systems is rooted in the broad police power of the state. Water is usually subjected to public control by state statutes or constitutions. Although the state's interest may be expressed in property terms, it is not one of ownership but of sovereignty. See Section III of this chapter. Individual interests in the right to use water may become private property which, like all other private property, is subject to the police power of the state. The definition of property rights, too, is the prerogative of the state. Whether a permit system provides adequate protection for earlier vested rights has been raised and, generally, resolved in favor of the state in the same manner as challenges raised by riparians whose rights were curtailed by the institution of appropriation law. See Section III C of this chapter.

b. *Separation of Powers*

Most state systems for administration of water rights include an adjudication process that casts an administrative body or official in a quasi-judicial role. All systems provide for court review either by appeal or as the last step in the water rights determination process.

Water users have challenged the mixed executive and judicial role of agencies. As early as 1900, the Wyoming Supreme Court ruled that the Board of Control's adjudication of relative water rights was primarily administrative. The court reasoned that the agency was actually determining evidence of title to the right; claimants were not seeking redress for injury. The court further held that even if the board acted judicially, the power was quasi-judicial, and thus a proper delegation to an administrator or board. Under most statutes a water user also has recourse to the courts if a state official's actions may impair a substantial property right. Farm Investment Co. v. Carpenter (Wyo.1900). Nebraska enacted a statute similar to Wyoming's, including a provision holding a decree to be final unless appealed to the courts. The Nebraska court upheld the law, stating that the duties of the agency were supervisory and administrative, not judicial. Crawford Co. v. Hathaway (Neb.1903).

Oregon has a mixed judicial and administrative system in which an administrative determination is made by the state engineer and filed in a court which presides over appeals, makes further modifications, and grants final approval. The Oregon Supreme Court held the duties of the engineer to be "quasi-judicial in their character," and the findings only "prima facie final and binding." *In re* Willow Creek (Or.1914). The U.S. Supreme Court held that proceedings before the Oregon engineer and court were not unrelated but part of a single proceeding, earlier stages of which are before the administrative agency and later ones before a judicial tribunal; that the preliminary proceedings merely paved the way for court adjudication; and "that the state, consistently with due process of law, may thus commit the preliminary proceedings to the board and the final hearing and adjudication to the court." Pacific Live Stock Co. v. Lewis (S.Ct.1916). See also United States v. Oregon (9th Cir.1994).

The Texas Supreme Court held unconstitutional a 1917 water rights statute, which was similar to Wyoming's, pointing out that although the state constitution in Wyoming was ample authority for such a system, Texas had no similar constitutional provision. The executive branch was given powers belonging to the judicial branch without the necessary constitutional mandate. Texas later adopted such a constitutional amendment and a system similar to Oregon's. It was found not to violate separation of powers or to constitute a taking. *In re* Adjudication of Guadalupe River Basin (Tex.1982).

3. *Permitting Procedures*

The first permit system was adopted by Wyoming in 1890. All appropriation states except Colorado have statutes requiring permits to appropriate water. The Wyoming act divided the state into four water divisions and established the office of state engineer to collect stream records, make surveys, and provide staff support to the Board of Control. The Board of Control adjudicates all claims and administers the permit system. Under most statutory permit systems a permit will be approved if an applicant follows prescribed procedures and if the state engineer finds that there is unappropriated water and that the appropriation is not detrimental to the public welfare.

a. *Filing*

In all permit states a formal written application for a permit to take unappropriated water must be made to the state engineer or an administrative body such as the Department of Natural Resources or Water Resources Control Board. This is almost always the exclusive way to obtain a water right, and must be done before any physical act such as digging a diversion ditch. The time of filing generally becomes the priority date if all later requirements are met.

Montana's water law is typical. Data that must be included under the Montana law include the name of claimant and watercourse, quantity of water, time of use, legal description of point of diversion, purpose of use, date of application to beneficial use, and any applicable support such as a map, plat or aerial photograph.

b. Notice

Typically a notice of filing the application must be published and efforts must be made to contact all affected parties, who have a fixed time in which to file objections. Objections are to be based on an allegation that statutory criteria for issuance of a permit are lacking.

c. Hearing

The administrative agency holds a public hearing on properly filed objections, serving notice of the hearing on the applicant and objector. The state engineer or equivalent official investigates factual data upon which the agency relies and reports to the agency on whether the statutory criteria were satisfied. The agency then approves, disapproves, or approves with modification the permit application. The applicant has a right to due process, i.e., to present any pertinent evidence. The agency's findings may then be appealed to the courts.

d. Issuance of Permit

The next stage of the process is issuance of a permit. A permit is not a water right but will ripen into one if all conditions of the permit are met. During a stipulated time period the permittee is required to construct diversion works, make a diversion, and apply water to a beneficial use. The application to beneficial use is the act that causes a water right to vest; the priority will then relate back to the act of filing. Typical permit conditions include compliance with the time periods stipulated and "due diligence" in completing a diversion project. All states allow extensions of time limits for cause.

Most responsible administrative agencies may impose permit conditions that dictate how the water right is to be exercised. The California statute, for instance, authorizes the State Water Resources Control Board to permit the appropriation for beneficial purposes of unappropriated water under "such terms and conditions as in its judgment will best develop, conserve, and utilize in the public interest, the water sought to be appropriated." Considerable discretion to fashion conditions is allowed. They will be set aside only if a court finds them to be unreasonable or not based on substantial evidence. East Bay Mun. Utility Dist. v. Department of Public Works (Cal.1934). In Bank of America National Trust & Savings Ass'n v. State Water Resources Control Bd. (Cal.App.1974), a permit condition requiring the applicant to keep a proposed reservoir open to the public for recreational uses was rejected. The court held that there was no substantial evidence in the record of the need for such a condition.

In addition to regular permits, temporary and seasonal permits are issued by some states. In California such permits create no vested rights and may be issued if there is unappropriated water available, and no harm to downstream users or unreasonable harm to the environment will occur.

The final document issued in the permit process in most states may be called a "license," "certificate," "certificate of appropriation," or "water right certificate." The administrator makes an inspection to see if the water has been applied to a beneficial use and the statute complied with. The certificate is similar to a deed in that it defines the extent of a property right in water. It also may be recorded like a deed.

4. *Statutory Criteria*

The permit procedures discussed above are to determine whether certain criteria set forth in the statute have been satisfied. In Montana the criteria require evidence of:

a.   a beneficial use;

b.   availability of unappropriated water at the time and period of use;

c.   no harm to prior appropriators;

d.   adequate diversion facilities; and

e. no interference with reservations of water for future use or other planned uses.

The requirement of available unappropriated water deserves comment. On many streams rights to divert water far exceed the quantity of water flowing in the stream. This is a result of two phenomena: (a) many users may depend on the same water, as downstream users divert water that has already been diverted and returned by upstream users; and (b) the most junior rights may be exercisable only in years of heavy flow or low senior usage. Thus, many streams in the West are "overappropriated." A finding that unappropriated water is available therefore does not mean that one will have a certain supply of water. Some states are stricter than others in preventing overappropriation. See Lower Colorado River Auth. v. Texas Dept. of Water Resources (Tex.1984).

5. *Public Interest Considerations*

The laws of most states authorize the agency to reject or condition applications not consistent with the public interest or public welfare. The New Mexico state engineer rejected an application for a proposed irrigation project that seemed too large for the available water supply and thus might result in high costs and uncertain supplies for those who bought land and the accompanying water rights. The state engineer was concerned that purchasers might be misled, and that a failed project might discourage investors in future water development enterprises. The state supreme court upheld the engineer's use of these broad policy concerns, specifically rejecting the applicant's contention that "public welfare" concerns should only include matters that are a "menace to public health and safety." Young & Norton v. Hinderlider (N.M.1910).

A Utah statute required the state engineer to determine whether proposed appropriations would interfere with a "more beneficial use" or "would prove detrimental to the public welfare." The Utah Supreme Court upheld rejection of an early application in favor of a later one because the interests of the public would be better served by the later appropriation (a federal water project) than by the earlier one (a private power plant). Tanner v. Bacon (Utah 1943).

In Washington public welfare considerations have been held to include environmental factors, not simply the effect of the proposed use on quantities available to others. Although these factors were not contemplated by the legislature when it passed the Water Resources Act, subsequent legislation showed an intention to include evolving notions of the public interest. Stempel v. Department of Water Resources (Wash.1973).

Western states have begun to charge administrative agencies with applying broad public interest factors in water permitting (and other related water determinations). Alaska has one of the most detailed state statutes requiring such considerations. Factors include: (1) benefit to applicant; (2) effect of resulting economic activity; (3) effect on fish and game and recreation; (4) public health effects; (5) possible loss of future alternative uses; (6) harm to others; (7) intent and ability of applicant; (8) effect on access to navigable or public waters.

Where states have public interest statutes that are relatively inexplicit as to the factors to be considered courts have directed water administrators to look to a wide variety of factors. Idaho's statute says only that the Director of Water Resources is to reject or modify a permit application if the appropriation "will conflict with the local public interest." The state supreme court held that public interest elements to be applied by the Director include those reflected in Idaho laws dealing with instream flows, water quality, water waste, and conservation. In addition, "common sense" argues for looking at the factors in the Alaska statute and other state laws. Shokal v. Dunn (Idaho 1985). The Nevada state supreme court, however, has refused to look beyond the state engineer's administrative definition of the public interest statute. Pyramid Lake Paiute Tribe of Indians v. Washoe County (Nev.1996).

It can be argued that an agency not only has authority but has a duty to reject applications for permits that may be contrary to the public interest. One court has applied the public trust doctrine to require "at a minimum, a determination of the potential effect of the allocation of water [to major energy projects] on the present water supply and future water needs of this State." United Plainsmen Ass'n v. North Dakota State Water Conservation Comm'n (N.D.1976). The ruling requires comprehensive water planning or some other method of weighing the effects of allocating substantial quantities of water to appropriators pursuant to state law.

The most extensive application of the public trust doctrine to limit a state's authority to grant permits to appropriate water was in National Audubon Soc'y v. Superior Court (Cal.1983). The court found that a state agency's 1940 permit to the City of Los Angeles to use water from tributaries to Mono Lake had been granted without consideration of the effect on public trust factors including fish, wildlife, and recreation. Thus the City's established rights to appropriate may be qualified by later agency restrictions to protect the fishery, wildlife, and recreational uses dependent on an inflow of fresh water to the lake. The decision is remarkable in that it effectively impresses every permit with a condition that allows it to be reviewed and modified if public uses were not adequately considered when the permit was issued. A later case held that the California State Water Resources Control Board, which has authority over both water allocation and water quality in the state, has a public trust duty to exercise its authority to condition water permits to accomplish water quality goals. United States v. State Water Resources Control Bd. (Cal.App.1986). Impacts on water quality appear to be among the most likely problems to incite an application of the public trust doctrine or an exercise of an administrator's authority to control appropriations in the public interest.

Other states also invoke the public trust doctrine. In Idaho it has been said to apply to all water rights, although it may not be considered by the court in a major general stream adjudication absent specific legislative direction. Idaho Conservation League, Inc. v. State of Idaho (Idaho 1995).

C. Adjudication

There are three general types of judicial procedures affecting water rights.

1. *General Stream Adjudications*

All states have adopted procedures for adjudicating the competing rights of all water users in a particular stream system. All persons claiming water rights in the system typically must be joined as parties. In some states, judicial proceedings may be initiated by the users, in others by a state agency and in some states by either users or an agency.

Today, general stream adjudications are proceeding in several western states to quantify and set the relative priorities of existing water rights throughout major watersheds. These are state-initiated adjudications that proceed according to rules set by legislatures. They typically require all water rights claimants to state and prove their water rights relative to all other appropriators. Legislatures have been motivated to pass these laws, in part by a desire to take advantage of a federal statute that requires the United States to participate in adjudication of its water rights if it is joined. Special legislation has been passed in recent years and general adjudications are now proceeding in major watersheds in Arizona, Idaho, Montana, Oregon, and Washington.

A state agency or special master typically serves as a fact-finder, gathering information, conducting surveys, and compiling claims. The initial hearings and decisions are generally made by an administrative body. The administrative determination of rights then is filed in a court which will embody the determination in a final court decree except to the extent findings may be altered in response to appeals from interested parties. There is usually a process for integrating new permits, issued after a general stream adjudication is commenced, into the decree.

2. *Validation or Review of Agency Permit Decisions*

Once an official or agency makes a determination it is final unless someone appeals. Appeals may first go to another level before proceeding to court. In most states the court engages in a trial de novo but most appeals are based on the administrative record.

3. *Conflicts Among Water Users*

One or more water users may sue other water users who allegedly violate their water rights. The decision generally binds only those who are parties. Administrative bodies in some states may have authority to resolve conflicts between individual water users. Decisions of an administrative agency are subject to judicial review either on appeal or as a required step in the process.

D. Regulation of Water Distribution

An administrative agency usually enforces established rights based on the relative priorities of appropriations. The manner in which appropriators use water is also subject to regulatory and administrative controls.

Wyoming's system is illustrative. The state engineer has overall supervision with division superintendents located in each of four water divisions. Each superintendent oversees several water commissioners who physically distribute the water. The commissioner's job, under the guidance of a superintendent and the state engineer, is to make sure the water of each stream is distributed in proper quantities at the right times to those who are authorized to receive it.

The commissioner opens, closes, adjusts, and locks headgates in accordance with a list of all appropriators in order of their priority in time, and is a streamside policeman with power to make arrests if necessary. As streamflow wanes in late summer, the commissioner closes headgates starting with the lowest priority (i.e., latest in time), to ensure that the earliest appropriators have access to the quantity of water to which they are entitled from available supplies. If streamflow increases, the commissioner can open gates and give juniors the benefit of the increase. Regulation of headgates requires no notice or hearing, because it is purely a ministerial duty of the water commissioner (not a judicial process). Hamp v. State (Wyo.1911).

The water commissioner also regulates reservoirs, including the exchange of stored water for direct flows. Commissioners report streamflow measurements and water usage to the state engineer. In this way data are centralized at the state level.

In Wyoming, an appeal from action of the water commissioner is taken first to the division superintendent, then to the state engineer, and finally to the district court of the county where the ditch in controversy is located.

E. The Colorado System

Colorado was the first state to provide special court proceedings for water rights controversies. The procedure was a refinement of the cumbersome adjudication process in which all claimants could be joined as parties to a lawsuit. Litigation in districts joined all claimants and allowed them to contest one another's claims. Before 1969, Colorado vested jurisdiction over all water rights adjudications in the district court of each county. The claimant petitioned for an adjudication and notice was given to all parties. The court then ordered the state engineer to supply a list of filings in good standing; the court also could seek additional information about diversion and storage structures from the water commissioner. At the conclusion of the proceeding, the court issued a decree. Water rights were determined without active agency participation. This produced blanket judicial decrees. New users were added to the decrees as they established appropriations.

Unlike the other western states, Colorado did not later create an administrative agency with permitting and regulation authority. Instead it retained a judicial system and charged it with administrative functions.

The Water Rights Determination and Administration Act of 1969, C.R.S. §§ 37–92–101 through 37–92–602, divided the state into seven water divisions that correspond to the seven major drainages. A division engineer is appointed for each division. "Water judges" are selected from among district court judges in each division and they have jurisdiction over water rights determinations. They function full or part time depending on the volume of water rights business. Applications for determinations of water rights are made to the clerk of the water court. The clerk prepares monthly resumes of applications that are sent to any potential party and published in local newspapers and other media. After an opportunity for statements of opposition to be filed by those objecting to the application, a referee conducts fact-finding. The state engineer and subordinate officials provide the clerk with a list of decreed and conditional water rights. The referee then approves, disapproves, or approves in part the application. In some difficult cases the referee refers the matter to the water judge.

All parties then have an opportunity to protest the ruling to the water judge. Rulings not protested are confirmed unless the water judge finds them to be contrary to law. Protested rulings may be confirmed, modified, reversed, or reversed and remanded. Once confirmed, the water right has a priority as of the date of filing the application. Plans for augmentation and changes in use follow a similar procedure. Appellate review from the judgment and decree of the water judge is available in the supreme court.

Division engineers compile and publish tabulations of all water rights in a division every four years, reflecting such matters as abandonment and conditional decrees awarded. The tabulations are subject to protests, on which the water judge conducts hearings. The state and division engineers regulate the distribution of water according to priorities and quantities decreed by the courts.

Colorado is the only prior appropriation state without a permit system, although the functions of water courts are quite similar to the permitting agencies. One difference in the Colorado system is that water users may begin using water before asking the court for a water right. This reflects an interpretation of a state's constitutional provision (which is common to several western states) declaring that "the right to divert the unappropriated waters of any natural stream to beneficial uses shall never be denied." In fact, the ability to exercise a constitutional right to divert water has little importance because it is always junior to all rights prior to the year the appropriator has it adjudicated. Therefore it is subject to the call of all users with adjudicated rights. (This is known as "anteda-tion.")

IX. TRANSFERS AND CHANGES OF WATER RIGHTS

Appropriative water rights may be transferred among water users subject to certain state law limitations. Transfer of water rights along with land is a routine matter. Water rights in most states pass with the land upon its conveyance un-less otherwise provided in the conveyance. And when land is divided, a pro rata portion of water rights may accompany each parcel. Stephens v. Burton (1976). In Colorado, the intention of the grantor determines whether water rights pass with the deed to land. Bessemer Irrigating Ditch Co. v. Woolley (Colo.1904). Rights may be granted sepa-rately from the land or by a reservation of the water right by the grantor upon conveyance of the land. Water rights, however, may effectively be made nonseverable by statute or severance may be al-lowed with conditions to protect other users.

Transfers for uses in locations, for different pur-poses, at different times, or involving changes in the points of diversion or return are more complicated, requiring protection of junior water rights under the so-called "no harm" rule. Some states have special restrictions on water use outside the water-shed of origin.

A decline in the economic importance of agricul-ture and urbanization of the West has created a demand for water to be shifted to uses that return higher economic benefits. Agriculture requires vastly larger quantities of water than municipal and industrial uses, so acquisition of irrigation water rights can yield plentiful water for such uses. And the typically early priority of irrigation rights makes them especially desirable. Municipalities sometimes temporarily lease rights they hold for anticipated future needs to others. See Section IV B of this chapter.

A. Transfers Generally

A transfer of water rights may be made by sale, lease, or exchange. A transfer of course may not exceed the quantity of rights held by the transferor. It may or may not be accompanied by a change of use (e.g., a different place or purpose of use). For example, if farm land is conveyed along with appurtenant water rights, there may be no change in the purpose, time, or place of use, or in the point of diversion or return. However, when water rights are conveyed separately (or where the original owner intends a different use), any or all of the above use characteristics may change, thus affecting the rights of other stream appropriators and triggering procedures for determining whether harm to others is sufficient to disallow a change of use.

B. State Restrictions on Transfers Apart From the Land

Some states restrict transfers for uses away from the land (Montana, Oklahoma, Nebraska, Nevada,

South Dakota, Wyoming). Arizona, Kansas, and North Dakota experimented with non-severance statutes but later repealed them. Laws restraining transfers apart from the land are based on the riparian-type notion that a water right is appurtenant. A likely motive for the laws was to prevent appropriators from making claims to water in amounts well beyond the quantity that could be used beneficially on their lands and then selling the early priority water right to others.

Wyoming's 1909 "no-change" statute provides *that no severance of water rights from land* may be made without loss of priority. This unfortunate rule, however, is riddled with exceptions (e.g., for domestic, transportation, steam power, industrial, and highway construction uses, pre–1909 rights, reservoir rights, and rotation of waters). Although the 1909 law remains on the books, a 1973 amendment authorizing transfers has negated its effect.

Nebraska's Irrigation District Act of 1895 makes irrigation water rights inseverably appurtenant to land. However, because the statute applies only prospectively, pre–1895 rights (very desirable because of their seniority) may be sold.

In Nevada, Oklahoma, and South Dakota, water rights are made inseverable as a rule, but may be severed if their use on the originally benefited land becomes economically infeasible. The Nevada statute limits only the transfer of irrigation rights; others are freely transferable. Montana prohibits a change in the purpose of use (of water rights in excess of 15 c.f.s.) from agricultural to industrial uses. In Arizona transfers of irrigation rights apart from the land are subject to approval of and conditions imposed by the Director of Water Resources. Arizona also subjects transfers of water rights outside the boundaries of irrigation districts or similar entities to the consent of the district.

In addition to statutory transfer restrictions, there are private restrictions on stock transfer imposed by mutual ditch companies and irrigation districts. See Chapter Eleven. These restrictions may appear on the face of stock or may be included in the company's by-laws or articles of incorporation.

C. Restrictions on Transbasin Diversions

Removing water from one watershed to be used in another, variously known as transbasin diversion or interbasin transfer, is generally permitted under the prior appropriation doctrine. Indeed, the seminal case of Coffin v. Left Hand Ditch Co. (Colo. 1882) involved a diversion of water out of the basin of its origin. The court recognized that the appropriation doctrine is fundamentally different from the doctrine of riparian rights in that it allows such diversions. A variety of state laws limit transbasin diversions by placing certain requirements on the diverter to protect the equities and interests of the area of origin. These limitations are in addition to restrictions imposed by the rules regarding changes in use that are discussed below. Restrictions on removing water from within a state may raise special problems under the commerce clause of the Constitution. See Chapter Ten, Section IV.

A transbasin diversion is often sought because growth and expansion occur where water supplies are inadequate. Great investments in diversion facilities are made in order to bring the water to the watershed where it is demanded. Southern California and Colorado's eastern slope have been able to flourish because of imported water. If rights are purchased from appropriators in the area of origin, the "no harm" rule applicable to changes in use provides some protection for existing appropriators. But the rule does not consider harm to the economy, ecology, lifestyle, and potential for future growth of the area where the water originates. Because these effects tend to be severe and lasting when there are massive exports of water out of a watershed, some states have enacted restrictions to protect the interests of areas of origin. Such protective legislation modifies prior appropriation law and adds costs to transfers, but is justified by public policy.

Legislation intended to protect an area of origin often attempts to safeguard present conditions including established water rights and streamflows for fish and wildlife. It also may attempt to provide for future development, but needs for this purpose are difficult to quantify. California allows transbasin diversions subject to the right of the area of origin to appropriate the water when it is needed, with an absolute priority over the exporter. California state law also reserves for the county of origin all the water that may be necessary for its development.

The largest transbasin diversions in Colorado are from the Colorado River basin west of the continental divide to Denver and other heavily populated areas in the east. The legislature enacted a statute to protect the western slope's "present appropriations of water and in addition thereto prospective uses of water for irrigation and other beneficial consumptive use purposes." Those who divert water from the western slope must show that future water supplies for the west slope "will not be impaired nor increased in cost." This is satisfied by providing "compensatory storage" to help meet future needs in the area of origin. See Colorado River Water Conservation Dist. v. Municipal Subdistrict, N. Colorado Water Conservancy Dist. (Colo. 1979).

A Nebraska statute authorizing interbasin transfers of 75% of the flow of major rivers in the state was interpreted to allow transfers to be denied if they are "contrary to the public interest." Little Blue Natural Resources Dist. v. Lower Platte N. Natural Resources Dist. (Neb.1980). Subsequently the statute was amended to set out the factors to be considered by the Director of Water Resources in deciding the public interest.

Texas law provides that interbasin transfers are allowed only if the water diverted is surplus to the reasonably foreseeable needs of the basin of origin for the next fifty years. Oklahoma requires that

sufficient reserves be established to meet present
and future needs.

D. Changes In Use

1. *No Harm Rule*

Whenever one seeks to change the point of diversion, or the place, purpose, or time of using a water
right whether or not a transfer of the right is
involved, special protections against harm to other
appropriators apply.

An appropriator who seeks to change a use or to
transfer a right to another for a changed use must
apply to the appropriate administrative body or
court for approval.

Changes in use may affect stream conditions
upon which other appropriators depend for their
beneficial uses. Of course a junior appropriator
may do nothing to impair a senior appropriator's
prior rights to water, but juniors are also protected
from changes made by seniors. The doctrine of
prior appropriation recognizes a right of junior appropriators "in the continuation of stream conditions as they existed at the time of their respective
appropriations." Farmers Highline Canal & Reservoir Co. v. City of Golden (Colo.1954).

Irrigation practices typically result in about half,
often more, of all water that is diverted returning to
the stream. Only a portion is actually consumed by
evaporation or by being drawn into plants and
retained or transpired into the atmosphere. The
rest either flows or seeps back to the stream from

ditches or fields or is caught in sumps, ponds, groundwater aquifers, and the like. The amount that does return to the stream—return flow—becomes available at certain times and places for others to divert. Changes in the point of diversion, or the place, time, or purpose of use must not cause material harm to the uses of other appropriators.

Not all actions that injure juniors are subject to the no harm rule. They include reuse or more intensive consumptive use of the water on the same land for the same general purposes (e.g., agricultural irrigation), changes in use of imported water (see Section VI B of this chapter) and, in some jurisdictions, certain changes in the point of return.

2. *Procedures*

An appropriator who wishes to make a change in use or transfer a water right to another who will use the right differently must seek permission for the change. In permit jurisdictions the decision whether a change in use will be allowed rests with a state administrative agency such as the office of the state engineer; administrative decisions are subject to review by state courts. In Colorado, a change of use is approved through a statutorily established court proceeding and evidenced by a court decree. In either type of jurisdiction, the main substantive issue in the change of use proceeding is whether the change violates the no harm rule.

In most states, the burden of proving that no harm will result is on the person seeking the new use. Other appropriators may contest the change on the ground that it will injure them. The holder of a conditional water right (see section IV B 2 of this chapter) who will be harmed may also contest the change. Rocky Mountain Power Co. v. White River Elec. Ass'n (Colo.1962). Once a prima facie case has been made, the burden is on the objector to refute the evidence and prove harm. In Montana the original burden of proving harm is on the objector.

Some states also authorize denial of a change on "public interest" grounds. The Utah statute specifically required the state engineer only to apply public welfare criteria to applications for new appropriations. The state supreme court held, however, that it would be unreasonable to allow the state's interest in protecting public recreation, natural stream environment, or public welfare at the time of an appropriation to be defeated on a change of use. Bonham v. Morgan (Utah 1989). The relevant considerations may include environmental, economic, and social effects of the transfer. The Idaho Supreme Court has said that the loss of a local tax base is not actionable harm. But under Wyoming's change in use statute the Board of Control may consider economic loss to the locality and the state. The Nevada statute allows the state engineer to consider the economic consequences to the state of changes to uses "involving the industrial purpose of generating electricity to be exported."

In one New Mexico case a change of water rights from agricultural to a proposed resort was found contrary to the public welfare. The decision was reversed on appeal because the public welfare statute did not at the time apply to changes, only new appropriations. Ensenada Land & Water Ass'n v. Sleeper (N.M.App.1988). Shortly after the trial court decision, the statute was extended to transfers of water rights.

3. Types of Changes

A change in use may take several forms, each with its own potential for harm to other appropriators. Changes may be made in the point of diversion (or point of return); in the place of use (or place of storage); in the purpose of use (e.g., irrigation or municipal); or in the time of use (e.g., seasonal or intermittent or continuous). Harm may occur either from depriving an appropriator of the quantity or quality of water that was available before the change or by increasing the appropriator's obligations to seniors. It is the possibility of harm, and not a certainty that it will occur, that must be proved.

Juniors are harmed to the extent that the quantity of water available to them is reduced. They may also be harmed if the change diminishes quality of the supply. Heine v. Reynolds (N.M.1962)(stream salinity increased by change).

Some potential causes of harm to other appropriators that allow juniors to object are illustrated by the following examples.

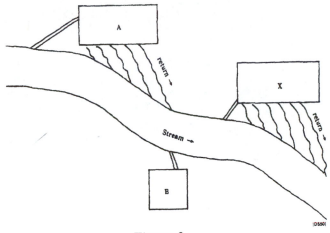

Figure 6

In Figure 6 senior A moves the point of diversion (and place of use) downstream to X, below junior B; B is deprived of A's return flow. The same result would occur if A transferred water out of basin.

The same type of change (senior moves downstream) but with no return flows, may harm B if it is a losing stream (e.g., due to seepage). The increased stream losses between points A and X may leave inadequate water for junior B after satisfying A. Haney v. Neace-Stark Co. (Or.1923).

In Figure 7 senior A moves the point of diversion upstream to point X. Before the move junior B could divert and use water, with the return flow supplying A. A's use at point X may deplete the stream leaving inadequate water to supply B. Vogel v. Minnesota Canal & Reservoir Co. (Colo.1910).

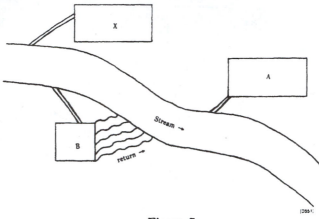

Figure 7

In the same example there may be another source of harm. If it is a gaining stream (e.g., flow increases downstream because of inflows from seepage or tributaries) between points X and A, senior A may have been supplied in part by the increased flow. After the change junior B may have to reduce use in order to make up for the increased flow no longer available to A. Crockett v. Jones (Idaho 1926).

In Figure 8 senior A moves the point of diversion upstream to point X. Junior C, who once benefited from the senior's call (i.e., was able to use return flows from water that the senior could prevent intervening junior B from using), now does not benefit if junior B (who is senior to C) uses the return flows before they reach C.

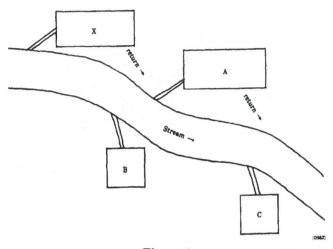

Figure 8

In Figure 9 senior A moves the point of diversion downstream to point X. B may have been supplied by A's return flow, leaving some water for C. After the change, B (who is senior to C) may be left with no water. B may now call C in order to get enough water.

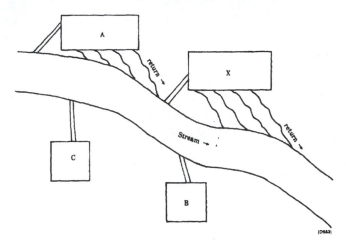

Figure 9

a. *Change in Point of Diversion*

One of the most common types of change in use is a change in the point of diversion (which may be accompanied by a change in the place of water use). An irrigator may want to divert through a new ditch or use a surface diversion instead of a well drawing on the same water source. Many of the examples above illustrate harm that can be caused by a change in point of diversion.

b. *Change in Place of Use*

A change in place of use must not increase consumptive use even if the amount diverted remains the same. Enlarged Southside Irrigation Ditch Co. v. John's Flood Ditch Co. (Colo.1949). Changes in place of use often change the place or timing of return flows from irrigation. Changing to out-of-basin uses will yield no return flows, making the new use 100% consumptive.

A change in place of use generally requires a severance of water rights from the land, so if a state has a statute restricting severance it may prevent the change.

A change in the place of storage, such as an alternative reservoir site, is a type of change in the place of use. The change may be permitted if the new reservoir is at a higher elevation with lower losses than the original site. Lindsey v. McClure (10th Cir.1943). But increased seepage and evaporation loss could harm juniors. Uses that involve a change from direct use to storage may affect both the timing of usage and amount of consumptive use.

Exchange statutes in several western states (including New Mexico, Colorado, and Utah) authorize agreements between water users (i.e., to furnish water at one point in the stream and withdraw at another). Exchanges are changes in the manner and place of use that are subject to the no harm rule. Almo Water Co. v. Darrington (Idaho 1972).

c. *Change in Purpose of Use*

A change in purpose of use typically involves a change from irrigation use to municipal or industrial use. Municipal uses are among the most consumptive since returns (usually sewage effluent) are a small percentage of the quantity diverted. Hydroelectric power generation and cooling are less consumptive than irrigation. Thus changes from irrigation to municipal use (City of Westminster v. Church (Colo.1968)) or from power generation to irrigation use (Hutchinson v. Stricklin (Or.1933)) may increase consumption.

The purpose of use (e.g., agriculture) is not changed if water is used in a new manner for the same purpose in the same place. Planting crops that consume more water or using different facilities to irrigate (e.g., sprinklers instead of flood irrigation) are not usually considered changes in the purpose although the manner of use is actually different and others may be harmed (e.g., by a reduction in seepage or elimination of return flows resulting from reduced application or increased consumption). This seems like a loophole in the no harm rule, but it is built on traditional assumptions of water users, especially irrigators, that they should be able to plant whatever they want and irrigate as necessary so long as the amount of water used does not exceed the amount allowed by a permit or decree. The prevailing rule remains: changes in the purpose of use that necessitate permission of an administrative agency or court and invocation of the no harm rule occur only when water is put to a different type of beneficial use.

d.   Change in Time of Use

A change in the timing of use can harm others. For example, irrigation water rights are seasonal (used only during the irrigation season), although municipal and industrial uses are typically year-around uses. Similarly, a storage right may permit constant diversion into the reservoir although actual uses are intermittent; a direct flow right is occasional, occurring only when there are present uses. A change in the timing of return flows is also a possible source of harm. The slow-moving character of seepage returning to the stream provides a form of "transient storage" which may furnish late-season return flows to juniors (thus extending the irrigation season).

e. *Change in Point of Return*

A change in the point of return of water may also cause harm to others. Ordinarily such a change accompanies other changes in use, as shown by many of the above examples. Although cases involving only a change in point of return are rare, one would expect the no harm rule to apply. But in Metropolitan Denver Sewage Disposal Dist. No. 1 v. Farmers Reservoir & Irrigation Co. (Colo.1972), the Court held that irrigators who depended on discharges of Denver's sewage effluent suffered no legal harm from Denver's change in the point of return when a new sewage plant was constructed.

The *Metro Denver* decision may be limited to the facts. The contest was essentially over who should pay to pump the treated sewage effluent back upstream to where the farmers could use it and perhaps the court did not want to interfere with the investment that the city had made in the new plant. Alternatively the court might have decided that, as a municipal supplier, Denver had a right to consume (or reuse) 100% of the water it diverted and therefore downstream users could establish no rights in waters that might return to the stream. See Arizona Public Service Co. v. Long (Ariz.1989) (city can market sewage effluent because it has unlimited right of reuse). It chose, however, to avoid the question of how much of the water diverted by Denver can be consumed.

In a later case, the Colorado Supreme Court in dicta reiterated the proposition that a change in the point of return is not subject to the no harm rule. City of Boulder v. Boulder & Left Hand Ditch Co. (Colo.1976). But the case was distinguishable from *Metro Denver* because a change in place of use was also involved. Instead of simply applying the historical use rule to the change in use (see discussion in the following subsection) to protect the junior (city) from harm, however, the court moderated the *Metro Denver* rule, saying it only applies to "waste water." Thus, there is no protectable right to the continued flow of "waste water" (water returning to stream in surface ditches) but there is a right to protection against changes in "return flow" (water seeping back to the stream), at least when triggered by a change in the place of use; presumably the distinctions will be applied in all Colorado change of use cases.

Most states have not addressed whether the no harm rule applies to changes in the point of return apart from other changes. Nor have states besides Colorado distinguished between waste and return flow.

4. Limits on Changed Use

A change in use will not be denied or enjoined if conditions can be imposed sufficient to protect junior appropriators from harm. To assure maintenance of stream conditions on which others are entitled to rely it may be necessary to restrict the new use. For example, a seasonally used direct-flow irrigation right may be transferred to a continuous storage use, provided diversions are restricted to the irrigation season, Brighton Ditch Co. v. City of Englewood (Colo.1951), and are made under the same conditions as the original direct-flow diversions, Colorado Milling & Elevator Co. v. Larimer & Weld Irrigation Co. (Colo.1899). An increasingly common condition requires bypasses or releases of water necessary to maintain streamflows or quality.

a. Historical Consumptive Use

A common restriction on a change in use is that the new use be limited to reasonably necessary historical consumptive use. Actual historical use may be shown by actual records of the amount of water diverted and the amount of water returned if they exist. Expert testimony is usually necessary, however. First, records are rarely adequate to demonstrate the amount of water that has been diverted and returned. Furthermore, actual usage may exceed the amount of water reasonably necessary to make beneficial use of the water for the purpose of the appropriation. Thus, historical use may depend on evidence of the amount of water that would have been reasonably required for the purposes to which it was devoted. Evidence would include soil conditions, proximity to the stream, crop water requirements minus average rainfall, and efficiency of irrigation. See Green v. Chaffee Ditch Co. (Colo.1962)(rights sold by farmers to city could not exceed amount of water farmers reasonably would have consumed, as established by expert testimony based on above factors).

Statutes, case law, and regulations restricting transfers to historical consumptive use are intended to prevent harm to others. The rules have been applied to restrict a change even if input on the stream of new use would be lower. For instance, in one case water had been taken to another watershed where it was used for irrigation, so the old use was 100% consumptive as to the watershed of origin. The new use, however, was entirely in the watershed of origin. One might have expected the change to be approved for the full amount "used" historically—all the water diverted. But the court limited the right transferred to the quantity of water that was consumed in the destination watershed (diversion less "returns") although none of the returns had actually reached the basin of origin. Basin Electric Power Cooperative v. State Board of Control (Wyo.1978). The decision may be explained by the fact the court was upholding a determination within the administrative discretion of the Board of Control.

Determinations of historical use are complicated by inadequacy of records and the expense of expert advice. The use of experts, then, can make changes

in use costly, impeding efficient changes (i.e.,
changes to higher productive uses). The cost of
proof may decide cases if parties are unable to pay
for the necessary expertise. See CF & I Steel Corp.
v. Rooks (Colo.1972)(objectors lost for failure to
refute applicant's expert testimony).

b. *Permitted or Decreed Diversion Right*

The amount diverted can never exceed the diversion right stated in a permit or decree. This is true
even if a change in use would result in no greater
consumption. If the historical consumptive use of a
decreed right of 200 c.f.s. was 100 c.f.s. (50% consumptive), the new user is entitled to consume 100
c.f.s. If the new use is only 40% efficient, however,
the new user would have to divert 250 c.f.s. in order
to consume 100 c.f.s. Since the changed use or
transferred right is also limited to the original decreed diversion right of 200 c.f.s., the new user will,
in fact, only be able to use 80 c.f.s. (200 c.f.s. x 40%
consumption).

c. *Other Restrictions*

It may be necessary to restrict a new use to less
than historical consumptive use. For instance, in a
change in point of diversion, the no harm rule may
dictate further curtailment to assure that the same
amount of water actually reaches those who depend
on it.

Other possible barriers to changes of use exist,
such as federal and state environmental pollution
laws (see Chapter Nine, Section V), minimum and

maximum streamflow requirements, land use restrictions, area-of-origin protection statutes and state anti-export statutes (see Chapter Ten, Section IV).

X. LOSS OF WATER RIGHTS

Water rights acquired by prior appropriation may be lost if they are not used. The statutes or applicable doctrines in most states provide that nonuse for a time coupled with intent to relinquish constitutes abandonment. Some states require forfeiture of rights for nonuse in spite of the appropriator's contrary intent. Appropriative water rights generally may not be lost by prescription because any water not used by appropriators in priority belongs to the stream, to be used for the satisfaction of rights of existing appropriators and for new appropriations.

A. Abandonment

Rights to use water established by prior appropriation will be abandoned and lost if they are not used for an extended time. Mere nonuse is not enough, however. One must intend to abandon the rights. Beaver Park Water, Inc. v. Victor (Colo. 1982). The burden of proving an intent to abandon is on the person attempting to establish abandonment, but an unreasonable period of nonuse will create a rebuttable presumption of intent to abandon. The period giving rise to the presumption is found in statute or case law. In Colorado, the state engineer publishes a list of abandoned water rights based on the statutory presumption arising from ten years of nonuse. Once a presumption of abandonment arises the rights holder may rebut it by showing facts or conditions justifying the nonuse. Economic, financial, or legal obstacles that frustrated attempts to use water may negate intent to abandon. Hallenbeck v. Granby Ditch & Reservoir Co. (Colo.1966). Economic infeasibility of the project, however, is not enough to overcome the presumption. CF & I Steel Corp. v. Purgatoire River Water Conservancy Dist. (Colo.1973). The distinction seems to be that in the former case water use was impeded by genuine economic difficulties and in the latter it was delayed for strategic business reasons. However, the Colorado court allowed the appropriator in one case to negate its intent to abandon with evidence that it was trying to sell the water right for which it apparently had no use. People *ex rel.* Danielson v. Thornton (Colo.1989).

Some states authorize administrative officials to initiate proceedings to declare abandonments as a way of curtailing paper rights that exist in excess of actual water use. E.g., Colorado, Montana, Texas, and Wyoming. An action may also be brought by a junior appropriator who stands to benefit. Abandonment can be raised in proceedings such as for a change in point of diversion. See, e.g., *CF & I Steel*, supra. Once a right is legally abandoned, the rights of junior appropriators become more reliable with the assurance that the abandoned senior rights cannot be asserted in the future. This also makes planning for water use throughout the basin more realistic.

B. Forfeiture

Forfeiture, unlike abandonment, does not require that the appropriator intend to abandon water rights by nonuse.   Involuntary loss of all or a portion of one's water rights is triggered simply by nonuse for a period set by statute.   Statutes that declare water rights "abandoned" without any requirement of intent are effectively forfeiture statutes.   The burden of proving nonuse is on the state (or other party) asserting forfeiture.   Rencken v. Young (Or.1985).   Forfeiture may be found where evidence is inadequate to prove intent to abandon. Jenkins v. State, Dept. of Water Resources (Idaho 1982).

Forfeiture statutes may provide for notice by a state agency or official that rights will be forfeited if nonuse is not cured within a statutorily specified grace period.   The New Mexico statute originally provided for automatic forfeiture after four years of nonuse.   State *ex rel.* Reynolds v. South Springs Co. (N.M.1969).   The law was amended to allow a one year period during which use can be recommenced or a showing made as to why it is impossible to put the water to a beneficial use at that time.

Some courts have held that the right is lost and cannot be revived once the period passes.   Baugh v. Criddle (Utah 1967).   In some states (e.g., Wyoming, Idaho, Nevada) however, the right continues to exist until there has been a declaration of forfeiture, Sturgeon v. Brooks (Wyo.1955), allowing additional time for use of the right or for proving an excuse for nonuse. No grace periods are allowed in some states. E.g., Oregon and South Dakota.

Forfeiture claims are usually initiated by statutory procedures but also can be decided in private litigation. Courts may defer to the primary jurisdiction of an administrative agency to decide whether there has been a forfeiture.

C. Adverse Possession

One may obtain another's rights in real property by taking actual, open, notorious, and hostile exclusive possession of the property. A few courts have ruled that a junior appropriator could adversely possess a senior's priority. E.g., Idaho, Montana, and Utah. However, rights held by prior appropriation generally cannot be lost to others by adverse possession. First, private individuals can obtain water rights only by compliance with statutory procedures. Furthermore, rights to use a public resource cannot be adversely possessed. Mountain Meadow Ditch & Irrigation Co. v. Park Ditch & Reservoir Co. (Colo.1954); People v. Shirokow (Cal. 1980)(claim to prescriptive rights not good against the state). Second, one's use of water cannot be adverse to others because everyone has a right to assume that any water use was pursuant to the priority system. Coryell v. Robinson (Colo.1948). This is especially true if the would-be adverse possessor holds some rights on the watercourse.

A junior appropriator who takes water to the detriment of a senior appropriator for an extended period may build a case for the senior's abandonment of the right. If nothing is done to prevent the junior's use, a court might find that the senior intended to give up the right. But the better view is that the junior would not take the senior's priority; at best the junior could establish a new appropriation in the abandoned water with a priority date no earlier than commencement of the junior's use.

XI.   ACCESS TO WATER SOURCES

Rights-of-way for ditches, canals and pipelines are of critical importance to both individual and corporate water users. Because most irrigated land does not border on a stream, bringing water to a tract may require building facilities on the land of one or more property owners. Even if land is adjacent to a stream, some use of another's land may be necessary in order to use a gravity flow pipe or ditch that must follow contours of the terrain. Recognizing the importance of access, both federal and state governments have acted to facilitate acquisition of rights-of-way across public and private lands.

A. Across Public Lands

At first virtually all lands in the West were public lands. Congress provided for ditch and canal rights-of-way across public lands in the 1866 Mining Act. In addition to recognizing the right of trespassers to establish water rights by prior appropriation on federal lands, the Act stated "the right of way for the construction of ditches and canals for the purposes aforesaid is hereby acknowledged and confirmed." The 1870 amendment to the Act made all patents of public lands and all homesteads "subject to any vested and accrued water rights, or rights to ditches and reservoirs used in connection with such water rights." These laws opened the way for construction of all necessary facilities without fear of later dispossession or interruption by the government or its patentees. See Section II A of this chapter.

Today, rights-of-way across public land are obtained by special permission. The Federal Land Policy and Management Act of 1976 (FLPMA), 43 U.S.C.A. §§ 1751–71, authorizes the Secretary of the Interior to grant or renew rights-of-way across public lands for water storage and distribution facilities (e.g., ditches, pipelines, and tunnels). Securing rights-of-way requires application to the Secretary (or the Secretary of Agriculture in the case of National Forest lands). Permits are granted for a fixed term and are subject to annual rentals and conditions on use deemed necessary to comply with mandates in public land laws, including such requirements as protecting fish and wildlife, recreational uses, biodiversity, and other environmental values.

B. Across Private Lands

1. *Status of Trespassing Appropriators*

Under the appropriation doctrine, use (not land ownership on a waterbody) is the basis of a water right; appropriators may thus take waters from lands they do not own. The first appropriations in the West were made by persons entering on the public lands without express authority. As indicated above, federal legislation validated the appropriative rights and use of lands for ditch rights-of-way by "trespassers" on the public lands. Lands conveyed to private parties were patented subject to rights of those who already had perfected water rights to use the land for ditch rights-of-way.

An 1890 act reserved to the United States rights-of-way for ditches and canals on all public lands patented after that date west of the 100th meridian. 43 U.S.C.A. § 945. A 1964 amendment to the act required the government to pay compensation for any such lands it actually used. Thus, many lands were impressed with rights-of-way not only for early private uses established before public lands were patented to private parties, but also for future uses. New appropriators whose water uses began after the land was privately patented and who were not acting with the sanction of the federal government generally had to reckon with private landowners when their diversions required crossing private lands.

A number of state laws and cases address whether appropriators may transport water across lands of others. Some state courts (e.g., Idaho and Oregon) have held invalid the appropriation of one who trespasses on the land of another to make a diversion. The right to contest the appropriation may be limited to the non-consenting landowner, however. More typically, trespassing appropriators may be subject to a trespass claim, but this will not defeat their water right. For instance, in Colorado trespass cannot be asserted to prevent perfection of a water right, but the trespasser must compensate the owner for the fair market value of using the lands and any resulting damage to the residue. See Bubb v. Christensen (Colo.1980). This is tantamount to a right of private condemnation, although the owner, if aware of the intrusion when it begins, could probably control the choice of a route across the land.

If a trespasser enters the land of another and constructs pipelines, ditches, or other facilities without the landowner's permission, and the facilities remain long enough, the use may ripen into a prescriptive right. The period of limitations varies according to state law.

2. *Purchase of Rights–Of–Way*

The most common way to obtain a right-of-way to convey water across private land is by purchase. Often the property owner can also be served by the water delivery facilities and an accommodation reached based on the benefits received. The right-of-way for a canal, ditch, or pipeline includes a secondary easement for necessary maintenance and repairs.

Grants of easements or rights-of-way, like other interests in land, usually must be in writing and conform to other conveyancing formalities. Yet it has been held that a landowner's oral permission to construct a ditch is valid as a license which the landowner is estopped to contest. See Gustin v. Harting (Wyo.1912).

3. *Condemnation of Rights–Of–Way*

Sometimes an owner whose land lies in the path of a canal, ditch, or pipeline is unwilling or unavailable to grant permission for use of the land. Western states have enacted statutes authorizing appropriators to condemn rights-of-way to transport water across private lands.

Private condemnation statutes have been challenged on the ground that they do not further a public use. The United States Supreme Court upheld Utah's grant of eminent domain power against a challenge that the law offended the due process clause of the fourteenth amendment. The Court recognized the great importance of water development under conditions prevailing in the West. Clark v. Nash (S.Ct.1905). Western state courts have upheld similar statutes. In Kaiser Steel Corp. v. W.S. Ranch Co.(N.M.1970) the Supreme Court of New Mexico said that any beneficial use pursuant to state law (coal mining in that case) would suffice to support a valid "public use." The only remedy of the landowner against the appropriator who crossed private land without permission was damages for inverse condemnation.

C. Appurtenancy of Ditch Rights to Water Rights

The right-of-way for a ditch and a water right are usually considered appurtenant to one another so that the conveyance of one carries the other with it. This does not prevent one from being sold apart from the other, however, if the parties express that intention.

XII. STORAGE

Without storage, beneficial use of water would be limited to short runoff periods throughout most of the West. Storage is an important way to maximize the use of scarce water resources.

On-channel storage means that the facility is physically part of the appropriated stream. Most major dams and projects are examples of on-channel storage; their function is to retain some of the natural flow, while allowing enough water to stay in the stream to satisfy rights of downstream appropriators. Off-channel storage requires diversion and transportation works to get water to the storage location away from the stream channel. There is no legal distinction between off-stream and on-stream storage rights. Retention of water in the streambed by artificial means constitutes a "diversion" for purposes of perfecting a water right.

A. Acquisition of Storage Rights

Permission to store water and permission to maintain a dam involve distinct issues.

1. Storage Water Rights

Some states make statutory distinctions between diversions for immediate use—"direct flow water rights"—and diversions for subsequent uses—"storage water rights." A right to use water directly from the stream does not entitle the user to store any water and a right to store water does not mean that water can be used directly from the stream. Handy Ditch Co. v. Greeley & Loveland Irrigating Co. (Colo.1929). Nevertheless, courts have often upheld storage of water appropriated under a direct flow right as a sensible conservation measure if no harm is caused to others. E.g., Ackerman v. City of Walsenburg (Colo.1970). The ability to capture and store unappropriated water beyond one's appropriation has also been upheld because it would otherwise go to waste. E.g., Federal Land Bank v. Morris (Mont.1941).

A permit or decree for a storage water right is obtained from the same agency or court that administers other water rights. The storage right is not complete until water is actually put to a beneficial use. Separate permits are required by some states for storage and for application to a beneficial use, e.g., Arizona, Nevada, Wyoming, and Nebraska. This approach recognizes that often the entity diverting and holding the water (e.g., reservoir company) is different from the entity or persons using the water (e.g., irrigators). Some states consider the two joint appropriators. Board of County Comm'rs v. Rocky Mountain Water Co. (Colo.1938).

2. *Permission to Construct Storage Facilities*

Besides perfecting a right to store water, one seeking to impound it in a reservoir must have permission to build the facility. Most states require plans for construction of dams and reservoirs to be approved by the same agency that administers water rights. The agency or official (e.g., state engineer or director of water resources) may consider factors related to the public interest such as safety, impacts on fish and wildlife, and aesthetics. Most states exempt small storage facilities like stock watering ponds from permit requirements.

B. Use of Storage Rights

The holder of a storage water right can use stored water for any beneficial purpose. Cf. Basey v. Gallagher (S.Ct.1874). Appropriative rights on a stream, whether for storage or direct flow, are governed by the same rules of priority that apply to other appropriations. Donich v. Johnson (Mont. 1926). Storage and direct flow water rights are integrated; neither is given preference. An exception is Nebraska, where water may not be impounded, even by holders of senior rights, when needed for direct irrigation.

Some states allow exchanges between appropriators. For instance, water stored downstream may be exchanged for direct flow diversions upstream.

Exchanges among rights holders maximize the use to which water can be put, allowing the benefit of storage to be shared by juniors (holding storage rights) with seniors (with no storage rights) who may have rights to direct flow at times when they do not need it. The seniors' water is stored in the juniors' reservoir and its use later shared. In Colorado an appropriator can devise a plan for augmentation that provides for such an exchange, which will be approved so long as others are not harmed. Exchanges are permitted in most states upon compliance with conditions imposed by an administrative agency. Stored water may also be used under a contract, lease, or other arrangement. E.g., Kearney Lake, Land & Reservoir Co. v. Lake DeSmet Reservoir Co. (Wyo.1970).

C. Limits on Storage

A widely applied limitation on holders of storage water rights is the "one-fill rule." The rule allows an appropriator to fill a reservoir only once annually and not to use it over the course of a year to store a cumulative quantity greater than its full capacity. Windsor Reservoir & Canal Co. v. Lake Supply Ditch Co. (Colo.1908). The purpose of the one-fill limitation was ease of regulating but its application can be terribly inefficient. A series of several fillings and drawdowns may be necessary to even out flows throughout the year. A small regulating dam can release many times its capacity during a year. This is prohibited whenever the one-fill rule is strictly applied. If applied to restrict control of

water by hydroelectric dams, the result could greatly reduce their utility.   In fact, there is a dearth of
cases except in the irrigation context.

Water diverted to a reservoir but not used may be
retained for future use by the appropriator.   Known
as "carryover storage," this practice helps balance
out wet and dry years.   Some states do not allow
the appropriator to use the amount of carryover
storage plus the reservoir's full capacity of carryover storage the following year;   the limit of one
filling still applies, with the amount carried over
debited against the single filling.

CHAPTER FOUR

HYBRID SYSTEMS AND OTHER VARIATIONS

Ten states employ a mixture of riparian and appropriation doctrine in their water laws. They include the three West Coast states (California, Oregon and Washington) and the six states that straddle the 100th meridian—the dividing line between the arid West and the relatively wet East (Kansas, Nebraska, North Dakota, Oklahoma, South Dakota, and Texas). These states flank a cluster of eight states that embrace the pure appropriation doctrine. (Alaska is the other appropriation state.) Mississippi also has a hybrid system. Hybrid states are sometimes said to follow the "California doctrine" because California developed such a system first and most fully.

There is no pervasive "doctrine" that fits all the hybrid states. California adopted a dual system from the beginning, but the others originally were riparian and later converted to a system of prior appropriation. Each hybrid state has its own mixture of the systems. Riparian rights are important in each, mostly for historical reasons, because substantial riparian water rights had been established by the time appropriation laws were passed. Appropriation law is more important today in the hybrid states since it is the basis of new rights. In California, Nebraska, and Oklahoma, however, riparians can still originate new uses superior to prior appropriators under certain circumstances.

This chapter considers several special water allocation schemes existing in the United States. Unique features of the water law of Louisiana and Hawaii are discussed, followed by a consideration of pueblo water rights, which have relevance in several southwestern states.

I. DEVELOPMENT OF HYBRID SYSTEMS

The historical roots of hybrid systems vary among jurisdictions. The common denominator is that each state recognized riparian rights from the start but also adopted the prior appropriation system because it was believed to be more suitable for allocating rights to use water. For states on the West Coast and central states that lie between higher elevation arid land and lower land with greater rainfall, neither the riparian system nor the appropriation system was entirely fitting; hence, they continued to recognize rights under both riparian and appropriation law—a "hybrid" system of water law. Hybrid states differ in the ways they have adapted to accommodate uses of water under the two rather inconsistent systems of water allocation.

A. California's Early Recognition of Both Appropriative Rights and Riparian Rights

In Irwin v. Phillips (Cal.1855), the dispute was between the owner of a canal supplying water to early miners located away from the stream and subsequent miners located along the stream. All were located on federal lands. The subsequent miners argued that their riparian location entitled them to use water without regard to earlier appropriations by the canal owner. The Supreme Court of California rejected this contention. Since the subsequent miners were not riparian landowners, they could not assert riparian rights to prevent the earlier miner from interfering with their use. The court concluded that among trespassers on the public domain, the rule of prior appropriation that was a custom among the early miners had become so firmly fixed as to be "looked upon as having the force and effect of res judicata." In reaching this conclusion the court noted that the state legislature had recognized canals for mining purposes as property subject to taxation, thereby implicitly approving the use of water by prior appropriation.

Shortly after the decision in *Irwin*, the California Supreme Court acknowledged the continuing viability of the riparian doctrine as between bona fide settlers and appropriators subsequent to the settlement. In Crandall v. Woods (Cal.1857), as in *Irwin*, the parties were all on the public domain. The defendant, however, had settled on a tract contiguous to a stream under the public land laws, but did not initially use any water. The plaintiff water company diverted water from the stream below the defendant to supply a nearby town. The defendant later started diverting water and the water company sued, claiming it had a valid prior appropriation. The court held that the defendant had settled under federal laws and was the absolute owner as against all but the United States. Thus the defendant was entitled to riparian rights subject only to the rights of appropriators who diverted water prior to the time he claimed his land. From the two cases, the rule emerged that between appropriators on the public land, the prior appropriator acquires the superior right, but a settler (with legal rights to land) who has not yet taken water could not be defeated by an appropriator whose water use began after the settler claimed the land.

The California Supreme Court later suggested in dictum that the rights of riparians whose land was patented (conveyed) to them by the United States after the Mining Act of July 26, 1866 could not be defeated even by appropriations made after the Act and before the patent. Lux v. Haggin (Cal.1886)(riparian plaintiffs whose land was patented before the Act held to have vested rights that would defeat any appropriator).

B. Federal Recognition of Appropriative Rights

The California Supreme Court assumed that water on federal land belonged to the federal government and passed with the land to settlers. Courts in Colorado and other appropriation states held that water law was entirely a state matter and that a federal patent carried with it no riparian rights. Did the Colorado doctrine states deprive landowners of riparian rights the federal government intended to convey to them? A few federal land statutes helped to clarify the situation.

The 1866 Mining Act, codified at 30 U.S.C.A. § 51 and 43 U.S.C.A. § 661, reads in relevant part:

> Whenever, by priority of possession, rights to the use of water for mining, agricultural, manufacturing, or other purposes have vested and accrued, and the same are recognized and acknowledged by the local customs, laws and decisions of courts, the possessors and owners of such vested rights shall be maintained and protected in the same.

By the Act, Congress recognized the validity of rights established under the appropriation doctrine that many western states had been applying on the public domain. The statute should have made clear that the rights of an appropriator on the public domain could not be defeated by a patentee of riparian land. To eliminate any doubt, the Placer Act of 1870 (amending the 1866 Act) said that future patentees of riparian land would take subject to the vested rights of appropriators.

Another federal statute important to western water law is the Desert Land Act of 1877, codified at 43 U.S.C.A. §§ 321–329. The law was originally intended as an incentive program in which the federal government gave desert lands to persons who irrigated them. After providing for establishment of the program, the Act stated:

> [T]he right to the use of water by the person so conducting the same on or to any tract of desert land of 640 acres shall depend upon bona fide prior appropriation, and such right shall not exceed the amount of water actually appropriated and necessarily used for the purpose of irrigation and reclamation; *and all surplus water over and above such actual appropriation and use, together with the water of all lakes, rivers, and other sources of water supply on the public lands and not navigable, shall remain and be held free for the appropriation and use of the public for irrigation, mining, and manufacturing purposes, subject to existing rights.* [Emphasis added]

The italicized portion of the Act was probably intended only to limit the amount of water an appropriator could claim. But the Supreme Court of Oregon interpreted it as removing riparian rights from all federal land patents. Hough v. Porter (Or.1908). In other words, a patentee who received a patent after March 3, 1877, acquired no riparian rights under the Oregon rule. South Dakota adopted the Oregon rule in Cook v. Evans (S.D. 1921). But the courts of Washington and California interpreted the Desert Land Act as applying only to specified desert lands and continued to hold that one who received a patent to riparian lands (other than desert lands) acquired riparian rights subject to the rights of prior appropriators. Still v. Palouse Irrigation & Power Co. (Wash.1911); San Joaquin and Kings River Canal & Irrigation Co. v. Worswick (Cal.1922).

The issue of whether the Desert Land Act extinguished all riparian rights on federal lands patented after March 3, 1877 was before the Supreme Court of the United States in California Oregon Power Co. v. Beaver Portland Cement Co. (S.Ct.1935). An Oregon landowner, whose property bordered on a stream, claimed riparian rights based on an 1885 patent, predating Oregon's statute subjecting all water in the state to appropriation. The Court upheld Oregon's interpretation of the Desert Land Act in Hough v. Porter (Or.1908), which abrogated riparian rights on lands patented after 1877, but left other states free to define water rights as they pleased. The Court said that federal land laws recognize that each state has "the right ... to determine for itself to what extent the rule of appropriation or the common law rule in respect to riparian rights should obtain."

C. Limitations on Riparian Rights

Unlike California, other hybrid states did not start out with dual systems of water law. Either by statute or adoption of the common law, each originally embraced only the riparian doctrine, then enacted legislation implementing a system of prior appropriation. Such statutes usually contained some provision recognizing the continued validity of vested rights of riparian landowners existing on the effective date of the act.

II. MODIFICATIONS OF RIPARIAN RIGHTS IN HYBRID SYSTEMS

All hybrid states limited the extent to which present riparian rights could be exercised and future riparian rights asserted. The ability of riparians to insist on the continued flow of a watercourse and to begin and cease using water as they pleased was incompatible with successful operation of an appropriation system.

A. Reasonable Use Limitations

In an early case, the California Supreme Court upheld the right of riparians to enjoin diversions by subsequent appropriators even in the absence of actual harm. Lux v. Haggin (Cal.1886). The practical difficulty with the rule was shown by Herminghaus v. Southern California Edison Co. (Cal.1926), where riparian landowners on the San Joaquin River, who relied on the heavy spring flows of the river to flood their lands, successfully enjoined the defendant from building an upstream hydroelectric power plant that would have deprived the plaintiffs of natural irrigation. *Herminghaus* led the California legislature to amend the state constitution in 1928. The amendment limited water rights "to such water as shall be reasonably required for the beneficial use to be served." Limiting riparian rights to reasonable uses was sustained as a valid exercise of police power in Tulare Irrigation District v. Lindsay–Strathmore Irrigation District (Cal.1935).

All hybrid states now follow some form of the reasonable use rule; thus a riparian cannot defeat an appropriation unless undue interference with the riparian's reasonable use of the water is proved. Some states legislatively or judicially adopted the reasonable use rule without the concern expressed in *Herminghaus* that made necessary a state constitutional amendment. E.g., Brown v. Chase (Wash.1923)(judicial adoption).

B. Extinguishment of Unused Riparian Rights

The essential conflict between riparian and appropriation systems was that riparian rights—being appurtenant to riparian land—do not depend on use. Appropriators had no assurance that their rights would not be defeated by formerly inactive riparians who suddenly decided to exercise their rights. This uncertainty provided little incentive for appropriators to undertake expensive water projects. As a result, all of the hybrid states have attempted to curtail unused riparian rights by statute.

Typically, unused riparian rights were eliminated by a statute adopting the prior appropriation system, but recognizing "vested rights." Riparians were sometimes required to obtain permits or file statements that reflected rights to the amount of water they actually put to use.

C. Constitutional Challenges

Legislation limiting or extinguishing riparian rights has generally been upheld when challenged as a taking of property without just compensation.

The 1928 California constitutional amendment restricting riparian rights to waters reasonably used was sustained. More substantial questions were presented by statutes that terminated unused riparian rights.

Kansas adopted a statute that said: "[s]ubject to vested rights, all waters within the state may be appropriated for beneficial use as hereby provided...." The statute also required riparians to obtain permits to preserve their vested rights, which were limited to water applied to a beneficial use at or within three years of the law's 1945 enactment. The constitutionality of the statutory scheme was tested when the United States refused to proceed with a major irrigation project that depended on appropriative rights under the statute unless the law was found constitutional. The Kansas Supreme Court upheld the legislation. State *ex rel.* Emery v. Knapp (Kan.1949).

The Kansas scheme is typical of others that limited "vested rights" to those applied to a beneficial use some time prior to passage of the statute or, in the case of works under construction at the time of enactment, within a reasonable time afterwards. Such laws have generally been upheld and compensation denied for extinguishment of unused rights. E.g., Hough v. Porter (Or.1908).

A few state courts had difficulties with laws limiting riparian rights in favor of a new appropriation system. In 1913, South Dakota's 1907 appropriation law was declared to be an unconstitutional taking of riparian property without just compensation. In 1964, a subsequently enacted system of appropriation in South Dakota was upheld in light of several intervening U.S. Supreme Court decisions distinguishing police power regulation from takings. Knight v. Grimes (S.D.1964).

Although California still nominally recognizes unused riparian rights, a 1979 decision interpreted the 1928 constitutional amendment to mean that legislatively authorized adjudication of water rights of all water users in an entire river system can limit riparian users to the amount of water currently being applied to a beneficial use, plus a quantified future right. In re Waters of Long Valley Creek Stream System (Cal.1979)(discussed in Section III B of this chapter).

Language in the Nebraska Constitution and water statute resembles language construed in other states to cut off future riparian claims, but the Nebraska courts have declared that riparian rights on lands patented before the 1895 Act have not been abolished and that riparian uses can still be claimed for these lands. Wasserburger v. Coffee (Neb.1966). Riparians are limited to a quantity reasonable for their purposes relative to the purposes of uses by appropriators.

The Oklahoma Supreme Court followed a similar path in its 1993 holding that a 30–year-old law adopting the appropriation system was unconstitutional insofar as it purported to extinguish unexercised riparian rights. In Franco–American Charo-

laise, Ltd. v. Oklahoma Water Resources Board
(Okl.1990), the court said that a riparian owner has
a vested property right to initiate or change reasonable uses of water at any time.   Since the statute
failed to protect those rights (except for future
domestic uses), it violated the takings clause of the
Oklahoma Constitution.   Thus, the rights of riparians to make future uses continues, limited (as in
Nebraska) only by the requirement of reasonableness.   The Oklahoma court refused to defer to the
legislative determination.   It held that reasonableness must be determined by administrative or judicial comparison of the relative reasonableness of the
riparian's new use and the uses of competing appropriators, based on the factors in Restatement (Second) Torts § 850A (discussed in Chapter Two, section IV A).   The legislature immediately acted to
clarify its intent to extinguish future riparian
claims, an effort that overcame the portion of *Fran-
co-American* that said rights could not be extinguished by implication.   But it could not overcome
the portion of the decision that said such an extinguishment was subject to a takings claim.   A trial
court in 1995 held that the 1993 Act is either
unconstitutional or does not apply to pre–1993 riparian claims.

III. ADMINISTRATION OF
HYBRID SYSTEMS

Because of the substantial differences between
riparian and appropriation systems, courts have
struggled to give effect to rights under both systems

of water law existing in a single jurisdiction. One of the most important differences is that in times of shortage riparians must cut back their uses ratably; early appropriators may take their full entitlement, placing the burden of shortages on junior appropriators. When courts must resolve disputes among competing riparians and appropriators they confront the inconsistencies between the two systems.

A. Resolving Disputes Among Water Users

In states where permits for riparian rights state a specific quantity, these rights can be treated as part of the hierarchy of appropriative water rights. If no fixed quantity is set, it may be necessary to quantify unused riparian rights (discussed in the next subsection). The priority date of riparian rights ordinarily is ahead of appropriators since appropriative rights were created in most states pursuant to a statutory scheme adopted to replace a riparian system.

California limits the circumstances in which an appropriator on public land can defeat a riparian. Thus, in California, a riparian will prevail over an appropriator except in cases in which water rights were appropriated *after* the 1866 Act and *before* the riparian's patent. See Lux v. Haggin (Cal.1886).

In Oklahoma and Nebraska, the courts have allowed competing rights of riparians and appropriators to be determined based on their relative reasonableness. The issue arises in Nebraska only as to riparian lands patented before the 1895 Nebraska Irrigation Act; prior appropriation prevails as to later patented lands. Wasserburger v. Coffee (Neb. 1966).

B. Adjudication of Unused Riparian Rights

Most appropriation states have procedures for adjudicating water rights among users. In hybrid states, riparians must be made parties to general adjudications to have their rights reflected in a final determination of all rights on a stream system. Riparian rights may be specifically quantified based on past usage and unused rights may be extinguished.

A number of hybrid states (Kansas, Oklahoma, South Dakota, and Texas) that have extinguished unused riparian rights have made exceptions allowing riparians to claim water rights for future "domestic" purposes that are superior to all appropriative rights. The quantities involved are small, so the uncertainties about unquantified, unused rights are minimal.

Although California nominally allows the future exercise of unused riparian rights, the right can be substantially limited by administrative decisions. In the case of *In re* Waters of Long Valley Creek Stream System (Cal.1979), a riparian owned several thousand acres, but was irrigating only eighty-nine when the State Water Resources Control Board began an adjudication. The riparian urged that unused riparian rights could not be quantified, but, if they were, they should include enough water to irrigate the entire tract with the same early priority date attached to the rights already in use. The Board awarded riparian rights to irrigate only eighty-nine acres and "extinguished" any future exercise of riparian rights for the other lands. On appeal, the California Supreme Court held that the Board exceeded its powers in abolishing unused riparian rights, but said their future exercise could be limited in "scope, nature and priority" to assure that uses were reasonable and beneficial (in accordance with the 1928 constitutional amendment). Thus, unused riparian rights may be put to any reasonable, beneficial use in the future, but may be presently quantified by the Board and granted a priority lower than all appropriations prior to the time riparian uses actually commence.

C. Prescription

Appropriation is the sole method of acquiring water rights in prior appropriation states; acquisition of a water right by adverse possession is generally not allowed. See Chapter Three, Section X C. In riparian states, upper riparians can gain prescriptive rights as against lower riparians if the lower owner is aware of the upper owner's prescriptive claim or suffers harm. The opposite is not true because a lower riparian using any amount of water left unused by the upper riparian cannot ever be adverse; the upper riparian could physically divert the water at any time. An upstream non-riparian may gain a prescriptive right as against a downstream riparian since any use by one without riparian rights is adverse. See Chapter Two, Section VII C.

Rules governing prescriptive acquisition of water rights in hybrid systems are illustrated by the case of Pabst v. Finmand (Cal.1922)(Figure 10). Four tracts of land were each owned by different parties. Pabst and Prior sued to quiet title to the waters of Eagle Creek. The California Supreme Court held that H.H. Finmand, a non-riparian, had acquired rights by prescription against both lower riparian plaintiffs by virtue of diversions for the statutorily required period of five years. This was so although the plaintiffs had not suffered actual harm. The court said, "the slightest use by the owners of these lands being notice to all riparian owners that a hostile right was being asserted, a prescriptive right was acquired by such adverse use on those lands." The court held that N.H. Finmand could not gain a prescriptive right unless the use caused actual harm to lower riparians. Since Prior's lands were only riparian to the north fork of the stream, N.H. Finmand's use from the south fork could not have harmed Prior. N.H. Finmand also failed to acquire a prescriptive right as against Pabst because "[i]n the absence of showing that the upper owner [N.H. Finmand] is using the water under a claim of prescriptive right, the lower owner [Pabst] has the right to presume that such owner is only taking that to which he is entitled as a riparian owner by virtue of his riparian right."

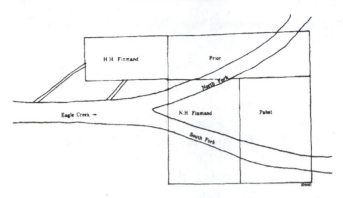

Figure 10

If a non-riparian acquires a prescriptive right in a hybrid system state, the right acquired is essentially a riparian right not subject to the appropriation scheme.

IV.　OTHER WATER LAW VARIATIONS

Some water law systems are not easily characterized as prior appropriation, riparian, or as a hybrid of the two. They include Hawaii's ancient system, remnants of civil law in Louisiana, and pueblo rights applicable in some parts of the southwestern United States.

A.　Hawaiian Water Law

Water law in Hawaii springs from the ancient Hawaiian system of land tenure. Traditionally, Hawaiian lands were held by chiefs in units known as *ahupua'as*. The typical *ahupua'a* was a wedge-shaped parcel that began at the top of the moun-

tains and widened toward the sea generally following watershed lines. Lands and waters were controlled by *konohiki* (land chiefs). Commoners were
allowed to work lands and raise crops but had to
give a share of what they produced to the chiefs
and, after unification of the islands under a single
monarch, to the king or queen. Rights to sufficient
water to cultivate taro (the mainstay of the Native
Hawaiian diet) were appurtenant to the land for use
of those who lived there. The *konohiki* in charge of
each subdivision of land allocated any surplus waters remaining after basic needs were satisfied.
Water distribution was based on recognition of the
mutual dependence of the *konohiki* and the commoners who produced crops for the *konohiki*.

At the urging of westerners, individual titles to
most of the land were established by a process
known as the Great *Mahele* (division). The most
significant accomplishment of the *Mahele* was to
make land titles (and certain "appurtenant" water
rights) alienable.

The Kingdom of Hawaii became a republic for a
while, then a United States territory, and finally a
state. Judicial decisions under Hawaii's various
governments announced principles of water law
that now apply to creation of individual, privately
held water rights. The decisions dealt with "appurtenant" and "surplus" waters.

Appurtenant rights are based on the amount of
water used for taro cultivation. Early cases responded to the water demands of sugar plantations

and allowed transfers of appurtenant rights, but only upon a showing by the party seeking the transfer that the change would not harm others in the exercise of their water rights or in their means of diversion. Kahookiekie v. Keanini (Haw.1891). Thus courts scrutinized changes in place of use, Peck v. Bailey (Haw.1867), and type of use or point of diversion, Carter v. Territory (Haw.1917).

Appurtenant rights also could be obtained by prescription if there was adverse use for the statutory period. Lonoaea v. Wailuku Sugar Co. (1895). Of course prescriptive rights cannot be obtained in waters on state-owned lands because adverse possession does not run against the government.

"Surplus" waters generally include all waters not needed to satisfy appurtenant water rights. Early courts disagreed about whether the rights to surplus waters belonged to the proprietor ("*konohiki*" or successor in interest) of the *ahupua'a* where the water originated or to the *konohikis* of all the *ahupua'as* through which the water passed.

Uncertainty also existed concerning whether "storm and freshet" waters were "surplus." An early case specifically included storm water as "surplus," holding its use to be within the control of the *konohiki* of the *ahupua'a* of origin. Hawaiian Commercial & Sugar Co. v. Wailuku Sugar Co. (Haw. 1904). But when a case arose concerning who was entitled to the storm waters that increased streamflow well beyond its normal levels, the territorial court did not follow its earlier dictum. Instead, it held that storm waters were to be divided between the bordering *ahupua'as* as they would be under the riparian doctrine. Carter v. Territory (Haw. 1917). The same court later reiterated its decision that surplus waters belonged to the *konohiki* of the land (*ahupua'a*) of origin, declining to say anything about the distinction in *Carter* between flood waters and other surplus waters (the parties had limited the issues by stipulation to "normal daily surplus waters"). Territory v. Gay (9th Cir.1931).

In 1973, the Hawaii Supreme Court made several major changes in existing law. The court applied riparian principles to hold that surplus water rights could not be used or transferred on any land except the riparian parcel and that appurtenant rights, by their nature, could not be used on other lands. The court also held that appurtenant rights could not be obtained by prescription. The court accepted the "natural flow" doctrine of riparian law in that it best fit the language of an 1895 statute vesting rights to free-flowing streams in "the people." McBryde Sugar Co. v. Robinson (Haw.1973). A short time later, the court changed its view, holding that the modern reasonable use test and requirement of actual harm to the plaintiff applied to riparian rights in Hawaii. Reppun v. Board of Water Supply (Haw.1982).

The *McBryde* court also held that an 1850 statute could not allow uses of surplus water away from the original land because the water did not belong to the landowner. Rather, it had been "reserved for the people of Hawaii for their common good in all of the land grants." Prescriptive rights were defeated because prescription is void against the state, which holds the water in trust for all the people.

The effect of *McBryde* was to prohibit parties who had acquired extensive rights from exercising water rights on their lands outside the watershed. This led to vigorous challenges. On rehearing, the parties urged that the court's decision amounted to a taking of their property rights in violation of the due process clause of the U.S. Constitution because it departed from earlier declarations of water rights. The court reaffirmed its decision.

The parties then took their cause to the federal district court, which enjoined the state from carrying out the state court decision. Robinson v. Ariyoshi (D.Hawaii 1977). On appeal of the *Robinson* case, the Ninth Circuit Court of Appeals certified several questions of state law to the Hawaii Supreme Court. Robinson v. Ariyoshi (9th Cir.1985). The most important was whether "the issue of who owned surplus water" was a "settled question in Hawaii law" before *McBryde*. The court replied that its earlier cases were in conflict about who was entitled to use surplus waters and *McBryde's* announcement of riparian doctrine for Hawaii had settled the confusion. Instead of adhering to the kind of riparianism that exists in other states, the court specially characterized Hawaiian riparian law as rooted in ancient Hawaiian custom giving the state, as trustee for the public, much greater authority to allocate Hawaiian riparian rights "than exists in other states." Robinson v. Ariyoshi (Haw. 1982).

The court explained that as successor to the monarchs and chiefs who formerly held all the lands, the state is obligated to assure a fair distribution of waters among all the people who put it to productive use. At the *Mahele* lands had passed to private parties subject to a reservation of rights in the monarch (now the state) to allocate water among all those needing it. The waters are held in a public trust for common usage of the citizenry, including diversion and use. This is analogous to the public trust doctrine, which obligates states to protect waterways for public uses such as navigation, recreation, wildlife, and fish. The state supreme court also said that Hawaiian rights are more akin to federally reserved water rights for Indian reservations (see Chapter Eight) than to true riparian rights. Reppun v. Board of Water Supply, supra.

During pendency of the *McBryde–Robinson* cases, the state constitution was revised to recognize the state's trust obligation to assure water resource use for the public benefit and to require establishment of a water resources agency to regulate resource use and conservation. In 1987, a sweeping new state water law was adopted, providing for a comprehensive state water plan, the designation of water management areas, and the protection of instream uses. Under the new law, existing and new water rights must have permits and the common law is largely supplanted once an area is designated as a water management area triggering the requirements.

One notable change from the common law as announced in *McBryde* and *Reppun* is that water use is not restricted to riparian or watershed lands.

B. Water Law in Louisiana

Although Louisiana is often listed as a riparian state, its system of water law is based on a civil code with French and Spanish origins; it is the only state in the Union that has a civil code system. The relevant rules for settling water disputes are found within the code, which specifies a scheme of regulation.   The courts are not bound by the principle of *stare decisis*, but may refer to common law precedents if they are on point.

The code sets forth rudiments similar to a riparian system, such as:

> Article 657: The owner of an estate bordering on running water may use it as it runs for the purpose of watering his estate or for other purposes.

> Article 658: The owner of an estate through which water runs, whether it originates there or passes from lands above, may make use of it while it runs over his lands. He cannot stop it or give it another direction and is bound to return it to its ordinary channel where it leaves his estate.

Article 657 is a nearly verbatim adoption of the French Civil Code, implemented by Napoleon. It is not clear whether the provision expresses the natural flow rule or the reasonable use rule. The early case of Long v. Louisiana Creosoting Co. (La.1915) applied a reasonable use rule in a water pollution context. The court said:

> [W]hether a use that pollutes a water course is a reasonable or an unreasonable use is for the judge or jury to determine from all of the circumstances of a case, including the nature of the water course, its adaptability for particular purposes, the extent of injury caused to the riparian owner, etc.

By statute, Louisiana has various types of water districts that supply customers with water for purposes such as domestic use, municipal use, industrial use, and irrigation. Municipalities also have statutory authority to maintain their own waterworks systems.

Until recently, groundwater in Louisiana was almost totally unregulated. The Civil Code states:

> Article 490: Unless otherwise provided by law, the ownership of a tract of land carries with it the ownership of everything that is directly above or under it.
>
> The owner may make works on, above or below the land as he pleases, and draw all the advantages that accrue from them, unless he is restrained by law or by rights of others.

Adams v. Grigsby (La.App.1963) held that water under a person's land is not owned until it is reduced to possession by pumping. The *Adams* decision was criticized for not providing incentives to conserve water. A 1972 act responded by authorizing the Department of Public Works to regulate wells producing in excess of 50,000 gallons per day. Smaller wells still appear to be governed by the rule of Adams v. Grigsby.

C. Pueblo Water Rights

In a few places in the Southwest pueblo water rights may be claimed under theories tracing to land grants and principles that were applied by the predecessor Spanish or Mexican governments. Generally, these rights recognized that municipalities could use all the naturally occurring water within their boundaries that was needed for their residents. Residents could use water in common with neighboring pueblos. Existence of pueblo water rights has been acknowledged in cases arising in New Mexico (Cartwright v. Public Service Co. (N.M. 1958)) and California (Vernon Irrigation Co. v. City of Los Angeles (Cal.1895)). They also have been the subject of claims in other states where such rights had originally existed (e.g., Arizona, Texas and Colorado). Today, however, their importance is small, having little recognition outside of California. They pertain mainly to the rights of cities in California and of Indian tribes (pueblos) in New Mexico.

Pueblo rights are traceable to rights recognized by the Spanish crown and the Mexican government. Spain ruled portions of the Southwest prior to 1821; the Republic of Mexico then governed the area until 1848. In that year, the territory was ceded to the United States by the Treaty of Guadalupe Hidalgo.

The treaty confirmed property rights then existing under Mexican law, including pueblo rights. Under Spanish law, water rights were held by municipalities as common property for their inhabitants. Grants of pueblo lands were intended to encourage settlement in the New World by facilitating growth of villages and agricultural production. In the case of the Indian pueblos, who for hundreds of years had inhabited parts of an area now in New Mexico, the grants seem to have had the dual purposes of evidencing respect for their aboriginal rights as governments and of defining the areas outside, on which settlement by others would be possible.

The pueblo right has special importance to some California cities. It has been held that use of the water is not required to keep a city's right alive; a successor city may displace long-established uses even if it has not historically used the water. Thus Los Angeles, as the successor to a pueblo right, was able to assert rights to meet its growing needs from groundwater supplies. The California Supreme Court held that the city's rights were superior to established rights of other appropriators (including other cities). City of Los Angeles v. City of San Fernando (Cal.1975).

Pueblo water rights extend to surface flows and groundwater, from the source to the sea, and to any amount of water reasonably required by the city's (or Indian pueblo's) inhabitants, including water for expansion or new uses, even if the entire supply is demanded.

Pueblo rights have been recognized in ongoing litigation concerning the rights of Indian pueblos. For these tribes, the pueblo right is similar in extent to Indian reserved water rights, discussed in Chapter Eight. See New Mexico v. Aamodt (10th Cir.1976)(certain Indian pueblos do not hold reserved rights, but may have comparable rights under Spanish and Mexican law). The *Aamodt* court held that the Indian pueblos have rights superior to all whose land titles were later than a federal law confirming the tribes' pueblo land titles. It said in later proceedings, however, that the amount of water to which the tribes are entitled depends on the amount of land irrigated in the period preceding that federal law. This limitation on future uses is not what one would expect under either the reserved rights doctrine or pueblo water rights as articulated in *Cartwright*. Although New Mexico courts have followed the California decisions, a New Mexico court of appeals decision argues that the pueblo water rights doctrine not only is disruptive of the appropriation system, by giving some cities unlimited time to put their waters to use, but also that the historical and legal bases of the *Cartwright* case, supra, are invalid and that it is ripe for overruling. State *ex rel.* Martinez v. City of Las Vegas (N.M.App.1994).

CHAPTER FIVE

RIGHTS TO USE THE SURFACE OF WATERWAYS

Rights in water are not exclusive in the same sense as other real or personal property rights. First, others typically share rights to use the same resource. Second, members of the public have rights to use the surface of many waterways. Public surface use of waters has deep historical importance. These rights are rooted in ancient Roman law and are reflected in the English common law.

Historically, waterways were chiefly valuable as avenues for commerce and for fishing and hunting by members of the public. These public rights have always qualified the rights of those who owned the beds and banks of the waterways. Landowners, whether they are governments or private parties, effectively hold the lands subject to the public's rights. This is a kind of "public trust."

Navigability of a waterway has become a legal benchmark for defining the realm of public use. This is because, of all the public uses, navigation has special commercial importance. And, in dividing sovereign prerogatives between the states and the national government, the Constitution gave commerce power to the U.S. Congress.

217

Apart from any rights held by the public, riparian owners have reciprocal rights and obligations allowing shared use with the public of land submerged beneath a particular waterway.

The principles in this chapter apply whether a state has a riparian, prior appropriation, or hybrid system of water rights. In each kind of jurisdiction, private rights to use water are limited to the extent necessary to allow the public to exercise its surface use rights as well as to allow individuals to exercise their private water rights.

I. PUBLIC RIGHTS IN NAVIGABLE WATERS

English common law gave all subjects rights to navigate and to make other uses of waterways such as fishing and hunting. Submerged lands that were susceptible to these uses were held by the Crown subject to public rights. Unlike other lands held by the monarch, Crown lands could not be used or conveyed by the monarch contrary to these public rights. Because of the nature of the public's uses of the waterways, these restrictions were held to apply to all lands affected by the ebb and flow of the tide.

Tidal influence may have described well the waterways that were most important to the public in the island kingdom of England. It fell short, however, for the United States where large navigable rivers go far inland beyond the point they are affected by the tides. Consequently, the Supreme Court rejected the "ebb and flow" test as the limit for admiralty jurisdiction in favor of looking at the navigable character of the river. The Propeller Genesee Chief v. Fitzhugh (S.Ct.1851).

"Navigability" thus became an issue in American cases involving not only admiralty, but also disputes over titles to submerged lands and, later, challenges to congressional powers under the commerce clause. The public uses that can be made of waterways—navigation, hunting, fishing, etc.—have become increasingly important in modern America. Since rights to make such uses may depend on who owns the bed of the waterway and whether it remains impressed with a public trust, decisions involving navigability for title are important.

A. Definitions of Navigability

1. *Federal Definition of Navigability for Title*

A federal definition of "navigable" waters determines title to the beds underlying streams and lakes. Federal classification as "navigable" also may inform the issue of whether congressional regulation of waters is proper under the commerce clause. Federal power to legislate concerning commerce based on navigability is developed more fully in Chapter Nine, Section II.

Litigation over title of submerged lands has arisen when both the federal government and a state claim title or between grantees when both sovereigns have attempted to transfer the same land. In some cases, oil or other valuable resources have been found in the bed. Generally speaking, if a stream or lake was navigable under the federal test, title to the bed passed to the state upon its admission to the Union.

The curious doctrine that granted new states title to ribbons of land through large expanses of federal public lands has origins in the common law. The original thirteen states took their sovereignty from foreign nations, principally England. Since the Crown held title to the beds and waters in all waters affected by the tide, the Crown's rights passed to the original states as England's successors. Then, upon formation of the United States the states ceded control of the waters flowing in navigable rivers. This was because in the commerce clause of the Constitution the states agreed to grant the national government the power to regulate commerce. Because commerce was then primarily waterborne, the clause was understood to establish national control of navigable waterways. Thus, control of the *flow* was necessarily surrendered by the states, but the states could retain title to the *beds*, subject, however, to the federal government's navigation servitude.

In Pollard v. Hagan (S.Ct.1845), the Supreme Court set out the principle that states acquired title to noncoastal tidelands upon admission into the Union. It said that prior to admission, tidelands were held in trust by the federal government for the people of future states. Later the Court held that *coastal* tidelands remained in federal ownership. United States v. California (S.Ct.1947). Congress responded by passing the Submerged Lands Act which turned over control of tidelands to the states.

Lands that pass to a state on statehood—public trust lands—must be held and conveyed subject to limitations for the benefit of the public. See Section II of this chapter.

The federal test of navigability for title is whether the waterbody was "navigable in fact" at the time the state entered the Union. In other words, the waterway must have been susceptible to being used as an "avenue of commerce" in its ordinary condition at the time of statehood. The Daniel Ball (S.Ct.1870). The Great Salt Lake was found to meet the test based on evidence that a few small boats used the lake for trade at the time Utah became a state. Utah v. United States (S.Ct.1971). The definition and rules for deciding whether a waterway is navigable are matters of federal common law. Hughes v. Washington (S.Ct.1967).

In addition to lands beneath navigable waters, the federal government also held in trust and conveyed to new states the beds of non-coastal, nonnavigable waters that were influenced by the tides. Phillips Petroleum Co. v. Mississippi (S.Ct.1988). These were Crown lands, too, but since they were not navigable the federal government did not assume admiralty jurisdiction or a navigation servitude over them. They remained, nevertheless, subject to the public trust for non-navigation purposes. Thus, the Supreme Court held that they too were held in trust by the United States until a state was formed, at which point they passed to the new state.

Submerged land beginning at the mean high water line belongs to the state. This line is determined by an average of the high water marks over all seasons. Along a navigable waterbody, riparian property ownership extends to that line; the state owns the bed of the river beginning at the line. The line also delineates the area in which the federal navigation servitude may operate to destroy private property interests without compensation. See Chapter Nine, Section I B.

Title to the beds of waters not navigable under the federal test usually passed from the federal government to riparian landowners. Under the law of a few states, such as Wisconsin and Iowa, the state took title to the lands beneath certain "nonnavigable" waters that had not been conveyed to private parties at the time of statehood. The states adopted their own tests of state navigability for this purpose.

2. *State Definitions of Navigability*

States may adopt restrictions on private or state-owned beds of waterways by statute or common law. These restrictions, and commensurate public use rights may be based on a state definition of navigability. States do not necessarily base their definitions of "navigability" on whether waterways can sustain commercial navigation. Some have used a "saw log" definition, asking whether a stream would allow passage of logs on their way to the mill.

Several states have adopted expanded definitions of navigability that are directly related to the stream's capacity for recreation—the "pleasure boat," People v. Mack (Cal.App.1971), or "recreational use" test, Arkansas v. McIlroy (Ark.1980). States following this approach include Arkansas, California, Idaho, Massachusetts, Minnesota, New York, North Carolina, Ohio, and Oregon. A waterway that is useful for rowboats, canoes, inflatable rafts, or the like is considered navigable and subject to public use. Property rights of riparians are qualified to the extent necessary to allow these public use rights. A Michigan court, on the other hand, has expressly rejected this approach, although the case dealt with private lakes that the court found to be too small for recreation. Bott v. Michigan Dep't. of Natural Resources (Mich.1982).

B. Rights of the Public to Use the Surface of Navigable Waters

Under the commerce clause of the Constitution the federal government can regulate navigation. Federal legislation is not constrained by navigability because commerce powers are broad. See Chapter Nine, Section II. Even in the absence of legislation, no private property owner can obstruct navigation. Federal law, however, has not dealt significantly with the permissible nature and extent of non-navigational public uses of navigable waterways because most navigable waterways are state or privately owned and are dealt with under state law.

To accommodate increased public demand for water-related recreational opportunities, some state legislatures and courts have defined a broad range of permissible public uses of navigable waters as defined by federal or state law. In Diana Shooting Club v. Husting (Wis.1914), a riparian owned the bed underlying a stream deemed "navigable" under state law. The defendant floated down the river in a small boat to hunt ducks and the riparian sued for trespass. The court ruled for the defendant, holding that the rights of hunting and fishing are incidental to the right of navigation. The court further held that riparian owners on streams navigable under state law have only a qualified title to the beds of those streams. The title is subordinated to a state's authority to secure for its people full enjoyment of navigation and other incidental rights. Ownership of the bed does not allow a riparian to prevent public use of the surface of a navigable waterbody for the purposes and in the manner permitted by state law.

II. THE PUBLIC TRUST DOCTRINE

Although each state took title to the beds underlying its navigable waters, it has been held that when such lands are in state ownership they are held subject to a public trust and cannot be conveyed unless it would promote a public purpose. This rule is known as the "public trust doctrine."

The leading case is Illinois Central Railroad v. Illinois (S.Ct.1892). In that case the Illinois legislature granted the railroad title to part of the bed of Lake Michigan in return for the railroad's promise to pay the state a percentage of its gross earnings from wharfs, piers, and docks to be built over the bed. The legislature later repealed the act, and the railroad claimed that the repeal was invalid. The state filed suit for a judicial determination of title to the submerged lands. On appeal the United States Supreme Court upheld the repeal and found the original grant to be invalid. The court reasoned that the state held title to the lands beneath the navigable waters of Lake Michigan in trust for the citizens of the state and could not convey the lands inconsistently with the trust.

Every state court that has considered the question (a total of 39) agrees that the state holds lands beneath navigable waterways in trust for the public. Most jurisdictions have set aside legislative attempts to defeat the trust by conveyance or relinquishment of the public's interests in the land. E.g., Arizona Center For Law in the Public Interest v. Hassell (Ariz.App.1991). This does not preclude a state from transferring the land so long as it remains impressed with a trust in favor of the public. Some states (e.g., Texas) have upheld transfers free of the trust. Where the doctrine applies, private uses will be scrutinized to determine if they are inconsistent with the trust. Kootenai Environmental Alliance v. Panhandle Yacht

Club, Inc. (Idaho 1983)(state lease of lake surface for construction of private sailboat slips).

The public trust doctrine has been interpreted by states to allow protection for a variety of public uses including navigation, commerce, fishing and hunting, bathing, swimming, and recreation. E.g., Marks v. Whitney (Cal.1971). States have also extended it to non-navigable waters and to contexts other than surface use. National Audubon Society v. Superior Court (Cal.1983)(limiting diversions under the prior appropriation system from non-navigable tributaries of a navigable watercourse).

III. STATE–RECOGNIZED PUBLIC RIGHTS OF SURFACE USE OF "NON-NAVIGABLE" WATERS

A number of states have recognized use rights in waters overlying privately owned beds that have recreational capacity without denominating them "navigable." Section I explains that some states have expanded their definitions of navigability to allow public recreational uses of waterways for recreational boating, fishing, and hunting even where beds are in private ownership. The rationale and result in states that base public use on recreational capacity are similar, but they avoid the sometimes difficult evidentiary problems of proving navigability.

Since colonial times in what is now Maine, Massachusetts, and New Hampshire, large, freshwater lakes known as "great ponds" (having a surface area over ten acres), although non-navigable, have been considered open to public use with a limited right of public access across private lands to reach the ponds. A Minnesota statute declares certain defined waters that are managed or accessible for public purposes to be public waters.

The modern approach is exemplified by Montana Coalition for Stream Access v. Curran (Mont.1984). In *Curran*, the court held that streambed ownership was irrelevant because "the capability of use of the waters for recreational purposes determines their availability for recreational use by the public." Although the river involved in the case was navigable, a case involving a non-navigable stream was decided by the same court a month later and it explicitly said that navigability for recreation (or any other purpose) was not an issue. After these cases, sweeping legislation specified extensive public rights in recreational streams of various types. Portions of the statutes that allowed camping and even construction of duck blinds below the high water lines of privately owned streams were held unconstitutional as was a provision requiring property owners to construct portage routes at their own expense.

The Montana court relied in part on a state constitutional provision that is similar to constitutional provisions in most western states, declaring all state waters to be "for use of its people ... subject to appropriation for beneficial uses." Wyoming cited such a provision to hold that riparian title on non-navigable streams is limited by a right-of-way for the water to pass and for the public to use it for navigation, hunting, and fishing. Day v. Armstrong (Wyo.1961). New Mexico follows the same approach.

A nearly identical provision in the Colorado constitution has been interpreted as having the opposite effect. People v. Emmert (Colo.1979). In *Emmert,* the court declined to read any right of public use into the portion of the constitution declaring that unappropriated waters are "the property of the public, and the same is dedicated to the use of the people of the state." The court said that the constitutional provision was "historically concerned with appropriation" and should not be used to limit the otherwise absolute property rights of riparians to use the surface. Thus, the public "has no right to the use of waters overlying private lands for recreational purposes."

Colorado is among a small minority of states that deny public use. Kansas has followed *Emmert,* refusing to accept the approaches of most other states. The court was influenced heavily by the legislature's failure to pass proposed public use bills a few years before. Kansas *ex rel.* Meek v. Hays (Kan.1990). Alabama, Pennsylvania, and Indiana also hold that riparians have absolute rights to exclude others from the surface. A few other states grant no public fishing or hunting rights in nonnavigable waters (e.g., Louisiana, Missouri, Virginia). Some old cases limit public rights to an easement for passage over privately owned beds (e.g., Connecticut, Illinois, Maine, Massachusetts,

New York, North Carolina, Tennessee). But most modern decisions allow at least some public recreational use.

Awaiting judicial decisions determining case by case which waters are subject to public use can cause uncertainty for property owners as to their rights and property values. Some states have opened private waters to the public by legislative act, allaying such uncertainty. A Minnesota statute lists as public waters various waterbodies including all large waterbodies, those that are classified by state agencies for uses such as fishing and those which are bordered or accessible by public lands. In Alabama and Pennsylvania such statutes have been held to effect a taking of vested property rights of the private owners of streambeds.

IV. ACCESS TO WATERWAYS FOR LAWFUL SURFACE USE

The public right to use the surface of waterways, whether they are navigable or are otherwise considered open to the public, often cannot be exercised without crossing private lands or touching the banks, sides, or bottoms of the beds. Generally the same principles apply to streams and lakes. There is, however, an additional issue concerning the right of members of the public to touch privately owned beds in the course of their surface use. Michigan and Missouri allow wading in the stream on privately owned submerged lands and the adjoining banks. Wyoming limits the use of streambeds to incidental contact necessary to exercise the right of flotation. In Montana the public can use the bed and banks of streams for recreational purposes and has the right to use upland areas to portage around obstructions.

A. Condemnation

States may take land by eminent domain to provide public access to waterways. Branch v. Oconto County (Wis.1961). Though there may be disputes over the amount of compensation due, there is little question that governments have the power to condemn easements and other rights of public access to waterways that are open to public use. The more difficult cases involve legislative and judicial decisions that such rights exist without the need to compensate landowners.

B. Implied Rights of Access

Several courts have held that riparian property bordering waterways that are open to the public is burdened with an easement of public access. They have employed a variety of theories.

1. Custom

Oregon has held that riparians can be prevented from fencing the dry sand areas adjacent to the ocean. State legislation declared the area between high and low tide lines to be a state recreation area. The court found that the public has an easement to use the dry sand area (above the high tide line) based on customs of the people going back to earliest times, citing principles for imposing limits on property based on custom set out by Blackstone. State *ex rel.* Thornton v. Hay (Or.1969).

The Supreme Court has held that police power regulation of private property that destroys all economically viable uses can be upheld only if the regulation proscribes uses that were not part of the property interests acquired in the first place. Lucas v. South Carolina Coastal Council (S.Ct.1992). Citing *Lucas*, owners of beach-front property in Oregon challenged the city and state's reliance on custom in *Thornton* to deprive them of the exclusive use of the dry sand area of their land. The state supreme court held that the landowners' title never included development rights that could interfere with the public's use of the dry sand area and that they were on notice of this long-standing custom when they took title. Stevens v. Cannon Beach (Or.1993).

Custom has also been cited as the source of beach access rights in Florida and Hawaii. The Hawaiian Supreme Court has relied on ancient Hawaiian usages of gathering and fishing to hold that the western concept of exclusivity does not universally govern property in Hawaii. Thus, developers of a beach resort must be denied construction and land use permits as necessary to preserve and protect native Hawaiian traditional rights of access to conduct customary activities. Public Access Shoreline Hawaii v. Hawaii County Planning Comm'n (Hawaii 1995).

New England statutes dealing with public use of great ponds allow public access across private land but have been interpreted to apply only to unimproved or unenclosed lands. These laws were based on colonial practices and are arguably rooted in custom.

2. Implied Dedication

Dedication is the donation of land or an easement for public access. It requires both an intention on the part of the landowners to dedicate and an acceptance by the public. The California Supreme Court has held that dedication of an easement of public access for recreational uses can be implied where members of the public used private land adversely for over five years. Gion v. Santa Cruz (Cal.1970). The doctrine has also been applied in New York.

3. Prescription

Wisconsin recognizes that a right to moor boats may be acquired by prescription. Prescription occurs when the public has used an access way openly, continuously, and adversely for the prescriptive period of time.

4. Public Trust

Other courts have applied the public trust doctrine as a rationale for a public right to cross private property and to use the dry sand area adjacent to the ocean. Matthews v. Bay Head Improvement Association (N.J.1984).

5. *Police Power Regulation*

Some coastal states impose extensive regulations upon property owners for the benefit of the public. Among the most extensive are those of the California Coastal Act. Conditions may be imposed on those seeking to build or modify structures within the coastal zone, including exactions of easements for view and for public access. The Act withstood constitutional attack where the exactions were related to the legislative purposes. Sea Ranch Ass'n v. California Coastal Comm'n (N.D.Cal.1981). However, the United States Supreme Court held that a condition requiring the provision of lateral access along the shoreline of an objecting property owner who was applying for a building permit was not tailored specifically enough to satisfy the stated statutory purpose of ensuring views of the ocean from behind the lots. Nollan v. California Coastal Comm'n (S.Ct.1987). Thus, there must be a reasonable nexus between the restriction and the public need. Where a city sought a public right of way on private land along a creek as a condition of allowing commercial construction on the land, the Supreme Court held that the city must also prove that the exaction is "roughly proportional" to the impact of the development on the public. Dolan v. City of Tigard (S.Ct.1994).

V. RECIPROCAL RIGHTS OF RIPARIAN OWNERS

A riparian owns the bed of a non-navigable waterway to its center. This means the area bounded by the centerline of a stream and by extension of lines to the center point of a lake from the points where the property lines of the riparian land meet the shore. Traditional property law principles recognize a landowner's rights in real property to extend "from heaven to hell"—that is, into the air space above as well as into the earth below. Under this absolute ownership concept, owners of riparian land on a waterway may exclude as a trespasser anyone seeking to use the water (or bed and banks) for recreational or other waterborne activities. Many early cases so held, but, as the above authorities in Section III show, the rule persists only in a few states (Alabama, Colorado, Pennsylvania, Indiana, and Kansas).

The rights of riparian owners overlying privately owned beds are qualified by the common right of other riparians to use all of the water surface. Under some state laws, they also may be subject to the public's exercise of surface use rights.

The general rule is that riparians may make reasonable use of water overlying the land of other riparians on the same waterbody. Although a technical trespass may be involved, the law has accommodated the practical need for mutual access to water resources in which several persons have a common interest. Most courts have held that all landowners surrounding a lake may use the entire surface if the use does not interfere unreasonably with the same rights of other owners. E.g., Johnson v. Seifert (Minn.1960); Snively v. Jaber (Wash. 1956).

The common right of the owners of land surrounding and beneath a waterbody may not apply to "artificial waters"—those created by structures (dams and dikes) rather than natural features. Anderson v. Bell (Fla.1983) (restricting owner of land that was flooded when lake artificially expanded after a dam was built from boating above lands owned by the dam owner). Furthermore, landowners adjacent to a pit mine that filled with water cannot assert riparian rights against the mine owner to prevent filling in the pit. Publix Super Markets, Inc. v. Pearson (Fla.App.1975). The Florida Supreme Court reached an opposite conclusion where the excavation had been named a lake and a subdivision built around it with covenants in the deeds that gave owners rights of access to the "lake." Silver Blue Lake Apartments, Inc. v. Silver Blue Lake Home Owners Ass'n, Inc. (Fla.1971).

The owner's right to use private land is subject to the common rights of others to use the surface. Because all riparians have rights to use a lake surface, it has been held that an owner of littoral land may not fill or build out into a lake on submerged land. Bach v. Sarich (Wash.1968). However, the court in that case said that the result might have been different if it had involved a "water-related" construction project (e.g., a dock or boathouse) and not an apartment house.

A property owner is prohibited from filling land if it obstructs the public right of navigation. One Washington case enforced this rule even where the level of a natural lake was raised by an artificial dam causing the land to be inundated part of every year. Wilbour v. Gallagher (Wash.1969).

In applying the reasonable use rule to non-navigable lake surfaces, the courts have held that a riparian (e.g., a resort owner) can permit guests to use the lake, but must limit their numbers and activities to prevent unreasonable interference with rights of other riparians. The general rule is that a riparian may grant permission, subdivide land, or convey riparian rights to non-riparians by easement or otherwise. This can multiply the numbers of people who have access to use a lake, resulting in problems as boaters and swimmers interfere with one another. They are bound by a rule of reasonable use. Thompson v. Enz (Mich.1967); Thompson v. Enz (Mich.1971) (construction of a series of canals and the granting of easements to permit public access to a small lake for recreational boating). The same rule applies if the state itself purchases or condemns lakefront land and opens it to the public. Only reasonable use by members of the public, as the state's licensees, will be tolerated. Botton v. State (Wash.1966).

CHAPTER SIX

GROUNDWATER

I. BASIC HYDROLOGY

A. How Groundwater Occurs

1. *Permeability of Rock Formations*

Occurrence and movement of groundwater are governed by the laws of physics and local geological conditions. Although groundwater can occur in the form of underground streams, most groundwater is percolating water stored in the pores, or interstices, of rock formations. The size of these interstices varies with the size of the rock particles; a bed of gravel has interstices visible to the naked eye, but clays have very minute particles and interstices. Interstices may be formed by geological processes at the time the rock was formed or created later by cracking or erosion.

Porosity is the measure of the amount of open space within rock. It is defined as the percentage of the rock's total volume occupied by pore space. Other factors being equal, the greater the porosity, the more freely water can move through the rock and the more water that can be stored within.

The force of gravity can cause water to move "downhill" through rock formations. Slowing this movement are the forces of *molecular attraction*. Molecular attraction is proportional to the surface area of the rock particles, which increases as their size decreases. To illustrate, compare the movement of water through gravel and through sand. The gravel is made up of large particles, so the surface area of all the particles is cumulatively smaller than the surface area of all the particles of sand. Thus, water moving through the minute interstices is slowed by powerful forces of molecular attraction. The porosity of a volume of sand may equal that of gravel, but the *permeability* of the sand (its ability to transmit water) is lower.

Although permeability varies across a spectrum, rock formations are grouped into broad categories, described as "permeable" or "impermeable." Whether water percolates through rock, and the speed at which it does so, are functions of the force of gravity and the permeability of the formation. Groundwater is often in permeable formations that are bounded and contained by impermeable formations.

2.   *Zones of Groundwater Occurrence*

Groundwater is found in strata that may be defined as the *zone of aeration* and the *zone of saturation*. In the zone of aeration, which is nearest the surface, moisture is present in the soil and accessible to the root systems of plants; but because it is held by molecular attraction, it cannot readily be captured by pumping.

Below the zone of aeration is the zone of saturation, in which groundwater saturates the interstices completely. In this zone, water flows in response to gravity and can be withdrawn by pumping. The upper boundary of the zone of saturation is the *piezometric surface,* or *water table*. Water is at atmospheric pressure at the piezometric surface. Underlying the zone of saturation is a layer of impermeable *bedrock*. Bedrock, under pressure from the formations above, has a very low porosity. Almost all usable groundwater occurs within two miles of the surface and is commonly within a half mile in depth.

3. *Aquifers*

Aquifers may be thought of as underground reservoirs. They are rock formations that yield water in significant quantities. Thus, a formation with low permeability may not be an aquifer, even if porous and saturated with water, because the water is liberated at a rate too slow to be of use. Aquifers may be confined or unconfined. Most common are *unconfined aquifers*, in which the water exists under normal atmospheric pressure. Unconfined aquifers must be pumped to withdraw the water. *Confined* or *artesian aquifers*, by contrast, are under a pressure greater than that of the atmosphere. This pressure is generated when the aquifer is squeezed between overlying and underlying impermeable strata. If the positive pressure is great enough, the water in a well may rise to the surface without pumping, but any pressure sufficient to raise the water above the top of the zone of saturation (water table) is sufficient to make the aquifer artesian. This often occurs when a portion of the aquifer lies above the point where the well (or spring) is located, in which case the pressure is caused by gravity.

A *perched aquifer* is an unconfined aquifer underlaid by an impermeable stratum that is perched above another aquifer. Perched aquifers are often hydrologically unaffected by withdrawals from the zone of saturation. Where perched aquifers outcrop on hillsides, springs may result. The term *spring*, however, applies to any concentrated discharge of groundwater that appears on the surface as flowing water.

Aquifers are initially filled with water either by geological processes occurring when the rock was created (*connate water*) or by subsequent sources such as rainfall (*meteoric water*). Typically, an aquifer is recharged by precipitation falling or flowing where the aquifer outcrops on the surface; it may also be recharged by surface or underground streams. The rate of recharge, like the rate of water movement, varies greatly and is a function of geologic conditions. Some aquifers get no recharge; others recharge so slowly that it takes millions of years to fill them.

Geologists call the amount of water an aquifer will yield without depletion the *"safe yield."* The term has also been used by economists, courts, and legislatures to describe rates of depletion in excess of recharge, but which are viewed as reasonable in light of current demands for the water. When withdrawals from any aquifer exceed its recharge, an overdraft or *mining* condition is said to exist. Some harmful effects of sustained overdraft are discussed in the next section.

Aquifers may be isolated from other aquifers and from surface streams. If aquifers are hydraulically interconnected, the term *groundwater basin* is used to describe the physiographic unit usually consisting of a large aquifer and one or more smaller aquifers.

If an aquifer is hydraulically connected to a stream so that groundwater withdrawals affect the stream supply, the groundwater is sometimes said to be *tributary* to the stream. Whether groundwater is tributary may have important legal consequences: sound management dictates that the tributary groundwater and the stream be managed as a single system. Thus, a court in a prior appropriation state may enjoin pumping from a tributary aquifer to prevent injury to senior appropriators on the stream. If groundwater use does not affect a stream, there can be no such harm and the groundwater need not be administered in conjunction with the surface water allocation system. Integration of groundwater and surface water uses are discussed in Section III of this chapter.

4. *Underground Streams Distinguished*

An *underground stream* has been defined as waters that flow underground within "reasonably ascertainable boundaries," and as "a constant stream in a known and well-defined natural channel." Hayes v. Adams (Or.1923). An underground stream, like *percolating waters*, is "groundwater," but it is generally subject to the law of surface streams rather than groundwater law. See Herriman Irrigation Co. v. Keel (Utah 1902). Factual determination of whether waters are percolating is often difficult, making the burden of proof onerous. The burden may be met by circumstantial evidence, such as vegetation growing above, indicating the course of the alleged stream. Additionally, the stream may be audible at the surface, or well withdrawals may produce downstream effects. Drilling and hydrologic studies are also used to satisfy the burden of proof.

B. How Wells Work

1. *Drilling and Pumping*

Water wells are commonly drilled by truck-mounted rotary drilling rigs. Drilling through layer after layer of rock is an expensive process. In addition, the deeper a well is, the greater are the pump-lift and attendant energy costs. Wells sometimes must be deepened because water tables are lowered by pumping in the area. The cost of deepening wells and of pumping from greater depths can force marginal water users out of business.

As the technology of groundwater diversion has developed, the character of use has changed. The spread of well-irrigated agriculture in the West was hastened by the invention of the windmill. Shallow aquifers could be tapped, giving irrigators a reliable supply in the face of uncertain surface flows and precipitation. Development of the high-pressure pump ushered in a new era of intensive groundwater use; deeper aquifers became accessible. In some cases, junior appropriators with deep wells drew down water tables beyond the reach of the seniors' shallower or less powerful pumps in the same aquifer or caused serious increases in the costs of pumping groundwater from greater depths.

2. Effects of Well Use

a. Cone of Influence

Once a well begins operating, a number of effects result from the water withdrawal. Water from the surrounding aquifer begins percolating through the formation to replace the water being withdrawn. This creates a *cone of influence*, a cone-shaped depression in the water table from which the water has temporarily been removed. The cone is inverted—its tip is at the point of withdrawal and its base is the surface of the water table. As the cone of influence broadens, it may affect the wells of neighboring users, forcing them to deepen or move their wells to avoid losing their supply.

b. Effects of Depletion

In addition to the localized cone-of-influence effect, the rate and extent of pumping also may affect the capacity and ability of the aquifer to produce water.

Salt water can contaminate groundwater as salty water from the ocean or underground deposits intrudes to replace the water withdrawn from an aquifer. Some coastal areas have dealt with salt water intrusion by injecting a barrier of fresh water into the zone of intrusion.

Depletion of a finite supply of groundwater may also cause *subsidence*—which is the sinking of the land surface overlying an aquifer. Subsidence occurs when certain formations (e.g., compressible, low-permeability clays) are unable to support the weight of overlying strata unless they are saturated with water. As the support provided by *hydrostatic pressure* is removed, the formation collapses irreversibly. The resultant sinking of the overlying land surface may damage buildings, highways, railroads, ditches, and wells. Natural structures may be harmed, aquifer storage capacity may be reduced, and cracks in the earth's surface may lead to erosion. Coastal areas may be flooded as they sink. There is some evidence that geological faulting may result. The most severe subsidence within the United States has occurred in Arizona, California, Florida, and Texas in areas experiencing heavy groundwater overdraft.

Subsidence, like other consequences of groundwater overdraft, is usually an economic externality of the pumper; that is, the cost of subsidence damage to others is not a part of the individual pumper's costs. Some jurisdictions provide legal remedies for such damage to help internalize the costs of subsidence. E.g., Friendswood Dev. Co. v. Smith–Southwest Indus., Inc. (Tex.1978)(subsidence damage caused by negligent pumping).

A variety of theories of subsidence liability exist: negligence, groundwater law principles, nuisance, and the obligation for subjacent support. Alabama has applied nuisance law where no liability would have attached under the state's common law of groundwater, which allows landowners to make any use of underlying water for which there is a "reasonable need." Henderson v. Wade Sand & Gravel Co., Inc. (Ala.1980).

A few states control subsidence as part of the groundwater management scheme. Texas confers powers over subsidence on groundwater conservation districts. Arizona's 1980 Groundwater Code authorizes establishment of Active Management Areas in regions affected by overdraft.

3. *Optimum Yield*

Probably the most significant effect of groundwater mining is the economic burden imposed on pumpers by a declining water table. Groundwater, a common-pool resource, is available to a number of individual users, each of whom may make unlimited use of it. A person who owns an entire aquifer might want to reduce current consumption to save part of the groundwater for future uses, obtaining the maximum economic benefit over time. If other users have access, however, little incentive exists to conserve for the future. The individual user who forgoes present uses takes the risk that others will consume any water saved; thus each individual is induced to pump as much water from the common pool as can be used for any purpose, even a wasteful or marginal use, before other pumpers use up the supply. This disincentive to conserve results in a "race to the bottom of the aquifer," preventing optimal economic utilization of the resource. Garrett Hardin has called the phenomenon the "tragedy of the commons."

Localized effects of overdraft can be significant to individual water users. As water tables fall, progressively deeper wells are required, resulting in increased drilling and pumping costs. Entities such as municipalities and large farms may enjoy economies of scale enabling them to pump from great depths; small, individual irrigators, however, are caught between high pumping costs and comparatively low economic return per unit of water applied. For an irrigator, the cost of pumping an acre-foot of water may be close to the benefit from an acre-foot of water applied to crops. Slight increases in cost can render further pumping uneconomical.

The groundwater rules applied will determine the obligation of the new pumper to the existing well owner. The newcomer may have to cease all pumping under a system of strict priority administration. The junior may also be required to pay the well-deepening and increased pumping costs of the senior or furnish the senior with water from the junior's well.

II. ALLOCATING RIGHTS IN GROUNDWATER

A. Nature of Rights

A number of legal rules and procedures address the difficult problems of establishing rights to use a common-pool resource such as groundwater. Rights and obligations pertaining to use of groundwater may be based on overlying land ownership, established uses, or the notion that water is a shared public resource. Rules adopted by a state's common law and legislation usually reflect more than a single theory of rights in groundwater, however. Jurisdictions that claim to follow one theory, invariably incorporate elements of others. Thus, a state may proclaim to recognize "ownership" of groundwater by an overlying landowner, but limit the owner to reasonable uses, provide special protections for earlier users against subsequent pumpers, and protect the public interest by prohibiting contamination of aquifer waters.

States in which the resource is relatively plentiful give little attention to allocation of legal rights in groundwater. But recent problems with groundwater pollution have caused even those areas to focus on rights in groundwater. Generally, one having a right to extract groundwater has a right to protect it from pollution by others. Statutory protections and administrative agencies dealing with pollution problems are usually separate from the mechanisms for allocating rights to use groundwater, however.

An integrated approach may be desirable as a practical matter.

1. *Rights Based on Land Ownership*

a. *Absolute Ownership Doctrine*

Under the absolute ownership doctrine a landowner has an unlimited right to withdraw any water found beneath the owned land. Also known as the "English Rule," the doctrine was set forth in Acton v. Blundell (Eng.1843). The court in *Acton* based its holding upon the ancient right of a landowner to the airspace above and the soil beneath the land and viewed groundwater as part of the soil. Another reason for the holding, however, seems to have been the mysterious character of groundwater; the primitive state of hydrology at the time made it difficult to establish a causal connection between withdrawals by a defendant and harm to a plaintiff. See Roath v. Driscoll (Conn.1850).

As scientists have come to understand groundwater better, legal doctrines have evolved. The absolute ownership doctrine was widely adopted in the United States during the 1850s. It is still said to be the law in Connecticut, Georgia, Illinois, Indiana, Maryland, Massachusetts, Mississippi, Rhode Island, and the District of Columbia. But nearly all of these jurisdictions temper its effects with regulatory legislation or common law interpretations.

The doctrine was rejected in a series of American cases, beginning in 1862 with Bassett v. Salisbury Mfg. Co. (N.H.1862). Courts found it harsh and impractical to recognize "absolute ownership" rights in groundwater because it leads to premature depletion of the resource and leaves groundwater users at the mercy of nearby high-capacity pumpers. Courts in some states have upheld legislation that treats groundwater as subject to appropriation on the ground that it is a public resource and not property of overlying landowners. State *ex rel.* Bliss v. Dority (N.M.1950).

Even malicious withdrawal of water for the purpose of injuring a neighbor was not actionable under strict application of the absolute ownership rule. Today, however, even states following the absolute ownership doctrine allow remedies for willful injury. In addition, a number of states that follow the English Rule impose liability for land subsidence caused by negligent pumping (e.g., Massachusetts). Many absolute ownership states subject groundwater use to regulation under some of the rules discussed below.

b. *Correlative Rights*

Under the correlative rights doctrine, like the absolute ownership doctrine, rights to groundwater are determined by land ownership. However, owners of land overlying a single aquifer are each limited to a reasonable share of the total supply of groundwater. The share is usually based on the acreage owned. The correlative rights doctrine was applied in Katz v. Walkinshaw (Cal.1903) *(reversed)*. In that case, the court ruled that in times of shortage, each overlying owner must limit withdrawals to a "fair and just proportion" of the supply—a proportion based on the ratios of the landowners' acreage overlying the aquifer.

California allows surplus groundwater (i.e., groundwater available in excess of a landowners' needs) to be used on other than overlying lands. Rights to export water are based on prior appropriation. The court in *Katz*, supra, held that as between two exporters, the doctrine of prior appropriation applies. In conflicts between overlying owners and exporters, an overlying owner is entitled to a reasonable share regardless of priority relative to the exporter, but any surplus is allocated according to priority. Other jurisdictions adopting correlative rights have not embraced the full *Katz* allocation scheme, but have only accepted the generalized notion of pro rata reductions based on land ownership.

California has introduced another appropriation concept, as well as incorporating a measure of public interest, into the law of correlative rights. In a case involving a basin subject to serious overdrafts caused by pumping for both overlying and export uses, the court held that all pumpers had used water contrary to the rights of one another. Consequently, the continuous adverse uses had resulted in "mutual prescription." City of Pasadena v. City of Alhambra (Cal.1949). Such rights are proportionate to actual historical use. The mutual prescription approach announced in *Pasadena* was developed to avoid the hardship of completely cutting off some large users such as municipalities and public utilities. But it resulted in a scramble to pump large amounts of groundwater in order to establish or prevent loss of prescriptive rights.

The mutual prescription doctrine was significantly qualified by the decision in City of Los Angeles v. City of San Fernando (Cal.1975). There, the court held that municipalities (which had stipulated to the mutual prescription approach in *Pasadena*) are exempt from prescription and required that owners be put on notice of the adversity caused by commencement of the overdraft. The court also altered the correlative rights allocation formula. Under the new formula, prescriptive rights against private owners are determined and a correlative rights allocation then made; prescriptive rights are then subtracted from each private owner's allocation. Any surplus remaining is allocated by priority of appropriation.

2. *Rights by Prior Appropriation*

Prior appropriation doctrine recognizes the best legal rights in the person who first begins using water. Some of the reasons for affording rights to early users of surface water apply to groundwater use. Investments in wells, irrigation equipment, land, and businesses that are based on an expectation of a water supply should be protected. Thus, the law has recognized special rights in established users of groundwater. The rules of liability discussed in Section II B of this chapter respond primarily to injury of existing users caused by a new user's pumping. Groundwater use permit systems usually protect equities of pumpers whose use predates the establishment of the permit system by giving them "grandfather rights" to the extent of their use. Permits for new uses are allowed only when they do not harm rights under earlier permits.

Allocation of rights in groundwater strictly based on prior use is not practical; a senior groundwater appropriator theoretically could demand that no pumping be allowed because virtually any new pumping causes some effect on existing wells. Appropriation doctrine also ignores the equities of individuals and the interests of society. It may be unfair to deny rights in groundwater to a junior pumper who owns overlying land and has no other readily available source. Most important, the state may have an obligation to protect and regulate use of a limited or nonrenewable public resource. This obligation would be frustrated by laws allowing the first users to monopolize rights in groundwater. In short, a strict application of prior appropriation could deprive other users—and society—of the ability to make full beneficial use of the resource.

States must determine the extent to which new uses will be allowed to interfere with established uses. Appropriators also must be limited in the uses they may make of groundwater in order to prevent an aquifer from being used too heavily. This may mean that no more than the average annual recharge can be pumped. Where there is little or no natural recharge, the state must decide whether the resource can be "mined" and, if so, at what rate and for what purposes. See Section II E of this chapter. Appropriation concepts are often reflected in statutes that modify the doctrine in order to set reasonable pumping levels for all or parts of a state. E.g., Alaska, Colorado, Idaho, Kansas, Montana, Nevada, New Mexico, North Dakota, Oregon, South Dakota, Utah, Washington, and Wyoming. The objective is to balance the interests in protecting senior users, optimize new economic uses, and assure a sustained supply.

3. *Groundwater as a Public Resource*

Private property notions do not inhibit state control of groundwater in most jurisdictions. Most states recognize no private ownership rights in groundwater and consider it subject to management as public property. Rights to use groundwater are typically created under permits granted by the state, usually with some recognition for the interests of overlying owners and established users. Rights are allocated by an administrative agency or official. Changes in the law ordinarily do not result in a taking if they deprive landowners or former users of the right to use groundwater. Town of Chino Valley v. City of Prescott (Ariz.1981).

The Colorado Supreme Court held that non-tributary groundwater is neither subject to the constitutional right of all citizens to appropriate water nor owned by the overlying owner. Thus the legislature is free to decide how to manage the resource. State, Dep't of Natural Resources v. Southwestern Colorado Water Conservation Dist. (Colo.1983).

In absence of (and in addition to) an administrative permit system, the exercise of private rights of landowners or appropriators is governed by the tort doctrines of nuisance and negligence, which impose liability for harm to other users and property owners.

States may exercise their police power in order to protect competing users and allocate the groundwater resource in the public interest. The police power is extensive enough to justify permit systems and strict regulatory schemes so long as any vested property rights are respected.

B. Rules of Liability

Most groundwater disputes arise when an existing pumper alleges that new or increased pumping by another is causing harm. The principal rules applied are described below. The rules of liability are influenced by and in turn reflect the theories defining the source of rights in the particular jurisdiction. Most states use permit systems (described in Section II D of this chapter) and thus avoid the complexities involved in litigation among groundwater users.

1. *No Liability Rule*

States that recognize property rights to groundwater in overlying landowners often allow pumping without liability to existing users. Theoretically, every landowner has a right to take whatever water may be pumped from the land by paying only those costs directly incurred (e.g., drilling, equipment, and electricity); no obligation is incurred for harm or expenses caused to others.

2. *Prior Appropriation—"Junior–Liable" Rule*

Many states, particularly those that adhere to the prior appropriation doctrine in allocating surface waters, impose liability on new pumpers for harm caused to existing pumpers with vested senior rights. This rule was applied in Utah in Current Creek Irrigation Co. v. Andrews (Utah 1959).

States have statutorily modified appropriation law to limit protection of seniors to reasonable pumping levels. To the extent such a limit does not apply to some wells (e.g., domestic), prior appropriation law may hold juniors liable for all harm caused to seniors. Parker v. Wallentine (Idaho 1982).

Few states impose a pure prior appropriation system on groundwater not hydrologically connected with surface water. But notions of priority may be built into statutory systems for groundwater allocation. Liability among well owners is based on the extent to which statutory rights to appropriate groundwater have been violated. Generally only "unreasonable harm" is actionable.

3. *Reasonable Use Doctrine*

The reasonable use doctrine was eventually adopted by so many American jurisdictions that it became known as the "American Rule." Adams v. Lang (Ala.1989). The reasonable use rule is nearly identical in purpose and effect to the rule applied to surface waters in modern riparian jurisdictions.

(See Chapter 2, Section IV A). A landmark case is Forbell v. City of New York (N.Y.1900).

The doctrine prefers uses on overlying land. Traditionally, any beneficial use on the overlying land (short of actual waste) was considered reasonable and any use off the land was considered unreasonable unless it was for purposes incidental to the beneficial enjoyment of the land. Higday v. Nickolaus (Mo.App.1971).

Where the correlative rights doctrine applies, the rule of reasonable use is further qualified. A well owner's reasonable use of water on overlying land could deplete an aquifer to the point that uses by others are difficult or impossible. The doctrine of correlative rights accommodates all overlying owners when the water supply is insufficient to meet the reasonable needs of all. Therefore, all users must ratably reduce their use of water so that each landowner gets a fair and just proportion of the supply.

4. Restatement (Second) of Torts § 858

The Restatement (Second) of Torts Section 858 is an attempt to balance equities and hardships among competing users. It imposes liability only for withdrawals that affect other users unreasonably. The Restatement approach differs from the reasonable use rule discussed above because it involves inquiries into the nature of the competing uses and the relative burdens imposed upon each party by a particular remedy. It differs from the correlative rights approach in that allocation of rights can depart from proportions of land ownership. Finally, the Restatement rule does not attach special significance to use of the water on overlying land.

No jurisdiction adheres exactly to the Restatement approach. However, most courts in reasonable use jurisdictions apply some of the Restatement considerations.

Section 858 is phrased as a rule of non-liability. It states that a well owner is not liable for withdrawal of groundwater unless the withdrawal:

　　a.　causes unreasonable harm by lowering the water table or reducing artesian pressure, or

　　b.　exceeds the owner's reasonable share of the total annual supply, or

　　c.　has a direct and substantial effect on surface supplies and causes unreasonable harm to legitimate surface users.

The first limitation requires a balancing test to determine "unreasonable" harm. It seems to require that a plaintiff's well be reasonably efficient in light of the type of use. A court applying the balancing test may inquire into such issues as relative wealth of the parties (e.g., municipalities vs. small farmers), relative ability to obtain financing, and relative value of the uses.

In Prather v. Eisenmann (Neb.1978), the court looked to the nature of use in determining the reasonableness of harm. In that case a high-capacity irrigation user was held liable for lowering the artesian pressure of a domestic well. The court interpreted the state preference statute to say that harm to domestic users caused by irrigation may be *per se* "unreasonable." In dicta the court noted that there would be no liability between domestic well owners for similar harm if there were an adequate supply deeper in the aquifer.

The second limitation in § 858 incorporates a "correlative rights" notion. In adopting this as an additional basis of liability, the drafters of the Restatement rejected the contention of the Wisconsin Supreme Court in State v. Michels Pipeline Constr., Inc. (Wis.1974) that high administrative costs militate against adoption of a correlative rights scheme.

The last limitation in § 858 contemplates administration of groundwater use in conjunction with surface appropriation systems, discussed in Section IV of this chapter.

5. *"Economic Reach" Rule*

The economic reach approach is similar to the Restatement in attempting to strike a balance between junior and senior rights. The leading case exemplifying this approach is City of Colorado Springs v. Bender (Colo.1961). In *Bender*, a senior groundwater appropriator sought to enjoin a junior pumper who interfered with the senior's shallow well. The court looked to the law of surface streams, which does not protect a senior's means of surface diversion against diversions by juniors unless it is reasonably adequate (a suggestion made by the Supreme Court in Schodde v. Twin Falls Land

& Water Co. (S.Ct.1912)). See Chapter Three, Section VII B 2. The court in *Bender* held that a senior well owner's well must be reasonably adequate in light of economics and historical use. This implies that an established domestic well need not be as deep as an irrigation well.

The *Bender* rule, like the Restatement, invites inquiry into issues such as wealth of parties and values of competing uses. The court observed that although seniors "cannot reasonably command the whole source of supply merely to facilitate the taking by them of the fraction," they "cannot be required to improve their extraction facilities beyond their economic reach, upon a consideration of all the factors involved." This rule has been applied in Idaho and Utah. Baker v. Ore–Ida Foods, Inc. (Idaho 1973); Wayman v. Murray City Corp. (Utah 1969). It reflects a policy compromise concerning the extent to which seniors should be protected against loss of pumping ability.

C. Economic Effects of Rules

Economics is useful in identifying the incentives for water use and conservation provided by various legal regimes for groundwater management. Groundwater use involves two kinds of costs: internal costs, borne directly by the individual, and external costs ("externalities"), passed on to third parties and the public. Internal costs of groundwater include costs of drilling and pumping (e.g., construction, equipment, electricity, pipe); external costs include harms to all users resulting from the withdrawal (e.g., costs of drilling deeper, buying more powerful pumps, or paying for more power to draw water from a lowered water table; a share of the value of water that will not be replaced). Every user inflicts "reciprocal externalities" on all other pumpers in the form of higher pumping costs and depletion of the physical supply.

If an individual pumper's comparison of costs and benefits includes only internal costs, decisions about whether and how much to pump will not take into account harm suffered by other pumpers and society as a whole. The law, by setting rules of liability, can internalize (impose on individual pumpers) some or all of the external costs. This affects the degree of demand placed on an aquifer since, theoretically, every prospective pumper will compare the marginal cost (additional cost of producing another unit of water) to the marginal return (additional value of crops or products from use of that unit of water) in deciding whether to pump. But many legal rules allow a pumper to externalize some of the marginal cost of producing water, yielding a net gain for the pumper, but deflecting that cost onto others, often to society's detriment.

This is not to say that a new pumper should internalize all costs resulting from pumping another unit of water. If that were the rule, the cost of new uses would be driven up artificially by inclusion of costs resulting from earlier pumpers' activities in the same aquifer. The law may seek to allocate to each pumper an appropriate share of the total marginal cost, including indirect pumping costs in order to achieve the most overall benefit for pumpers. Presumably, at that point the optimum or "best" decision is made for society since water will not be "wasted," i.e., more water produced than will yield a net gain or less water produced than could be used to yield a net gain.

Legislatures or courts may choose to adopt rules that fix liability on new pumpers for all costs, impose no liability on new pumpers (senior and junior pumpers paying only their own direct expenses), or impose liability in a way that considers factors like priority and efficiency. Theoretically, users will adapt to any rule to achieve sound economic results. But some rules may be "better" at producing socially desirable results because transactions may be costly, information about the cause of impacts difficult to obtain, and some individuals resistant to change.

If no liability is imposed on new pumpers for the resulting harmful effects on others, each user pays only the internal costs of pumping; established users will either have to adjust their uses (deepen their wells, etc.) or compensate new users to prevent those effects. Rapid and uneconomic exhaustion of the aquifer often results.

The junior-liable rule that fully protects vested senior rights will discourage juniors. All the seniors' costs are passed on to the junior, including external costs partially attributable to the seniors' own use (the water table would decline due to the seniors' use even without new junior pumping).

Further, the seniors' inefficiency can be protected by this system and juniors forced to compensate them for improving their means of diversion.

The rule of the Restatement (Second) of Torts § 858 holds a junior liable only for unreasonable harm to seniors. Determination of reasonableness may involve many factors, including value of the competing uses, efficiency of competing wells, and wealth of the parties (e.g., economies of scale and ability to finance improvements). The Restatement rule has potential for correcting the inequity of the junior-liable rule by making seniors responsible for a share of the marginal costs attributable to their pumping (thus achieving desired incentives for optimal resource allocation). The balancing test is subjective, however, and far-ranging enough to consider non-economic factors; results may be dictated by equities, not just by economic effects.

D. Permits

Permit systems are administrative means to establish and protect rights to use groundwater consistent with other state goals. Rights embodied in permits can be based to some degree on land ownership, use, and public interest and may include conditions that reflect any one or a combination of the rules of liability discussed in Section II B of this chapter. Groundwater statutes establishing permit systems were enacted in an attempt to replace piecemeal litigation between water users with a unified administrative scheme. The central objective of permit systems is to regulate development and use of groundwater so that it is used most beneficially. Such systems also provide for public knowledge and community control of pumping activity.

Permit requirements vary depending upon the source of water. States commonly apply separate permitting procedures to different types of groundwater; many distinguish groundwater connected with (i.e., "tributary" to) surface streams and lakes. Florida and Minnesota have permit systems that are among the most comprehensive in the nation. Most western states require a permit for all groundwater withdrawals, excepting small domestic and stock watering wells. Other states require permits only for withdrawals of groundwater from certain sources. For example, California requires permits only for withdrawals from underground streams or the underflow of surface streams (although special restrictions apply in many areas such as municipal water districts and where there are adjudicated rights in a groundwater basin). Texas requires no permits for groundwater withdrawals (except from the Edwards Aquifer), but provides for voluntary formation of local management districts.

Statutory restrictions and permit requirements often are not imposed until overdraft problems develop. Many states have designated "critical areas" where permit requirements and other regulations apply. Although economic tools, such as pump taxes could be used to remedy such problems, permit systems administered by a state engineer's office, or its equivalent are far more common. Most permit requirements include criteria designed to prevent overdraft and protect existing wells.

There are two types of permits, well permits and permits evidencing a water right, and both are usually required.

1. Well Permits

Permits are often a prerequisite to well drilling. Well drillers must also be licensed and report information on geological structures, locations, and depths of aquifers for all wells drilled.

Information on applications for well permits is mandated by statute or administrative rulemaking. Required data typically include: type of use and amount of water to be withdrawn, legal descriptions of well location and land on which the water is to be used, type of well, and description of geologic strata through which it is drilled. Most states have laws governing well construction, such as the requirement that all wells be cased, or sealed, as they pass through other water-bearing formations. This requirement permits migration of pollutants into or from another aquifer and accidental tapping of other water-bearing formations. Other than the casing requirement, however, there is little regulation to prevent the well from producing contaminated water or contaminating other waters. Proximity of wells to one another also is regulated.

2. Permits Evidencing a Water Right

A separate permit may be required to use water. In evaluating applications for water rights, administrators are primarily concerned with whether the granting of additional water rights will impair existing pumpers' rights. Determination of "impairment" is based in part upon hydrologic data on aquifer recharge and the extent of existing uses. Administrators also make value judgments as to the permissible rate of aquifer depletion, usually guided by statutory criteria. Such criteria reflect policy choices made by the legislature in reconciling priority of use rights with rights of overlying owners, economic efficiency, and other social goals.

Statutes often specify the type of public notice and hearing required and provide procedures for potentially injured parties to file objections. Many provide for appeal and judicial review of administrative decisions to grant or deny water rights. Permits may contain conditions on well use designed to protect existing rights. Once a prospective user's well and water use permits are issued, the user must proceed with reasonable diligence to drill the well and apply the water to a beneficial use. The right vests when the water is put to use, and a certificate is usually issued evidencing it. Permits are subject to loss by abandonment, forfeiture, or violation of conditions.

E. Statutory Limits on Pumping

Every jurisdiction provides some protection for existing uses. Many states also statutorily limit the rate or volume of groundwater pumping. Several states have enacted laws to deal with areas having special groundwater pumping problems.

1. Protection of Existing Rights

Most statutory systems regulating groundwater include some measures to protect existing wells. Potential interference is possible from any new well, so absolute protection is not contemplated. The goal is to prevent "unreasonable" interference. Therefore, an agency or official weighs the inequities that would result if the state authorized new wells that would interfere with lawfully established older wells. Statutory systems are designed to bring order and reliability to groundwater management; protection of existing wells is an important means to that end.

In some states, a statutory permit system has replaced groundwater rights based on appropriation or land ownership; protections are often built into the statute for wells predating its enactment (even those that would not have been authorized under the statute) as well as for those permitted under the statute.

The 1965 Colorado Groundwater Management Act seeks to reconcile protection of vested appropriative rights with full economic utilization of groundwater. The statute employs a "modified" appropriation doctrine to govern administration of designated basins. In contrast to the pure appropriation doctrine, under which a new use would be denied if any harm resulted to seniors, the statute requires refusal of a permit only if unreasonable harm to senior rights or unreasonable waste would result. Unreasonable harm is defined to include "the unreasonable lowering of the water level, or the unreasonable deterioration of water quality, beyond reasonable economic limits of withdrawal or use." Criteria for determining unreasonable harm or waste include geologic conditions, average annual yield and recharge rate of the supply, priority and quantity of existing claims to the water, proposed method of use, and all other appropriate factors. Existing well owners are required to have reasonably deep and efficient wells. The Colorado Groundwater Commission has complex regulations to implement its vague statutory mandate. E.g., Fundingsland v. Colorado Ground Water Comm'n (Colo.1970)(upholding rule denying new permits that would result in 40% depletion of aquifer by all wells within 3 mile radius in 25 years).

New Mexico case law has addressed the question of what constitutes impairment of existing rights in a critical area. In Mathers v. Texaco, Inc. (N.M. 1966), the New Mexico Supreme Court rejected the argument that any pumping whatsoever by juniors in a closed basin constitutes impairment, stating that a lowering of the water table is not impairment *per se*. But in City of Roswell v. Reynolds (N.M. 1974) the court upheld conditions on use imposed by the State Engineer to protect seniors, stating that "it does not follow that the lowering of the water table may never in itself constitute an impairment of existing rights."

2. *Legislative Schedules for Groundwater Mining*

Several states have provided for controlled mining of aquifers so that depletion occurs over a predictable number of years. The term "safe yield," in its strictest sense, means a level of withdrawals that does not exceed recharge. In the case of aquifers that are not rechargeable or which take many years to recharge appreciably, the concept has been modified so that "safe yield" refers to a level of withdrawals that will allow depletion of an aquifer over a period thought to be socially optimal.

The choice of time period reflects policy judgments. For example, a long depletion period preserves groundwater for future uses, but requires more severe curtailment of present withdrawals; thus it imposes a hardship on well owners who must invest large sums in well drilling and irrigation equipment. By contrast, a shorter period allows larger withdrawals for the benefit of current users, but may allow depletion so rapid, for instance, that an established irrigation economy fails suddenly as puumping costs exceed economic returns from the water. Usually a compromise is reached under which investors have time to recover their equipmentcosts and aquifer life is also prolonged. Oklahoma's 1972 Groundwater Management Act allows a comparatively rapid 100% depletion within 20 years. In Nebraska, local districts may establish their own timetables for depletion. Pumping in nontributary aquifers outside designatedbasins in Colorado must provide for a 100 year aquifer life.

3. Critical Area Legislation

Even where there are no statewide problems of groundwater overdraft, there may be localized overdrafts that demand strict management. Many western states statutorily provide for identification and management of "critical areas" in which new well drilling and pumping may be severely curtailed or prohibited. Western states providing for designation of critical areas include Arizona, California, Colorado, Hawaii, Idaho, Kansas, Nebraska, Montana, Nevada, New Mexico, Oklahoma, Oregon, Texas, Washington, and Wyoming. Critical areas are commonly regulated by the state engineer's office or an equivalent administrative body and tend to be geographically defined by the boundaries of an aquifer or groundwater basin.

Requirements for critical area status vary. In Montana, Oregon, and Wyoming a critical area may be designated if withdrawals from the basin exceed recharge (the definition of "overdraft"). In Colorado, an overdraft condition need not be shown to establish an area as a "designated groundwater basin," if the basin is non-tributary or located in an area where groundwater has been the principal water source for fifteen years prior to the application for designation. Kansas and Nebraska allow formation of groundwater districts by local option.

Critical area legislation also varies in the remedy applied to correct the overdraft. For example, under the Idaho Groundwater Management Act, groundwater is deemed unavailable and appropriation permits denied where further withdrawal would: (1) affect present or future use of any groundwater right, or (2) cause overall withdrawals to exceed recharge. This statute was held to prohibit junior pumping if it would involve mining of groundwater. Baker v. Ore–Ida Foods, Inc. (Idaho 1973).

Colorado, Nevada, and Washington statutes also provide for pumping reductions, but the reduction is made on the basis of priority; senior appropriators may continue to pump, while juniors are shut down. Oklahoma's 1972 Groundwater Management Act adopts a doctrine of "correlative rights" similar to California's doctrine. Scarce supplies are allocated based on land ownership.

Kansas allows formation of local groundwater management districts by petition of local residents. Management plans are subject to approval by the Chief Engineer of the State Department of Water Resources. Each local district applies its own standards for well spacing and safe yield.

Phoenix and Tucson in Arizona are the largest metropolitan areas that depend heavily on groundwater. Years of unregulated pumping led to severe overdrafts. Accordingly, Arizona's 1980 Groundwater Management Act contains the strictest controls of any state statute. It provides for establishing "active management areas" that now encompass eighty percent of the state's population. These areas may be designated if overdraft exists, withdrawals threaten to create subsidence, or groundwater quality is threatened by saltwater intrusion. The management goal for critical areas is to achieve safe yield (withdrawals not in excess of recharge) within forty-five years.   To reach this goal, the state director of water resources is required to formulate a management plan including: mandatory conservation by "reasonable reductions" in per capita use by municipalities and individuals, pump taxes with revenues earmarked for expenses of administration and augmentation plans, retirement of irrigated lands, and a requirement that new subdivisions demonstrate an assured water supply for 100 years (or have a contract for Central Arizona Project water).

III.   CONJUNCTIVE USE

The term "conjunctive use" refers to the joint use or management of groundwater and surface water sources.   It is especially important if the two sources are hydrologically interconnected.   The term sometimes also refers to use of two unconnected sources to maximize available supplies.   Joint management of connected surface and groundwater sources is the only reasonable way to deal with what is in fact a single resource. Nevertheless, laws in many states govern water use from wells and streams separately, ignoring the fact that they may derive from the same source.   As discussed below, an increasing number of states are managing interconnected groundwater and surface sources as a single system.

In some instances, conjunctive use involves influencing or compelling water users with rights and access to both wells and surface sources to adjust their use of each to an optimum mix. In other situations, the vested rights of surface and groundwater users must be observed, but regulated in a manner consistent with maximizing overall beneficial uses. One promising approach is to create a water management agency with powers over conjunctive use. There is often political resistance, however, to giving agencies substantial powers to tax, incur bonded indebtedness, own property, take legal action, and exercise broad administrative powers.

A. Regulation of Groundwater Connected With Surface Sources

1. *Interaction of Groundwater and Surface Water*

Groundwater is often hydrologically connected to surface streams. For example, seepage from a stream may charge an underlying aquifer. The surface flow of a stream may "ride piggyback" upon the groundwater contained in the aquifer beneath the stream. Or, a stream may be fed by seepage from aquifers. See Section I A of this chapter. In these situations, stream water use may diminish water in the aquifer and withdrawals of groundwater may diminish surface flow. Some states call such interconnected groundwater sources "tributary."

Although the scientific community has long recognized the interconnection of groundwater and surface water, the law has been slow to catch up. Some early cases enforced rights based on this truth. Smith v. Brooklyn (N.Y.1899) (riparian entitled to prevent interference with streamflow from use of groundwater). Laws of many states, however, are still founded on the misconception that the two types of water exist in isolation from one another; thus, they mandate separate regulatory systems for groundwater and surface water.

Several states, including California, Colorado, New Mexico, Utah, and Washington, administer groundwater sources affected by or affecting surface flow as part of the surface appropriation system. The 1973 Report of the National Water Commission recommended wider adoption of this approach. Some states do not treat tributary water as part of the surface system, but empower regulatory agencies to impose special conditions on groundwater withdrawals that interfere with surface rights. E.g., Oregon. The Arizona Supreme Court, however, has ruled that tributary groundwater should be treated as part of the groundwater system (and therefore controlled by the landowner subject only to reasonable use limitations) rather than as part of the surface water regime. In re Gila River System (Ariz.1993).

Timing and magnitude of the effect of well pumping on streamflow are expressed by the United States Geological Survey as a "stream depletion factor." Since groundwater may percolate very slowly through aquifers, there is often a delay between groundwater withdrawals from a connected aquifer and their effect on the surface stream. In addition, the effect may be less in amount than the groundwater withdrawal. The stream effect is defined as a percentage of the streamflow (not of the amount withdrawn). For example, a thirty-day, five percent stream depletion factor means that the pumping will diminish the streamflow within thirty days by an amount equal to five percent of the streamflow. Calculation of stream depletion factors involves use of computer models and stream depletion contour maps.

The length of the delayed effect of well pumping on streamflow determines how far in advance of the needs of senior surface rights holders junior well-owners must be shut down. It also determines when juniors will be allowed to pump, despite the fact that a senior surface user is deprived of water, under the "futile call" doctrine (see Chapter Three, Section V C). The length of delay also helps define which waters have a sufficient hydrologic connection to be conjunctively managed since stream effects remote in time may be considered de minimis.

2. *Definition of Hydrologically Connected ("Tributary") Groundwater*

The word "tributary" refers to groundwater that has a hydrologic connection with a surface stream that is sufficiently direct to warrant legal attention. Tributariness may have important legal consequences, and proof is often difficult and expensive. To simplify fact-finding, Colorado courts have adopted a "presumption of tributariness." Safranek v. Limon (Colo.1951). The courts have ruled that where pumping would not affect a stream for over 100 years the water was nontributary, but that where pumping would affect a stream within 40 years, the water was tributary. District 10 Water Users Ass'n v. Barnett (Colo.1979). A Colorado statute now defines non-tributary water as water, "the withdrawal of which will not, within one hundred years, deplete the flow of any natural stream at an annual rate greater than one-tenth of one percent of the annual rate of withdrawal." As a practical matter, the presumption operates in favor of stream appropriators since the expense of proof is borne by proposed junior groundwater users.

3. Conjunctive Use Management

Interrelation of ground and surface supplies gives flexibility to users with access to both. A senior stream appropriator may be able to "follow the source" and get a more reliable supply by sinking a well to tap water flowing under the stream. This procedure was approved in Templeton v. Pecos Valley Artesian Conservancy Dist. (N.M.1958). An owner of senior water rights who was unable to divert sufficient surface water because flows had been diminished by groundwater pumping, sought to drill a well in the alluvial aquifer supporting the stream. The court held that the well used the same water from a deeper source, so it had the original surface priority rather than a recent priority as of the time the well was drilled. The "follow-the-source" rule allows surface appropriators to tap deep aquifers that feed more shallow aquifers. Langenegger v. Carlsbad Irrigation Dist. (N.M. 1971). The water in the supplemental well must, however, be from the same source as the original diversion. Consistent with the recognition of the interconnection of groundwater and surface water, the state engineer has a duty to deny a groundwater permit if pumping would interfere with vested surface rights. Albuquerque v. Reynolds (N.M.1962).

Colorado, which integrates management of tributary groundwater with surface sources under prior appropriation law, allows wells as alternate points of diversion for surface sources. A Colorado statute even requires seniors who have both wells and surface diversions to use their wells as alternate points of diversion before they "call the river" (require upstream juniors to shut down). It is not clear how much expense courts will require seniors to bear in operating or deepening a well as an alternate point of diversion. It is likely that the Colorado courts will follow the same approach they use in well interference cases: require the senior's well to have a reasonable economic reach before a junior will be shut down. See Section II B 5 of this chapter.

Conjunctive management can take advantage of the delayed stream effects of pumping that may allow months between the time of withdrawals and the time a surface user feels the effects. In states with flexible administrative policies, the junior may continue to pump so long as the senior is provided with sufficient supplemental water to prevent harm to appropriative rights.

Stream effects may not only be delayed, but the magnitude of the measurable stream effects may be less than the amount withdrawn from the tributary aquifer. For example, the withdrawal of five acre-feet from an aquifer underlying a stream may reduce streamflow by only two acre-feet; other sources of recharge make up the difference at least for a long time or in the immediate vicinity. In this situation, a pumper may furnish seniors on the surface stream with a substitute water supply of sufficient quantity and quality, thereby making a much larger supply of groundwater available. In the example given, the pumper might withdraw five acre-feet while bypassing two acre-feet directly into the stream to avoid stream depletion effects on surface water users, a technique known as "bypass pumping." Its effectiveness is limited by the physical recharge to the aquifer and by possible effects on adjacent wells. Stored or imported surface water may also be used to satisfy surface priorities, thus allowing greater amounts of groundwater to be pumped without adverse effects on senior rights in the connected stream.

The Colorado 1969 Water Rights Determination & Administration Act provides for conjunctive management by means of "augmentation plans." Junior appropriators may satisfy senior rights by use of a comprehensive plan that protects senior priorities. It is common to replace the seniors' water with groundwater although plans use a variety of augmentation methods including development of new diversion and storage facilities, alternative points of diversion, water exchange projects, substitute supplies, and development of new sources of water. The plans are subject to terms and conditions designed to protect senior appropriators and must be approved by the Colorado State Engineer. Typically, augmentation plans are entered into and costs shared among groups of junior appropriators threatened with curtailment if priorities were strictly enforced. Some augmentation plans are administered by a central water manager, who relies on hydrologic studies and computer models to formulate a basin-wide water budget. Although there is some risk to seniors that their rights will not be satisfied because hydrologic data may be in error or the plan will fail for other reasons, the validity of augmentation plans was upheld in Cache LaPoudre Water Users Ass'n v. Glacier View Meadows (Colo. 1976).

4. *Regulation of Tributary Groundwater: The Colorado Example*

In Colorado, the State Engineer administers tributary waters as part of the system of surface priorities. Junior well owners are subject to shutdowns in the event of a senior call, but the Colorado Supreme Court has mandated that the State Engineer's power to protect senior rights be used judiciously in order to maximize economic use of water. In Fellhauer v. People (Colo.1968), the court set aside an order of the engineer shutting down junior wells because it was not shown that seniors would benefit. This is the tributary groundwater equivalent of the "futile call" doctrine (Chapter Three, Section V C). For example, if a junior's pumping does not affect streamflow within twenty days, and if a senior's use would end within the twenty days (e.g., at the end of the irrigation season), the junior is allowed to continue pumping. Recognizing the inefficiency of strict priority administration, the court in *Fellhauer* noted the beginning of "a new drama of maximum use and how that use may constitutionally be integrated with the protection of vested rights."

Fellhauer's mandate of maximum use and acceptance of the futile call doctrine for groundwater was reaffirmed by the Colorado Legislature in the 1969 Water Rights Determination and Administration Act. The Act recognized vested water rights of well-owners, but effectively required appropriators to have a reasonably efficient means of diversion. No one is permitted "to command the whole flow of the stream merely to facilitate his taking of a fraction."

The Colorado State Engineer has adopted a "zone system" for administering wells in tributary aquifers. Pumping zones are based on the delay between groundwater withdrawals and streamflow effects. Wells can then be shut down in advance of anticipated senior calls on the river, with wells in the most distant zone shut down soonest, then wells in the next zone, and so on, according to the timing of expected effects on streamflow and senior needs.

The system was approved as a fair and reasonable administration scheme in Kuiper v. Well Owners Conservation Ass'n (Colo.1971). The court later went further and said that the State Engineer can require seniors to develop well water before calling juniors. Alamosa–La Jara Water Users Protection Ass'n v. Gould (Colo.1983).

B. Imported Supplies and Intensive Management: The California Example

Southern California's rapid population growth long ago created demands exceeding the capacity of local supplies. Large aquifers were overdrafted and threatened with saltwater intrusion and subsidence. Local water users responded by implementing a unique water management system based on increasing the physical supply and managing for conjunctive use.

The Metropolitan Water District (MWD) was formed by an act of the state legislature in 1929 to meet the supplemental needs of its public agency members—several southern California municipalities and municipal water districts. MWD imports water from northern California and the Colorado River and wholesales it to MWD members, who then distribute it to local users and water companies. Some imported water recharges aquifers from spreading basins or injection wells and it is later withdrawn from storage by pumping.

To manage and distribute imported water and to integrate its use with naturally occurring groundwater, southern California has engaged in a two-step process. First, groundwater rights of everyone in a particular basin have been adjudicated. Once basins have been adjudicated, special water districts are formed to manage basin-wide development and use of water. Pumping allocations are made among users and pumping assessments levied to provide for purchase of imported water to fulfill the needs that are not met by local supplies.

Some southern California districts use market mechanisms to adjust uses of groundwater and imported water in southern California. The Orange County Water District (OCWD) buys imported water from MWD and then allocates imported water and groundwater by pricing incentives, attempting to achieve an economic solution to conjunctive use problems. A basin-wide goal is set for the proportional use of groundwater and more expensive imported MWD water. Users who pump more groundwater than the indicated proportion of their total entitlements are subject to a special pump tax equal to the difference between the cost of pumping an acre-foot of groundwater and the cost of buying an acre-foot of MWD water. Thus, everyone effectively pays the same for an acre-foot of water, whether groundwater or MWD water.

IV. GROUNDWATER STORAGE

Storage capacity greatly enhances flexibility in water planning decisions. Erratic surface flows can be accumulated through the year and released as needed. The conventional method of storage is impoundment of surface waters behind a dam, creating a surface reservoir. Aquifer storage avoids many of the high costs and environmental effects as well as evaporation losses and pollution problems of surface reservoirs. Southern California uses underground storage in conjunction with its importation of waters from the Colorado River and the northern part of the state. Arizona has recently adopted its own program to enable it to store Central Arizona Project water underground and pump it as needed.

Imported water may be introduced into an aquifer by several methods. Natural recharge may be augmented by imported surface water. Water may be placed directly into the aquifer through injection wells or may be spread on the overlying lands to allow waters to percolate down.

Despite its advantages over surface storage, underground storage may be infeasible unless the importer has legal rights in the stored supply. A public agency will be reluctant to undertake an expensive importation scheme unless it has the right to reclaim, and exclude others from taking, waters it has captured or imported and stored.

In California, which has taken the lead in developing underground storage and administering the stored water in conjunction with surface uses, the importer/storer has firm rights in the stored supply. In City of Los Angeles v. City of San Fernando (Cal.1975), the court held that the City of Los Angeles has the exclusive right to recapture imported water it adds to the groundwater basin. The right is limited to imported water and to storage by public agencies. Similarly, Washington has held that commingling stored and naturally occurring groundwater does not cause the stored water to lose its separate identity. Jensen v. Department of Ecology (Wash.1984).

In Alameda County Water Dist. v. Niles Sand & Gravel Co. (Cal.App.1974), the water district was engaged in a groundwater storage program. Niles pumped water out of its sand and gravel pit which was hydrologically connected to the storage aquifer. The dewatering operation drew down the level of the stored water in the aquifer while the water district was attempting to recharge it to prevent salt water intrusion. The court enjoined pumping, ruling that the storage plan was within the police power of the water district and that the district had a "public duty" to maintain the water level. Thus the gravel company's use was burdened with a "public servitude" in favor of storage. In *Niles* the court also ruled that the burden on the gravel pit owner did not constitute a compensable taking. Similarly, the Nebraska court held that a state law recognizing rights to store and recover water in the aquifers under the lands of others was not an unconstitutional violation of the rights of overlying property owners. Central Nebraska Public Power & Irrig. Dist. v. Abrahamson (Neb.1987).

The cases support the existence of three types of storage rights: (1) the right of a public agency to import and store water without obligation to overlying landowners, (2) the right to protect the stored water against use by others, and (3) the right to recapture the stored water.

New Mexico has followed a contrary line of reasoning in cases holding that once imported water percolates into an aquifer, it becomes public water subject to appropriation. Kelley v. Carlsbad Irrigation Dist. (N.M.1966). The New Mexico approach, if strictly followed, could frustrate efforts to develop groundwater storage.

Statutes in several states facilitate storage. California statutes provide that underground storage is a beneficial use for which surface supplies may be appropriated and that private parties may not acquire rights in stored water as against storage entities. Similar statutes are in effect in Arizona (Central Arizona Project water), Nebraska (water incidentally or intentionally stored by projects), Utah (provides for appropriation of water for storage), and Washington (stored water held out from appropriation).

An issue unresolved in some state laws concerns priorities among those using groundwater storage. The issue may arise if several public agencies are competing for the limited storage capacity of a groundwater basin. Priorities could be embodied in storage agreements negotiated between competing public agencies.

V. CONTROLLING GROUNDWATER CONTAMINATION

Federal laws limit, mostly indirectly, the discharge or use of materials that may cause pollutants to enter groundwater. Some states also have laws to prevent groundwater contamination. Common law remedies are also available to well owners to redress aquifer pollution.

A. Regulation of Groundwater Pumping

Groundwater extraction can cause pollutants to migrate from a contaminated aquifer into a relatively pure one. Improperly constructed wells and wells that draw out water in large quantities or at high rates can attract contaminated water into the aquifer. The sources of contaminated groundwater include seawater intrusion, other saline or otherwise naturally contaminated waters, land disposal of pollutants, waste injection wells, surface storage and activities, and runoff from agriculture, city streets, and industry. The use of extracted groundwater can also cause pollution. If groundwater is already contaminated its application to land or other uses can affect other aquifers or surface sources.

Only a minority of states deny or condition well permits to prevent groundwater contamination by, for instance, controlling the rate and extent of extraction. In states like Arizona, Colorado, and Kansas, criteria for imposing permit conditions in certain districts or critical areas include prevention of groundwater contamination. However, critical areas are rarely designated specifically to deal with contamination problems.

State permitting agencies often examine the effects of an application for a new well or for a change in well location to see if it will draw saline or other lower quality water into parts of an aquifer used by existing pumpers. If serious degradation is likely, the agency may deny or condition the permit. But, minimal increases in the rate of intrusion or concentrations of pollution may be considered reasonable and the permit granted in the interest of allowing full development of water resources. Stokes v. Morgan (N.M.1984).

Virtually no jurisdictions deny the right to use groundwater because the use, as opposed to the extraction, of water will cause contamination. The Oklahoma Supreme Court has ruled, however, that an agency decision to allow withdrawal of fresh groundwater to be used in a waterflood operation (spreading water in old oil fields to help produce secondary recovery of oil) required a finding that it would not cause "waste" by either pollution or depletion. Oklahoma Water Resources Bd. v. Texas County Irr. and Water Resources Ass'n, Inc. (Okl. 1984).

B. Regulation of Polluting Activities

1. State Regulation

Most states have long regulated well construction. The oil producing states also control oil and gas drilling and production to prevent saline water from getting into freshwater wells. Most states are now adding new regulatory programs, many in response to federal incentives or requirements.

Comprehensive groundwater quality laws must regulate land use and other activities, in addition to well construction and use, because land-based activities are the major sources of contamination. Some laws classify aquifers according to the uses that can be made of them and allow more or less pollution to occur in order to protect the actual or anticipated uses. States that have enacted somewhat comprehensive groundwater protection laws include Arizona, Florida, and Wisconsin.

It is rare for the same agency that regulates groundwater allocation to regulate polluting activities. Thus, there can be interagency conflicts. E.g., Matador Pipelines, Inc. v. Oklahoma Water Resources Bd. (Okl.1987) (Corporation Commission has exclusive authority over pollution so Water Board did not have jurisdiction to order clean-up after break in oil pipeline).

2. *Federal Regulation*

Federal regulation of groundwater quality has not pursued a fixed strategy, but there are many environmental laws that have the effect of protecting groundwater.

The Clean Water Act, described in Chapter Nine, Section V A, controls discharges of pollutants from point sources. Although the Act has not been applied specifically to protect groundwater it does regulate many industrial and other activities that are sources of groundwater contamination. The Surface Mining Control and Reclamation Act (SMCRA), 30 U.S.C.A. §§ 1201–1328, regulates coal mining activities begun since 1977 in order to prevent water pollution.

Non-point sources, irrigation return flows and runoff from farming, construction activities, city streets, and mine sites can cause pollutants to seep into aquifers and run down wells. Although the Clean Water Act requires states to develop plans to control these sources, there are no sanctions for failing to implement effective programs.

The Safe Drinking Water Act, 42 U.S.C.A. § 300h, has a wellhead protection program that provides for designation and protection of wells and wellfields used to extract drinking water. This program motivates some control of non-point sources. The Act includes an underground injection control (UIC) program that requires permits and adherence to certain standards. It also regulates disposal of liquid waste, including some hazardous wastes, that is injected into deep wells. States are allowed to take over the administration of these programs.

Protection of groundwater necessitates control of dumps and, in many cases, clean-up of old sites. The law that most directly protects groundwater quality is the Solid Waste Act, also known as the Resources Conservation and Recovery Act (RCRA), 42 U.S.C.A. §§ 6901–6991i. RCRA controls every aspect of hazardous waste generation, transportation, storage, processing, and disposal. It also sets guidelines for state regulation of other nonhazardous wastes. The Act also regulates underground storage tanks (such as gasoline tanks).

Past disposal of wastes causes contamination of many groundwater resources and threatens others. The Comprehensive Environmental Response, Compensation, and Liability Act (CERCLA), 42 U.S.C.A. § 9605, also known as the "Superfund," establishes a federal program to clean up hazardous substances in inactive or abandoned sites. CERCLA creates a cause of action against almost anyone connected with past disposal activities for damages to resources. The resource most frequently harmed is groundwater. See Utah v. Kennecott Corp. (D.Utah 1992)(setting aside CERCLA consent decree as giving inadequate protection to state's groundwater).

Indirect protection of groundwater results from legislation controlling the production and use of toxic substances. The Federal Insecticide, Fungicide, and Rodenticide Act (FIFRA), 7 U.S.C.A. §§ 136–136y, requires federal registration of pesticides and other chemicals regularly applied in farming. It also allows the Environmental Protection Agency to limit the distribution, sale, or use of pesticides in order to protect the environment.

C. State Judicial Remedies

Most state courts entertain liability suits by well owners against persons, including oil well owners, whose activities cause pollution of water wells. Some state laws, like Oklahoma's Oil Well Pollution Act, create special rights of action. Common law remedies for groundwater contamination include nuisance, trespass, and negligence suits. Mowrer v. Ashland Oil & Refining Co. (7th Cir.1975); City of Attica v. Mull Drilling Co. (Kan.App.1984).

Some cases involve questions of whether federal statutes and programs preempt state programs and actions. The outcome depends on a reading of the individual federal statute to determine if Congress intended to preempt state laws. E.g., Attorney General v. Thomas Solvent Co. (Mich.App.1985) (CERCLA did not preempt state public nuisance suit). In some cases, state remedial programs and causes of action will be allowed as a way of making pollution control more effective. In others, Congress intended, for instance, not to burden interstate commerce with varying requirements.

CHAPTER SEVEN

DIFFUSED SURFACE WATERS

Watercourses are subject to the applicable state water allocation system—riparian, appropriative, or hybrid. Diffused surface waters are generally those waters that have not yet joined a watercourse, such as runoff from rainfall. Different rules apply as people seek to use or avoid these diffused surface waters.

Naturally occurring water can make land less valuable or useful unless it is channelled, controlled, or drained. A landowner responding to such concerns may direct surface flow toward another's land, creating conflicts between landowners. Generally one may take reasonable measures to protect property or persons from harm.

Another issue, arising mostly in arid areas, is whether a landowner may take and use surface flows unrestrained by state laws concerning appropriation of water. The laws of most jurisdictions, although differing in rationale, allow unrestricted use of diffused surface waters captured on a landowner's property.

I. WATERCOURSES AND DIFFUSED SURFACE WATERS DISTINGUISHED

A. Watercourses

Theoretically, almost all waters may be included in the definition of a "watercourse." A great river includes tributaries, which in turn include not only small streams, but also gullies and washes that channel rainwater and snow melt from throughout the watershed. A watercourse may also include underground water that is hydrologically connected with surface water. But there are limits to the confidence with which science can trace water destined for streams and lakes, and to the state's practical and political ability to impose controls on water use. Thus, there are accepted criteria for defining "watercourses" that come under state regulation and allocation.

States generally seek to exert authority over "natural watercourses." A natural watercourse is usually defined as a body of water flowing in a defined channel with bed and banks. Most states require water to be present for a substantial portion of the year in order to qualify as a natural watercourse, but some states will consider dry streams or lake beds to be "natural watercourses." Water flowing in a surface depression only as the result of rainfall or snowmelt usually is not considered to be in a watercourse (see Chapter Three, Section VI A). States differ on whether underground water is treated as part of a watercourse.

B. Diffused Surface Waters

Surface water not in or connected with a "watercourse" is considered "diffused surface water." The Restatement (Second) of Torts § 846 defines this as "water from rain, melting snow, springs or seepage, or detached from subsiding floods, which lies or flows on the surface of the earth but does not form a part of a watercourse or lake." Diffused surface water usually includes water flowing in draws, swales, gullies, ravines, and hollows. It may also include water in puddles, depressions, marshes, and small ponds. A spring may not be considered diffused surface water if it runs directly into a stream or has a large enough flow to constitute a stream. Generally, if water flows with some frequency and historical regularity, and carves a recognizable channel or reaches a lake or pond having some permanency, it is considered to be in a watercourse. Floodwaters, usually considered to be in a watercourse, become diffused surface waters when they lose their connection with a stream, such as by overflowing the banks and settling elsewhere.

II. PROTECTION FROM DAMAGE BY SURFACE FLOWS

Some of the earliest reported cases dealing with water have to do with drainage. The law allows landowners to protect or develop their land even if it causes drainage problems for others. An upper landowner may augment natural drainage to make marshy land useful, divert flood waters to protect land or buildings, or fill, build on, or pave land as part of developing it. In each case drainage patterns are altered, affecting lower landowners. Lower landowners can raise their land level or construct dikes, buildings, or other obstructions to the flow of surface waters that back water up onto the lands of upper landowners. Disputes often arise if avoided water cannot be diverted directly into a watercourse without causing harm to others. American jurisdictions have historically split between two rather extreme and opposite rules to resolve such disputes: the "common enemy doctrine" and the "civil law doctrine." Today, most jurisdictions follow a rule of reasonable use.

Water other than diffused surface water may have to be disposed of or drained from one's land. For instance, a person using water diverted from a stream or lake (*e.g.*, for irrigation or to power a mill) may need to dispose of the unconsumed water, often referred to as "tail water." Tail water is not diffused surface water and ordinarily may not be drained across the land of another without permission, which is usually accomplished by acquiring an easement or right of way. Cf. Loosli v. Heseman (Idaho 1945). The right to drain tail water, however, can also be acquired by prescription.

Water impounded on one's land, such as in a reservoir, is treated under special rules. A landowner who builds a dam or otherwise backs up water (whether or not it is diffused surface water) and causes another person's land to be flooded is subject to action for trespass. However, if the flooding is continuous and satisfies the relevant statute of limitations, the landowner may gain a prescriptive right to flood the land. Government entities with the power of eminent domain may be subject to an inverse condemnation suit and be liable for compensation.

Dam owners must also protect the property of others in maintaining a reservoir and in releasing water from it. Many jurisdictions impose absolute liability for harm caused by artificial storage of water, such as when a dam breaks. Rylands v. Fletcher (Eng.1868).

A. Common Enemy Doctrine

The common enemy doctrine holds that landowners may take any action they see fit in order to avoid diffused surface waters without incurring liability to others. Such actions include building a barrier to water flowing down from adjoining land, such as a dike along one's upper boundary, or altering natural drainage patterns by a system of berms, ditches, or pumps to keep it out of a basement or away from a field. The doctrine may also allow development of drainage systems to augment natural drainage. Excavations may be made for drains and channels to collect and divert flows or accumulations of water. The only limitation is that one may not store surface water (as in a dam or reservoir) and then release it upon another.

The doctrine is sometimes called the "Massachusetts rule" but it has since been rejected there. The doctrine has been attributed to the common law of England where, as in much of the eastern United States, development or agricultural use of land may depend on avoiding surface runoff and draining saturated land. In England, where drainage was early centralized by statute under a system of common drains, no clear common law developed and decisions contain some support for both the common enemy and civil law doctrines.

The absolute right of landowners to use their lands as they please, as embodied in the common enemy rule, ignores an equally important and reciprocal principle in our jurisprudence: landowners must use their property in a manner that does not harm others. Very early it became apparent that although the doctrine encouraged development of property needed for a growing nation, unhindered development often came at the expense of other owners. It also promoted nasty drainage contests among landowners and breaches of the peace.

Nearly all states that purport to follow the common enemy rule today have modified it to include the familiar tort concept of reasonableness. Courts have altered the rule by holding that deflection or other activity causing surface water to flow onto the lands of another must be in good faith, not be negligent, and not cause substantial harm. Jurisdictions that employ a modified common enemy doctrine are: Arizona (as to floodwaters), Arkansas, Nebraska (up to the point water enters a natural drainage way), South Carolina, and the District of Columbia. In addition, courts in New York, Oklahoma, Virginia, and Washington invoke the doctrine but have modified the rule so extensively that they effectively apply the reasonable use rule (discussed below in Section II C of this chapter). The Massachusetts court has indicated an intention to follow the rule of reasonable use in future cases. See Tucker v. Badoian (Mass.1978). In spite of the anomaly presented by the doctrine in its unmodified form, it is still controlling in Maine, Indiana, and Montana. See Argyelan v. Haviland (Ind.1982) (suggesting that channelling water onto a neighbor's land would not be covered by the rule).

B. Civil Law Doctrine

The civil law doctrine, traceable to the Code Napoleon, entitles every landowner to have the natural drainage maintained. Each owner has a reciprocal duty to refrain from damming, channelling, or diverting diffused surface waters that would change or increase drainage in ways that would adversely affect others. The rule thus places a servitude upon adjoining lands for natural drainage. The civil law rule is unsuited to settled areas because it prevents most development. For example, construction of a building or paving a parking area displaces natural runoff and would not be permitted under literal application of the doctrine; in rural areas, cultivation for agricultural use often depends on altering the natural drainage pattern.

Although the language of the few reported cases is often ambiguous, the following states appear to follow the civil law doctrine without significant modifications: Florida (as to unimproved land),

Georgia, Kansas, Louisiana, Michigan, New Mexico, Tennessee, Texas, and Vermont.

As with the common enemy doctrine, courts have modified the civil law doctrine to fit the society it is supposed to serve. Several states have incorporated notions of reasonableness into the civil law doctrine to allow for some alteration of natural drainage patterns. Colorado and Iowa allow deviations that do not change the quantity or manner of flows. Maryland insists that its "reasonableness of use" test is but a qualification of the civil law, though the outcomes are hard to distinguish from a reasonable use rule.

In addition to employing reasonableness concepts, some states have incorporated elements of the common enemy doctrine. For instance, Arizona has generally followed the civil law doctrine for diffused surface waters but has held that "floodwaters" are subject to the common enemy rule.

Some states have made "reasonable use" exceptions to the civil law doctrine to accommodate development in urban areas where lots are typically small and close together. They include Alabama, Florida, Ohio, Pennsylvania, and South Dakota. Idaho makes an exception allowing reasonable use as to waters discharged into a natural streambed.

Nebraska, which generally follows the common enemy rule, applies the civil law to require lower owners to bear the burden of any waters that are in a natural drainageway, including those that have been put there artificially in the exercise of "good husbandry." In Oregon, an exception has been allowed for agricultural drainage if required for "good husbandry" and water that is in natural channels. Illinois permits artificial drainage if it is necessitated by good husbandry. In Texas the civil law doctrine applies to private parties while the reasonable use rule applies to municipal corporations.

C. Reasonable Use Doctrine

Permitting landowners to affect natural drainage in ways that are reasonable under the circumstances creates both benefits and burdens. The existence of reciprocal rights, however, increases uses that may be made of all property, to society's benefit, and enhances land values. Thus, courts have crafted numerous exceptions to temper the common enemy and civil law doctrines such as when they allow landowners to disregard the property of others or restrict landowners so much that they tend to stifle development.

The reasonable use doctrine is embodied in the Restatement (Second) of Torts §§ 822–831, 833. It has become the majority rule as courts have rejected or modified the common enemy and civil law doctrines. Some states purporting to follow one of these doctrines have so modified it that the principles of the reasonable use doctrine in fact control.

The reasonable use doctrine was first invoked to determine rights in cases involving interference with diffused surface waters in New Hampshire. Bassett v. Salisbury Mfg. Co. (N.H.1862). It now appears to be followed in more states than either of the other doctrines. The states that follow the doctrine are Alaska, California, Connecticut, Delaware, Florida (improved land), Hawaii, Kentucky, Massachusetts, Minnesota, Mississippi, Missouri, Nevada, New Hampshire, New Jersey, New York, North Carolina, North Dakota, Missouri, Ohio, Oklahoma, Rhode Island, South Dakota (urban areas only), Texas (municipal corporations), Utah, Virginia, Washington, West Virginia, and Wisconsin.

In applying the reasonable use doctrine, courts generally balance the gravity of harm against the utility of the conduct. To determine the gravity of harm, a court may consider the extent and character of the injury, the social value of the activity harmed, the suitability of the harmed use to the location, and the difficulty that the injured party would have had avoiding the harm. In evaluating the utility of the conduct, courts may consider the social value of the activity for the location, the impact on the activity if compensation for harm were required, and the difficulty to the person harmed of avoiding injury.

Often "reasonableness" criteria will not point clearly to a particular result. Several jurisdictions that employ the reasonable use doctrine also refer to the common enemy or civil law doctrine. For example, in California the reasonable use doctrine is considered to be a modification of the civil law doctrine previously used. The California Supreme Court, discussing considerations of reasonableness in deciding disputes over diffused surface waters, said there must be a case by case judgment. Keys v. Romley (Cal.1966). If the conduct and uses of both parties are reasonable and necessary, the burden of any harm will fall on the landowner who changes the natural drainage system, a result that is consistent with the civil law rule.

D. Public Control of Surface Drainage

1. *Public Drainage Projects*

For centuries, England has administratively regulated surface drainage. In the United States, there are numerous special districts that administer drainage projects. Drainage projects are typically formed under state law after a local election or petition showing consent of a majority of affected landowners. The projects are usually publicly financed, and assessments are made against all property benefited, whether or not all individual landowners have consented. Such projects can increase the agricultural capacity of drained lands and provide "new" land for buildings and other improvements. Indeed, many thousands of acres of marshes and swamplands in drainage districts have been reclaimed for productive use.

Special statutes governing drainage districts generally exempt them from restraints imposed by the various doctrines discussed above. But if private property rights are taken or if others are damaged, compensation must be paid.

2. Public Restrictions on Draining Wetlands

Marshy areas, sometimes considered useless in the past, are important habitat for migratory waterfowl and other types of birds, fish, and wildlife. Drainage may have an adverse effect on recreational opportunities, increase fluctuations in streamflows, cause flooding problems, and lower groundwater levels. Consequently, many states and the federal government have passed laws regulating private activities that would impair desirable qualities of swamps, marshes, and other wetlands.

State and local control of private land use for environmental protection is surely a proper exercise of police power. Although restrictions may interfere with an owner's ability to put land to the most lucrative use, they do not amount to a taking vulnerable to constitutional challenges or claims for compensation. See Just v. Marinette County (Wis. 1972); but see State v. Johnson (Me.1970).

Section 404 of the Clean Water Act, 33 U.S.C.A. § 1344 (see Chapter Nine, Section V A) requires that a "dredge and fill" permit be obtained from the Army Corps of Engineers before constructing a project affecting any wetlands or other "waters of the United States." The definition of "waters of the United States" is so broad as to include remote reaches of the tiniest streams that eventually flow into a navigable stream. Before issuing a dredge and fill permit, the Secretary of the Army must find that there will be no unacceptable effects on fish or wildlife or their habitats and that values protected in other federal statutes will not be impaired. As administered, the Act is a major limitation on drainage or other such activities in wetlands. States may apply to administer the federal permit system, but must follow federal guidelines and standards. Coverage of § 404 is so broad that there is no room for conflicting state or local regulation. However, the Clean Water Act expressly allows states to impose more stringent standards than those in the Act.

III. USE OF DIFFUSED SURFACE WATERS

Diffused surface waters subject to capture are generally not regulated by the state; thus no one can demand continuation of their flow. A landowner is entitled to impound and use such waters at will, but if a higher landowner intercepts the waters, the lower landowner has no remedy.

A. Right to Capture Diffused Surface Waters

Most states recognize an absolute right of landowners to any diffused surface waters on their lands, including waters from ravines and gullies, rainfall, snowmelt, and any standing water. This entitles them to dam, store, use, or sell the water and consequently to prevent it from flowing to adjoining lands. The unlimited right to capture diffused surface waters is in accord with the rationale of the common enemy doctrine: a landowner owns all water above and below the land and may deal with it without incurring liability to other landowners. Broadbent v. Ramsbotham (Eng. 1856). The civil law doctrine of natural flow would seem to allow adjoining owners to demand that surface waters be allowed to flow unimpeded. Nevertheless, the rule of capture has been embraced in virtually all civil law jurisdictions as well.

Only a few states attempt to regulate or restrict a landowner's use of diffused surface water. Generally, no legally enforceable rights or responsibilities arise concerning use of diffused surface waters, except to the extent that avoidance rules (discussed in the preceding section) may apply. Water rights usually cannot attach until water has joined a watercourse.

B.   State Control of Use of Diffused Surface Waters

States seeking broad control of waters are likely to define diffused surface waters narrowly, since watercourses are subject to state regulation. A few states recognize no distinction between water in watercourses and diffused surface waters for the purpose of regulation. This is done by express, all-inclusive legislation or by interpretation of constitutional or statutory language defining the state's authority.

A Texas statute explicitly exerts state control over all "storm water, floodwater, and rainwater of every river, natural stream, canyon, ravine, depression, and watershed in the state" by making it the "property of the state." The Texas Supreme Court limited the effect of the statute by holding that it cannot apply to lands granted (presumably to private owners) prior to the effective date of the law because the right to such water had vested in the landowners.   Turner v. Big Lake Oil Co. (Tex. 1936).   The decision relies on the statute's reference to state "property" as an assertion of ownership.   Typically, such language in statutes and constitutions refers to a state's sovereign power over water.   If interpreted in this way, the Texas law should have been held valid as an extension of police power over all diffused surface water.   Other Texas decisions have expanded state control of diffused surface waters by relaxing the definition of watercourse to include any water found present at times and in quantities that make it "practicable and valuable to irrigate therefrom."   Hoefs v. Short (Tex.1925).

A Utah constitutional provision asserting jurisdiction over all waters in the state has been interpreted by the state supreme court to preclude use of diffused surface waters outside the state regulatory scheme.   Richlands Irrigation Co. v. Westview Irrigation Co. (Utah 1938).   The court held that all water destined for a stream is effectively part of the stream.

Colorado's Constitution provides that "natural streams" are within the state's power.   This has long been judicially and legislatively extended to surface water.   All water tributary to a natural stream affects the streamflow and the courts presume that all flowing water is tributary.   A statute asserts that all "water ... which is in or tributary to a natural surface stream" is public property subject to appropriation in accordance with the state constitution. Even precipitation has been claimed as subject to state control. Case law indicates that capture and use by a Colorado landowner of diffused surface water destined for a stream is not allowed. Nevius v. Smith (Colo.1929).

The Colorado and Utah approach is based upon the realization that streamflow depends on runoff. Although this may seem to deny property rights to landowners, in fact water rights in surface waters can be perfected and assured by complying with state appropriation law, by which one acquires an enforceable water right that is not subject to the whims of other landowners. Whether strict state control of surface waters would prevent minimal uses such as small stockwatering ponds (or even rainbarrels) has not been decided; if the use is trivial the case probably will not arise. Thus, the lawful use of even a small stockwatering pond created on a natural stream by human effort depends upon the landowner's conformity with the state's prior appropriation system.

Some riparian states regulate diffused surface waters by subjecting them to the reasonable use doctrine (e.g., New Hampshire and Minnesota). A statute in Iowa affirms the right of a landowner to use diffused surface waters, but the right is conditioned on a continuation of minimum flows necessary to protect the rights of lower water users (presumably on a watercourse that depends on the surface flow).

Most states afford all landowners a right to capture waters outside a natural stream. The rule is embodied in statutes of some states (e.g., Indiana and South Dakota). Oklahoma and North Dakota expressly exclude diffused surface waters from state control. In Arizona and New Mexico the omission of diffused surface waters from the definition of waters subject to appropriation effectively excludes them from state control. Most states confine control to "natural streams" or use similar terminology construed to mean "watercourses" as opposed to diffused surface waters. A few states (e.g., Nevada and Oregon) claim control over all waters, but only Utah and Colorado actually extend control to diffused surface waters. Many jurisdictions simply have not yet dealt with the issue of a landowner's right to use diffused surface water.

CHAPTER EIGHT

FEDERAL AND INDIAN RESERVED RIGHTS

I. RESERVED RIGHTS DOCTRINE

The reserved rights doctrine was created to assure that Indian lands and public lands set aside by the government for a particular purpose would have adequate water. The doctrine recognizes rights to a quantity of water sufficient to fulfill the purposes of the reservation of land. Although most water rights in the western United States have priority based on when they first were put to a beneficial use, rights on federal and Indian lands have a priority dating back to at least as early as the reservations were established even if water use begins long after others have appropriated waters from the stream.

To quantify these rights, Congress has consented to joining the United States as a party in state court stream adjudications. Generally, however, reserved rights are not subject to state law.

A. Origin of the Doctrine—*Winters v. United States*

The reserved rights doctrine is rooted in the Supreme Court decision in Winters v. United States

(S.Ct.1908). That case was a conflict between Indians of the Fort Belknap Reservation in Montana and nearby non-Indian settlers over waters of the Milk River. In 1888, the Indian tribes agreed to cede territory to the United States that was part of the lands reserved by them in an earlier treaty and to be confined to a relatively small reservation. The federal government induced settlers to take up homesteads on the ceded lands. The homesteaders began using water from the Milk River for irrigation, perfecting their water rights under Montana law. A short time later, the Indians began diverting large quantities of water for irrigation. The settlers diverted water upstream from the Indians, preventing them from getting sufficient water. The United States then brought suit against the settlers on behalf of the tribes.

The Supreme Court held that although the settlers had established rights under state law and had begun using water before the Indians, the Indians held a prior water right. The right was based on an implication drawn from the circumstances. Because it was government policy to make the Indians "pastoral and civilized people" and because the reserved lands were arid, the Court found it inconceivable that either the Indians or the government would agree to the vast land cession unless enough water was reserved to make the remaining lands useful. Although the agreement was silent on the subject, water rights were found to exist by "necessary implication." Further, the Court had to reconcile the conflicting implication that the government had intended settlers to cultivate the ceded lands, which purpose would be defeated by denying the settlers' water rights. The Court applied the established rule of construction that ambiguities in an Indian agreement or treaty should be resolved in the Indians' favor to compensate for the typically unequal bargaining positions of the Indians and the United States.

It was many years before the full impact of the landmark case was realized because few Indian tribes asserted their rights. Although Indians theoretically held rights under the *Winters* doctrine to waters developed by others, they lacked facilities to divert and distribute the waters and legal representation to assert their rights.

Indian tribes are in a fiduciary relationship with the federal government, that causes them to look to it for protection of their property and assertion of their legal rights. However, the federal government invested heavily in water development projects that enabled non-Indians to use vast quantities of water subject to inchoate Indian rights. Thus, a conflict of interest may arise when the federal government represents tribes. The Secretary of Interior plays a dual role as administrator of the Bureau of Reclamation and trustee for Indians, but must exert uncompromised efforts to secure sufficient water to the Indians, not simply seek an accommodation between the interests. Pyramid Lake Paiute Tribe v. Morton (D.D.C.1972). Nevertheless, once the government has represented Indians in a water rights adjudication, third parties can rely on the determination; the Supreme Court has refused to modify such determinations even if the tribes were inadequately represented. See Nevada v. United States (S.Ct.1983).

Once asserted, Indian reserved rights can have an important impact on the quantity of water available to non-Indians in the future. Arizona v. California (S.Ct.1963) held that reserved rights extend to protecting future reservation uses and is not limited by the population or needs of the Indians.

The Indian reserved right is not extinguished except by express legislation, even after the reservation is terminated and the land sold off, so long as there is a continuing purpose to be served. United States v. Adair (9th Cir.1983)(tribe retained unextinguished fishing rights).

B. Application to Federal (Non–Indian) Lands

The reserved rights doctrine has been extended to public lands reserved for a particular governmental purpose. The rationale of *Winters* concerning Indian reservations is apt: if Congress authorizes creation of a park, wildlife refuge, national forest, military base, wilderness area, or other reservation of public land that demands water for its success, reserving the land implies an intention to reserve sufficient water to carry out the congressional purposes.

Congress has legislative power, under the property clause to reserve waters from appropriation when it sets aside federal lands.   The question is whether a reservation of federal land, silent as to water rights, should imply a reservation of water rights. The Supreme Court held in Federal Power Comm'n v. Oregon (S.Ct.1955)(the *Pelton Dam* case) that a *reservation* of federal land for particular purposes (not merely the existence of public land available for homesteading or other dispositions) removed water sources on that land from appropriation pursuant to state law.   The decision foreshadowed the Court's unequivocal decision, announced eight years later in Arizona v. California (S.Ct.1963), that the reserved rights doctrine applied to federal lands.

Courts imply a reservation of waters in each reservation of federal public lands to the extent necessary to fulfill the purposes of the reservation. Thus, the Supreme Court upheld the government's claim to the amount of water in a limestone cavern at Devil's Hole National Monument required to preserve the habitat of the pupfish, a prehistoric species mentioned in the proclamation setting aside the monument.   Cappaert v. United States (S.Ct. 1976).

The quantity of water reserved is limited to the amount necessary for the reservation's specific purposes.   Only purposes encompassed by the grant of congressional authority at the time the reservation was set aside will be considered.   In United States v. New Mexico (S.Ct.1978), which involved reserved rights for a national forest established in 1899, the Supreme Court rejected government claims of reserved rights for instream flows needed for wildlife, recreation, aesthetics, and stockwatering because purposes stated in the 1897 Organic Act of the Forest Service included only furnishing a timber supply and protecting watersheds. Reserved water rights may be created for instream flows, however, when Congress creates a wilderness area because the purposes of the Wilderness Act include preserving lands in their natural condition. See Sierra Club v. Yeutter (10th Cir.1990).

C. Federal Power

No Supreme Court decision has questioned the existence of federal power to reserve water from appropriation under state law. Rather, the persistent question has been whether, in the absence of an express reservation, Congress intended to exercise its powers.

1. *Constitutional Bases*

Congress has power to reserve water for use on public lands under the property clause of the Constitution, art. IV, § 3, which authorizes it "to dispose of and make all needful Rules and Regulations respecting the Territory or other Property belonging to the United States."

In United States v. Rio Grande Dam & Irrigation Co. (S.Ct.1899), the Court upheld the ability of Congress to regulate the flow of a non-navigable stream that affected the navigable capacity of navigable waters. The navigation power was also cited in Arizona v. California (S.Ct.1931). However, the property clause, mentioned in dictum in *Rio*

Grande, is the most commonly cited source of power for federal reservations of water. Water rights can also be reserved in the exercise of other federal powers, such as the defense power (in the case of a military installation or a dam needed to generate electricity for defense purposes).

Reservation of water for Indian reservations is generally based on the Indian commerce clause, art. I, § 8, cl. 3, granting Congress the authority "to regulate Commerce ... with the Indian Tribes," but also may be based on the treaty power, art. II, § 2, cl. 2, which is sometimes cited as authority for establishing Indian reservations.

2. *Exercise by Congress or the Executive*

Close questions arise concerning whether Congress intended to exercise its power and, if so, whether it intended to supersede the operation of state water law.

Congress can take the water rights it needs for federal purposes in the exercise of its eminent domain power. This requires paying just compensation to persons holding rights established by state law, since those rights constitute property. But, if Congress reserved water for future federal uses at a time before private rights were established by appropriation, no compensation need be paid.

Congress exercises its power to reserve waters whenever it sets aside land for purposes that require water. The land can be set aside by an act of Congress, a treaty, or an executive order made pursuant to a delegation by Congress of authority to the President. Arizona v. California (S.Ct.1963). Although Congress may not have considered whether it was delegating authority to reserve water when it gave the executive the authority to establish Indian reservations, national forests, or other reservations, courts have had no trouble finding an implied reservation of water rights based on the establishment of executive order reservations.

D. Relationship to State Water Law

The federal government has long deferred to state law in the allocation of water, even on public lands (see Chapter Three, Section II). The 1877 Desert Land Act was interpreted in California Oregon Power Co. v. Beaver Portland Cement Co. (S.Ct.1935) as confirming a federal policy of recognizing only those water rights on public lands that were perfected according to state law. Yet, the Supreme Court's reserved rights doctrine acknowledged the prerogative of the federal government to remove water from availability for state law appropriation and to establish and exercise water rights in ways that may not be in accord with state law.

States never had power to alienate rights to water needed for federal uses on public lands. Federal recognition of state-perfected water rights did not abdicate the federal property interest in unappropriated waters (waters not yet allocated to private parties) on the public lands. A state's authority to allocate rights in water, then, applies to all waters in the state except those that the federal government reserves for itself before they are appropriated.

State law cannot interfere with federal property rights or defeat federal purposes and programs. The supremacy clause limits state control of water to the extent it conflicts with an exercise of federal power. The effect of federal preemption in this area especially concerns state water law administrators and holders of state water rights because federal reserved water rights often remain unused for many years and exist in uncertain quantities. This creates a possibility of disruption of a state's water rights system and displacement of state water rights holders that are economically dependent on those rights.

1. *Prior Appropriation*

The prior appropriation doctrine, operating in most western states, recognizes water rights based on historical beneficial use. That is, the earliest user has a right to use the amount that has been continuously diverted, superior to rights of subsequent users. Each user is ranked according to when water use began, with the earliest continuous users securing the highest priority rights. See Chapter Three. All water rights holders who began their uses after a reservation was created have rights lower in priority than the reservation. The federal government can enter the picture at any time to assert its unusual water rights; if a stream is fully appropriated, rights junior to the federal reservation may become worthless when substantial federal rights are asserted. Thus, anyone who established rights after the date public land was reserved for a particular use holds rights subject to a degree of uncertainty. The value of those rights depends upon the quantity of prior rights, the potential size of federal uses, and the available supply. Federal rights are limited to quantities needed to fulfill the "purposes of the reservation."

A federal use may be the basis of a reserved right even if it does not constitute a beneficial use under the state definition; the federal government need not comply with the state system of water administration to exercise a reserved right. In addition, the federal government cannot be restrained or regulated by state law in exercising its reserved water rights to carry out federal purposes.

2. Riparian Rights

Winters and other reserved rights cases arose where the prior appropriation doctrine was applicable. The government "priority" for uses on a reservation as of the date the reservation was established fits into a system of ranking of rights by date. But under riparian water law, no special significance attaches to the order in which people began using water. See Chapter Two. Generally, every landowner bordering on a stream has a right to use a reasonable quantity of water. In times of shortage, available supplies are shared by all riparians.

The courts have not decided how the concept of reserved water rights applies in a riparian jurisdiction. If the federal government must share the burden of shortage equally with other users no assurance exists that federal purposes can be carried out. One solution would be to exempt the government from sharing shortages, imposing the burden only on private riparians. But this may be unfair to the early riparians.

Professor Eva Hanks has recommended a solution without building in unfairness: allow the federal reservation its full use; allow riparians whose ownership predates the reservation the share they would have gotten if all water users, including the government, had shared the shortage equally; limit riparians who acquired rights after the reservation was established to shares diminished further by apportioning among them the burden caused by the government's taking its full water needs.

II.   PRIORITY OF RESERVED RIGHTS

A.   Date of Reservation

The federal government obtains a water right with a priority as of the date a reservation is established—the date of the statute, executive order, agreement, or treaty setting aside the reservation. Private rights existing on a stream when a reservation is established are superior to the reserved rights of the federal government; federal reserved rights are superior only to subsequently established private rights. This greatly limits the federal government's rights for newer reservations on heavily or fully appropriated streams.

B. Early Priorities Based on Aboriginal Indian Rights

Many Indian treaties are grants of land from tribes to the United States. If a tribe is seen as reserving all rights except those specifically granted away, priority may attach to the reserved right at some time in prehistory. Some lower courts have so indicated, but the Supreme Court has not yet decided the question. Whether the priority date of an Indian reservation is the date of the treaty or time immemorial is usually of little consequence, however; most Indian reservations were created before other rights were established. On the other hand, the rationale for the earlier, immemorial priority would not apply to Indian reservations established unilaterally by the government from land not aboriginally held by the tribe.

III. QUANTITY

A. Purposes of the Reservation

The quantity of water subject to federal or Indian reserved rights is limited to the quantity necessary to fulfill the purposes of the reservation. The amount may change over time as needs change so long as they are within the original purposes for establishing a reservation.

1. *Limitation on Quantity Reserved*

The Supreme Court, in Cappaert v. United States (S.Ct.1976), said that the government impliedly reserved "only that amount of water necessary to fulfill the purpose of the reservation, no more." In United States v. New Mexico (S.Ct.1978), the Court said that the purposes to be considered in imposing this limitation are the specific purposes for which the land was reserved.

2. Determining Purposes

The Supreme Court in *New Mexico* required a "careful examination" of the purposes for reserving land to determine the quantity of water reserved "because the reservation [of water] is implied, not expressed, and because of the history of congressional" deference to state water law. The Court examined the language and legislative history of the Forest Service Organic Act and its predecessor bills to find that at the time of the Act Congress had two primary purposes for authorizing establishment of national forests: timber production and watershed protection. The Act did not refer to fish and wildlife or stock watering. The Court contrasted the Organic Act with legislation expressing concern for wildlife (such as the National Park Service Act). Subsequent legislation such as the 1960 Multiple Use Sustained Yield Act broadened the administrative mandates for national forests to include wildlife, recreation, and range but did not reserve any additional water for existing forests. United States v. City and County of Denver (Colo.1982). The Supreme Court, however, might reach a different result in a case concerning a forest reservation made after enactment of legislation expanding the national forest purposes.

The Colorado Supreme Court held that the United States could present evidence to support a claim that certain instream flow rights were necessary to provide water for channel maintenance. United States v. Jesse (Colo.1987). If minimum flows were necessary to prevent the "watershed" purposes of the National Forest from being entirely defeated, then they could be granted. On remand, however, the water court held that the purpose could be satisfied in ways other than by asserting water rights.

The only court to confront the question held that reserved water rights are created when a wilderness area is established. However, the decision was vacated on appeal because the issue was not "ripe." It was not clear that harm to the wilderness character of the area would be so great and immediate as to violate the preservation mandate of the statute. Sierra Club v. Yeutter (10th Cir.1990). In that case, the government was resisting the attempt of a conservation organization to force it to claim reserved rights. It is likely that if the agency had claimed reserved rights for the wilderness area the court would have deferred to the exercise of its discretion.

3. *Indian Reservations: Practicably Irrigable Acreage*

In Arizona v. California (S.Ct.1963), the Supreme Court found that "the only feasible and fair way" to measure the reserved rights of the five Colorado River tribes was based on the amount of water needed to irrigate all of the Indians' practicably

irrigable acreage (PIA)—a very substantial amount
of water. A state court adjudication applying the
PIA method (as described in section VI A) was
upheld by the United States Supreme Court. In re
Rights to Use Water in the Big Horn System (Wyo.
1988), affirmed by an equally divided court, Wyoming v. United States (S.Ct. 1989) (*Big Horn*).

The broad purposes of Indian reservations differ
from the rather specific purposes of federal reservations. Typically, documents establishing Indian
reservations recite general goals such as encouraging "the habits of industry" or "advancing the
civilization of the Indians." Nearly every Indian
reservation was intended to be a homeland where
Indians could remain self-governing and become
economically self-sufficient. These purposes may
justify numerous water uses, including: furnishing
municipal supplies; supporting economic endeavors
such as agriculture, mining, and recreation; and
sustaining fish, wildlife, and natural vegetation.

In *Big Horn*, the Wyoming court said that the
purpose of the reservation was purely agricultural,
notwithstanding several references to a "permanent
homeland" in the treaty in question. Thus, it
refused to recognize reserved rights for fisheries,
mining, industrial, or wildlife purposes. The U.S.
Supreme Court did not review this portion of the
decision.

B. Use for Other Than Original Purposes

Once Indian reserved water rights have been
quantified, they may be put to uses other than

those for which they were quantified. For example, the Indian reservations along the Colorado River are entitled to certain quantities of water based upon their irrigable acreage. But the tribes may apply the water allocated to them to industrial purposes. Arizona v. California (S.Ct.1979).

A divided decision of the Wyoming court in a later phase of the *Big Horn* case held that water rights quantified based on practicably irrigable acreage could not be changed to instream flow uses for fish without complying with state law procedures for change of use. In re Rights to Use Water in the Big Horn River System (Wyo.1992). It was not appealed.

IV. WATERS RESERVED

Reserved water rights are probably available to federal and Indian lands from every source now reasonably accessible to the reservation. Of course, the water must have been unappropriated at the time of the reservation.

A. Waters Bordering on or Traversing Reservations

In cases like *Winters* where a stream borders an Indian reservation or where streams run through reservations, selection of the particular land probably was influenced by proximity to water, implying a reservation of water from that source.

B. Waters Beyond Reservation Boundaries

A reservation is not necessarily deprived of the benefit of reserved water rights simply because there are no water sources within its boundaries or because those located there are inadequate for reservation purposes. Thus, in Arizona v. California (S.Ct.1963), the Supreme Court upheld an allocation of water from the Colorado River to the Cocopah Reservation some two miles away; water from the river had been delivered to the reservation by an irrigation canal for several years before the decision. Reservations of water-short tracts may have occurred for many reasons. For example, Indians may have chosen to retain an area where most of them lived, ceding lands between their residential community and water sources. Or, a national monument may have been created on a small tract dependent on a water source elsewhere.

Almost all states (except the original thirteen, Texas, and Hawaii) were created largely out of the public domain, where the government had control of virtually all waters. At the sufferance of the United States, private rights in those waters were created pursuant to state or territorial law. The reserved rights doctrine holds that the government impliedly withdrew its consent to creation of private rights each time it earmarked public lands for a specific federal purpose to the extent necessary to fulfill that purpose. Thus, the fact that a reservation was detached from water sources does not prove an absence of intent to reserve waters some distance away. Judicial references to such rights being "appurtenant" to reserved lands apparently refer not to some physical attachment of water to land, but to the legal doctrine that attaches water rights to land to the extent necessary to fulfill reservation purposes.

The question whether a non-adjacent source may be used if on-reservation water is available may be influenced by practical considerations (such as ease of delivery or water quality) that make a distant source more practicable. If the government or a tribe elects one source from among several, a court is likely to defer to its exercise of discretion in making such a choice; but if the choice is unreasonable, a court can be expected to intervene.

C. Groundwater

It appears that the doctrine of reserved rights applies to groundwater. In Cappaert v. United States (S.Ct.1976), the Supreme Court upheld an injunction against groundwater pumping by a private water user who had perfected water rights after establishment of a nearby national monument. The purpose of the monument—preservation of the desert pupfish—would have been jeopardized by continued pumping. The habitat of the pupfish was threatened when the water level of a pool in a limestone cavern, which was hydrologically connected with the source of the private user's well water, dropped as the user pumped. The Supreme Court in *Cappaert* said, "we hold that the United States can protect its water from subsequent diversion, whether the diversion is of surface or groundwater." A federal district court has found that the "same implications which led the Supreme Court to hold that surface waters had been reserved would apply to underground waters as well." Tweedy v. Texas Co. (D.Mont.1968). Since at least 1953, the Department of the Interior has taken the position that the doctrine applies to groundwater on Indian reservations.

The state court in *Big Horn* held that reserved rights did not extend to groundwater, but this decision was not reviewed by the Supreme Court.

V. TRANSFERS OF RESERVED RIGHTS

By their nature, reserved water rights exist for the fulfillment of reservation purposes. In some situations, this may dictate that waters be used by private parties on the reserved public lands or Indian lands, such as a concessionaire operating a lodge in a national park or a lessee of irrigated tribal land. Contractual arrangements for use of reserved water rights on or off an Indian reservation may also fulfill the broad purposes of such reservations.

A. Users of Public and Indian Lands

Persons using the public lands for private purposes do not exercise reserved water rights and must perfect water rights in accordance with applicable state law. Reserved rights can arise only when public land is reserved—withdrawn from entry and dedicated to a specific federal purpose—and may be exercised by private individuals only while they are engaged in activity that fulfills the federal purpose. Federal purposes that might be fulfilled by private entities (who incidentally may profit from their role) include operation of a commissary at a military base, road building or other construction on any type of reservation, and operation of a concession in a national park.

Ordinarily, lessees and permittees who use public or Indian lands for profit and whose activity is not necessary to the federal purpose must establish their own water rights under state (or tribal) law. But under some circumstances, a lease of reserved water rights may be appropriate. Leasing of Indian lands for use or development by others, itself fulfills the intent of the federal Indian lands leasing program and federal economic development goals for Indians. Indian water rights, like other real property interests of Indians, may not be conveyed without congressional consent. Leasing of Indian lands, including the right to use water, is allowed by statute, but no general consent has been given to leasing water rights apart from land.

B. Individual Indian Allotments

The General Allotment Act of 1887 fostered a policy of dividing up tribal lands into individual holdings. The purpose was to convert Indians from their nomadic ways to agricultural pursuits; it was thought that the most efficacious way to do this was to give each Indian a parcel to farm. Lands not allotted were "opened" to homesteading by non-Indians. Other allotment schemes embodied in treaties and legislation had similar approaches and objectives. Allotments were to be held in trust by the United States for twenty-five years, during which they could not be taxed and could not be sold or otherwise alienated without consent of the Secretary of the Interior. The trust period was legislatively extended for fixed terms several times. Ultimately, Congress realized the Act had been a failure and the trust period was extended for an indefinite duration. The Allotment Act was early amended to permit leasing of allotted land and land sales with the approval of the Secretary. These provisions resulted in many non-Indians occupying reservation lands.

Nothing in the General Allotment Act partitions a tribe's water rights as it did with tribal lands conveyed in severalty to individual Indians. Grey v. United States (1990). Section 7 of the Act empowered the Secretary to promulgate regulations to "secure a just and equal distribution" of irrigation water among reservation Indians. 25 U.S.C.A. § 381. This provision merely confirmed that allottees have a right to use some share of tribal water rights. United States v. Powers (S.Ct.1939).

In Colville Confederated Tribes v. Walton (9th Cir.1981), the Ninth Circuit Court of Appeals interpreted the Allotment Act as giving individual allottees a right to use a share of the tribe's reserved water rights. A non-Indian purchaser of an allotment can take the right to use a share of the tribe's reserved water with a priority date as of the creation of the reservation. The result may be rationalized on the ground that Congress, in making allotments alienable, intended the Indian seller to derive full value from them, including the value of the reserved water right. The *Walton* approach can be criticized as giving allotment purchasers an advantage over their neighbors whose lands were homesteaded; they get rights superior to most other private water users. This disrupts state law water allocation schemes, provides an incentive to transfer Indian lands to non-Indians, and divests tribes of their reserved water rights in a piecemeal fashion without congressional authorization. The Ninth Circuit's rule in *Walton* was followed by the Wyoming Supreme Court. In re Rights to Use Water in the Big Horn River System (Wyo.1995). The same court rejected the argument that non-Indians owning unallotted lands within a reservation should be entitled to use water with the tribe's priority date.

C. Uses Outside Indian Reservations

The purposes of establishing Indian reservations include making Indian tribes economically self-sufficient. Treaties and other laws setting aside reservations and more recent federal legislation encourage economic development and resource use. Although many tribes develop reservation resources for profit, few have marketed water off the reservation.

Absent federal legislative permission, tribes probably cannot sell, lease, or exchange their water rights because they are interests in real property subject to restraints on alienation established by federal Indian law. Congress has not yet given any blanket approval to Indian water leasing or other marketing arrangements. The idea has long been suggested as a way of removing some of the uncertainty created by the existence of reserved rights. The 1973 report of the National Water Commission recommended that leases of Indian reserved water rights be allowed to enable non-Indians to make efficient use of water resources not immediately needed by Indians.

One device for off-reservation marketing, a deferral or exchange agreement, secures a tribe's promise not to use its water for a period, allowing undisturbed use by holders of non-Indian junior rights. As with a lease, this type of agreement may not be valid without congressional authorization. It can benefit non-Indian users and, by encouraging profitable use of reservation resources, it can fulfill the purpose of the reservation. The deferral agreement is attractive from the standpoint of efficient water use because it moves water to higher, more profitable uses. Recent reserved water rights settlements anticipate off-reservation leasing and other arrangements for non-Indian water use.

VI. QUANTIFICATION

In the prior appropriation system, ideally the priority dates and quantities of everyone's rights are known. This information, together with information on annual and seasonal flows, enables water rights holders to predict how much water may ordinarily be diverted. Incorporating reserved water rights into state water law schemes presents difficulties. First, the quantities of rights impliedly reserved are without an easily definable limit. Second, holders of reserved rights, the United States and Indian tribes, are immune from suit by virtue of their sovereign status, frustrating state efforts to adjudicate their rights or to regulate their water use. These difficulties have been partly resolved by a congressional waiver of federal sovereign immunity and by negotiated settlements, legislation, and litigation setting numeric quantities for reserved rights.

Once a quantity has been set for tribal reserved rights, that amount together with the reservation's priority date can be integrated with the schedule of private water rights. Those whose water rights were perfected after the reservation was established can discover the magnitude of potential senior water claims. The government or an Indian tribe may not in fact use its entire entitlement, but knowledge of the full quantity of reserved rights that might be asserted allows others to make wiser decisions about their own uses.

The courts have not resolved the problem of how to make the doctrine accommodate future uses as it was intended. Reservation purposes may demand varying amounts of water in the future. A military base may expand its population or functions; increased knowledge of habitat needs of fish and wildlife may change the instream flows required for a wildlife refuge; new types of recreational demands in a park may demand deeper or faster water. The problem of varying water needs is especially great in the case of Indian reservations where the purposes are usually broad—ensuring a permanent homeland and livelihood for the tribe.

A. Adjudication

The most common method of quantification is by adjudication. A court applying the "practicably irrigable acreage" standard of Arizona v. California (S.Ct.1963), would hear evidence on soil characteristics, hydrology, engineering, and economics. Land that is "irrigable" (i.e., capable of supporting sustained agricultural activity without long-term deterioration in quality) is identified. Then, the physical and financial feasibility of constructing necessary water delivery systems must be determined. The quantity of water required can be calculated based on average demand in the area for total practicably irrigable acreage.

1. *Suits by the United States*

The United States can initiate a quantification of reserved rights by bringing suit against all other water users from the same source or against the relevant state or states in their *parens patriae* capacities. Several federal court cases seeking quantification of federal and Indian reserved rights have been initiated in western states. The most notable was Arizona v. California (S.Ct.1963), brought as an original action in the Supreme Court by Arizona under a prior commitment of the United States that it would intervene to assert federal and Indian rights. That case dealt with a congressional act allocating rights to Colorado River water among several states (see Chapter Ten, Section III). The federal government procured an adjudication of the quantities of reserved rights for Indian reservations and wildlife refuges that are deducted from the respective state allocations.

The Supreme Court has indicated that once a quantification has been made, it will not ordinarily be disturbed. Changing needs must be met by changing the type of use made of the quantity of water adjudicated for the reservation, but the quantity is fixed. In 1983, the Supreme Court said the allocation of water to the tribes in *Arizona* could be increased only if a court were to find that the irrigable acreage had changed because of a survey error or by a redetermination of reservation boundaries. The Court rejected claims that the tribes' share of the water should be increased because the United States had failed to claim water for all the lands on the reservation now known to be irrigable. Arizona v. California (S.Ct.1983). The interest of non-Indians in certainty of water rights adjudications was found to be sufficiently great to preclude reopening the issue of practicably irrigable acreage.

The Court's concern with reliance of others on water rights adjudications was also the basis for the decision in Nevada v. United States (S.Ct.1983). The Pyramid Lake Paiute Tribe claimed the United States did not press a claim for water needed to maintain a fishery although fishing was the reason the reservation was established. Instead, they said, the government secured most of the water for a reclamation project for irrigation of lands owned by non-Indians who competed with the Indians for water. The effect of the Court's decision was to bind Indians to determinations in stream adjudications in which they are represented by the United States government, even if the government's advocacy was weak, incomplete, or compromised by a conflict of interest.

2. *Joinder of the United States in State Court Actions—McCarran Amendment*

Because the United States may not be sued without its consent, Congress must waive governmental immunity for a particular action or a general class of cases. Immunity can be waived to the extent the United States submits itself to suit by joining voluntarily as a party.

Indian tribes also enjoy sovereign immunity. Although tribes may be able to waive immunity from suit if the subject matter is a contract or other business transaction, a tribe's general waiver without congressional consent may be invalid. This is because tribal property, including water rights, is held in trust by the federal government. But if a tribe exercises its right to initiate a federal lawsuit invoking the equitable jurisdiction of the courts to determine its rights, a court may find a valid waiver of sovereign immunity.

The United States has waived its sovereign immunity by a statute commonly known as the McCarran Amendment.   43 U.S.C.A. § 666.   The statute specifically consents to joinder of:

the United States as a defendant in any suit (1) for the adjudication of rights to the use of water of a river system or other source, or (2) for the administration of such rights, where it appears that the United States is the owner of or is in the process of acquiring water rights by appropriation under State law, by purchase, by exchange, or otherwise, and the United States is a necessary party to such suit.

Thus, when private parties go to court to adjudicate water rights throughout a stream system, they may join the United States.   The inability to do so would leave uncertainty in the outcome of a general adjudication of a stream in which the United States might have a substantial claim, especially if it is on behalf of Indian tribes.

The McCarran Amendment authorizes joinder of the United States only in a comprehensive adjudication of water rights in a stream system.   This includes ongoing proceedings in Colorado's water courts (United States v. District Court In and For the County of Eagle (S.Ct.1971)) and even state agency proceedings that are adjudicative in nature and are overseen by the courts (United States v. Oregon (9th Cir.1994)).   It does not subject the government to state court jurisdiction in private suits to decide priorities between the United States and particular claimant.   Dugan v. Rank (S.Ct. 1963).

The McCarran Amendment's consent to joinder of the United States applies to suits in state or federal court, but, as a practical matter, it is only used in state court proceedings because federal cases usually are not initiated by others to adjudicate water rights.

Federal court jurisdiction does exist if the United States initiates suit, and the McCarran Amendment does not preclude adjudication of the government's water rights in that forum. Although there is concurrent jurisdiction, the Supreme Court has upheld district court dismissal of a federally initiated action filed even before the United States had been joined in a parallel state court proceeding.   Colorado River Water Conservation District v. United States (S.Ct. 1976)(*Akin* case).   That case involved "exceptional circumstances," however.   Although the federal suit was filed only six weeks before the United States was served in the state court action, the state proceedings concerning the stream system in question had been ongoing and some 1000 other parties, though not the United States, were already before the state court.   In the short time involved, nothing had occurred in federal court.   The state court proceedings were comprehensive; the federal court action was piecemeal.

The Amendment's language refers only to federal "rights by appropriation under State law, by purchase, by exchange, or otherwise," but the court in

Eagle County found that the word "otherwise" included reserved rights.

The water rights of Indian tribes are not federal property, but are rather private rights held by the United States as a fiduciary for the tribes. Consequently, it has been argued that they do not come within the consent to be sued under the McCarran Amendment, which applies only to rights of which "the United States is the owner." But in the *Akin* case, the Supreme Court ruled that Indian reserved rights are also covered by the Amendment because, "bearing in mind the ubiquitous nature of Indian water rights in the Southwest, it is clear that a construction of the Amendment excluding those rights from its coverage would enervate the Amendment's objective." *Big Horn* was the first state case to adjudicate fully the claims of an Indian reservation under the McCarran Amendment.

The Court has recognized that the McCarran Amendment does not waive the immunity of a tribe and that tribes may bring their own suits to adjudicate water rights. But it has held that concurrent federal court proceedings initiated by the tribe are subject to dismissal under *Akin* if the same rights are at stake in state proceedings. Arizona v. San Carlos Apache Tribe (S.Ct.1983). The *San Carlos* case involved the states of Montana and Arizona, both admitted to statehood under enabling acts that reserved jurisdiction and control over Indian lands to Congress. The Court held that the McCarran Amendment removed the jurisdictional bar of the enabling acts.

Once the government is joined, it must adhere to state procedural requirements.   United States v. Bell (Colo.1986) (failure to claim water source specifically precludes later filing for priority dates as of date of reservation).   The Supreme Court has held, however, that the Act's waiver of sovereign immunity does not allow a state court to collect statutorily required filing fees from the United States.   United States v. Idaho (S.Ct.1993).

Attempts to get a court to order the government to claim reserved rights when officials have exercised their prosecutorial discretion not to do so have been unsuccessful.   In Sierra Club v. Yeutter (10th Cir.1990), the district court required the agency to show that its wilderness preservation mandate could be satisfied without reserved water rights.   In Shoshone-Bannock Tribes v. Reno (D.C.Cir.1995), the tribes failed to show a legal limitation on the Attorney General's discretion.   But see Pyramid Lake Paiute Tribe v. Morton (D.C.1974), where the court found an abuse of discretion in failing to claim and protect an Indian tribe's reserved rights.

B.   Other Methods of Quantification

Another means of quantifying reserved rights is by negotiated agreement.   Some agreements involve federal rights, but most focus on Indian rights. Such agreements must be approved by Congress if they limit or allow others to use Indian reserved rights.   Since 1982, negotiated settlements have been reached with some 20 tribes in 10 states. Settlements typically not only quantify Indian rights, but also provide funds (federal plus state cost sharing) or water sources (often from a new or existing federal project) to enable tribes to use water without infringing on established non-Indian uses. Many settlements allow for limited marketing of Indian water on and off the reservation. Some provide "development funds" to the tribes. In addition, a settlement may deal with matters like efficient use, conservation, environmental concerns, and interstate compact obligations. Negotiation avoids many of the tremendous costs involved in litigation and is more likely to reach a solution tailored to the needs of the parties.

Broad federal legislation has also been suggested as a means of quantifying reserved water rights. Although Congress has had numerous proposals before it for quantifying or modifying reserved rights, none has passed. The complex factual variables and the strength of political views involved in the process indicate that quantification may best be reached by negotiation or litigation for individual reservations.

C. Regulatory Authority

Although the federal government has deferred most control of privately held water rights to the states, the doctrine of intergovernmental immunity prevents a state from regulating water rights held by the United States or Indian tribes absent congressional consent.

On federal lands, the presumption is that state regulatory authority may be exercised to the extent that it does not interfere with specific congressional mandates or purposes. On Indian reservations, the general presumption is that state regulation does *not* apply, at least as to Indian land, unless Congress authorizes it; there are several exceptions that depend on whether land is owned by non-Indians and the impacts of the regulation.

1. *Preemptive Power of the Federal Government*

Congress may exercise its constitutional powers to preclude the operation of state law. If such a power is found in the Constitution and is exercised it prevails over state law pursuant to the supremacy clause of the Constitution, art. VI, cl. 2. But whether Congress intended to preempt state water law is a difficult question because there is rarely specific legislative language. Typically, a court must search for indicators of congressional intent. For instance, if the state definition of beneficial uses does not permit a federal use necessary to the purpose of reserved land, state law will be preempted. Thus, if a state does not recognize that use of water for instream flows in a National Park is a beneficial use, the court would analyze the issue of intent to preempt. It would look at the purposes of the park as set out in the Park Service Organic Act, the statute designating the particular park, and other statutes and legislative history. This would probably be a relatively easy case since parks are established to "conserve the scenery and natural and historic objects and the wildlife therein and to provide for the future enjoyment of the same...."

State law thus would be preempted to avoid impeding fulfillment of federal purposes.

Requirements of filing reports with the state engineer, registering water rights, and other ministerial acts would not be preempted. Courts have noted the federal policy of deferring to state water law. That policy might influence a court to find that state regulation should prevail if it places a relatively insubstantial burden on federal programs or policies. See California v. United States (S.Ct. 1978), discussed in Chapter Nine, Section IV D. Whether the government can be required to release stored water to clear channels or to control chemical concentrations, depends on what impact the requirements will have on the government's ability to carry out federal purposes or programs.

2. *Tribal Self–Government*

The right of Indian tribes to govern their members and territory stems from their aboriginal sovereignty, which has never been extinguished. Congress has power to terminate tribal governing powers, but it has generally not exercised these powers in ways that have affected tribal jurisdiction to regulate Indian water rights. In 1953 (one year after the McCarran Amendment), Congress enacted Public Law 280, giving certain states jurisdiction over criminal matters and civil causes of action on Indian reservations. The Act excepted any jurisdiction over "alienation, encumbrance, or taxation of any real or personal property, including water rights, belonging to any Indian tribe." 28

U.S.C.A. § 1360(b); 25 U.S.C.A. § 1322(b). See also 18 U.S.C.A. § 1162(b); 25 U.S.C.A. § 1321(b). The tradition of Indian self-government is embodied in numerous treaties between the federal government and tribes, as well as in statutes and policies stressing tribal self-determination and strengthening tribal governments. The only significant area of state jurisdiction Congress has allowed over Indian water rights is the McCarran Amendment's authority to adjudicate Indian water rights in state proceedings. See Section VI A 2 of this chapter.

The existence of a tribal government within a reservation serves to reverse the presumption generally applicable to public lands that favors applying state law unless a federal policy is frustrated. When non-Indians are involved, however, there are additional considerations, discussed below.

Regulation of Indian water use is solely with the tribe unless Congress acts to allow federal or state jurisdiction. One federal statute, § 7 of the General Allotment Act, allows the Secretary of the Interior to adopt rules "to secure a just and equal distribution" of water for agriculture among reservation Indians (25 U.S.C.A. § 381), but no regulations have been adopted under the statute. Section 7 does not limit a tribe's authority to regulate water use except that Secretarial regulations could prevent the tribe from making an inequitable allocation of agricultural waters.

Several Indian tribes have adopted water codes to regulate water allocation and use on their reservations. These codes and other tribal regulatory actions are binding upon Indians using reserved rights on an Indian reservation both because Indian reserved rights are tribal property and because of the tribe's sovereignty over its members and territory. Tribal regulation would also govern Indians exercising rights established by prior appropriation within the reservation. Sovereignty over activities on the reservation is the basis for the tribe's jurisdiction.

More difficult questions arise when an Indian tribe or a state seeks to assert jurisdiction over non-Indians using water on a reservation.

Use of reserved rights in conjunction with a lease or other consensual use of tribal or allotted land is generally subject to tribal regulatory authority. State regulatory authority is precluded because of the tribe's sovereignty over Indian property within its boundaries.

One must distinguish between regulation of water used pursuant to reserved rights and water in excess of these rights—"surplus water." Rights to use surplus water on the reservation may be established under state law. Whether the exercise of those rights by non-Indians may be regulated by the state depends on whether exercise of state authority has been preempted and whether tribal self-government would be infringed. A tribe has a clear interest in consistent, unified management of the resource throughout the reservation. Concurrent state jurisdiction can conflict with tribal water management policy. But if the tribe lacks a system of water resources allocation and regulation, it will have difficulty arguing that its interest in unified regulation is infringed by state regulation.

It is more likely that a court will find state regulatory jurisdiction of a stream that runs for most of its course through lands outside the reservation than one that is entirely or mostly within the reservation. Compare Colville Confederated Tribes v. Walton (9th Cir.1981)(state regulation preempted where stream within reservation) with United States v. Anderson (9th Cir.1984)(state regulation not preempted over stream that touched reservation for part of its course).

Other important factors are the degree to which the water source is relied upon for reservation uses and the existence of federal irrigation systems on the reservation. Recent case law suggests that a state presumably could regulate the non-Indian exercise of appropriative (or "surplus") water rights on non-Indian lands unless to do so would affect the political integrity, economic security, or health and welfare of the tribe. Montana v. United States (S.Ct.1981).

VII. "NON–RESERVED" FEDERAL WATER RIGHTS

The federal government can hold rights under state law in addition to holding reserved rights.

The United States may need to acquire rights pursuant to state law if, for example, the uses for the water go beyond the reservation's purposes (i.e., stockwatering in a national forest) or water rights are all held by private parties because the reservation was established after such water were appropriated. Further, the federal government may acquire rights under state law because Congress directs it to or because of an executive decision to do so. So long as Congress has acted under constitutional authority, there is no question about its power to acquire such rights. A question arises when the United States seeks to appropriate or use non-reserved water rights in ways that are not authorized by state law.

State law may not restrict acquisition or use of water rights so as to hamper a federal program. Thus, in California v. United States (S.Ct.1978), the Supreme Court held that the state could condition use of state water rights acquired by the United States for a federal reclamation project, but any conditions that conflicted with congressional directives on how the project was to operate would not be valid. A careful examination of the relevant statutes is required to determine Congressional intent to allow the land manager to appropriate and use water inconsistently with state law. Only when a federal program or congressional mandate is frustrated is state law preempted; state law must be complied with as far as possible.

CHAPTER NINE

FEDERAL CONTROL OF WATER AND WATER DEVELOPMENT

I. FEDERAL POWERS

State law generally controls the use of water, but the federal government has assumed a significant role in water allocation because of its financial support of major water development projects, the need to carry out programs and policies for the public lands, the desirability of national regulation of environmental quality, and the primacy of the federal government in matters concerning navigation and international treaty obligations. As the federal role in water resource development has grown, so have tensions between state and federal sovereignty. Conflicts tend to be more severe in the western states because of water scarcity and the concentration of federal lands there.

Waters within state boundaries, even on the public lands, are managed and allocated according to state and local laws absent some preemptive exercise of congressional power. The Supreme Court decided in California Oregon Power Co. v. Beaver Portland Cement Co. (S.Ct.1935) that private persons taking title to public lands take only water rights perfected according to state law because estates in land and water were severed by the 1877 Desert Land Act (if not by earlier manifestations of federal deference to state water law). Nevertheless, federal power over water is paramount when Congress chooses to exercise a constitutionally based power that requires water. The courts have recognized federal authority to deal with water resources under a variety of powers: commerce power (and its subsidiary, the navigation power), property power, and treaty power. Even the defense power has been invoked to uphold the federal government's construction of a hydroelectric dam that provided power to munitions plants. Ashwander v. Tennessee Valley Auth. (S.Ct.1936). The question is rarely whether power exists, but rather whether Congress intended to exercise its power to displace state law.

The preemptive federal power to reserve waters from appropriation pursuant to state law in order to carry out the purposes designated for public lands is discussed in Chapter Eight. This chapter is concerned with other uses of federal power that may affect the ability of the states to deal with water resources.

A. Navigability and Congressional Power

1. *Historically*

Use of waterways has played an important part in the exploration, settlement, and economic development of America. Lewis and Clark's exploration of the Louisiana Purchase lands relied partly on river transport, as did the early westward movement of settlers. Before the advent of the railroads and modern motorized transport, waterways provided the most feasible means of shipping freight. Large cities grew on the banks of the nation's rivers nourished by these natural arteries of commerce. Accordingly, there is strong federal interest in assuring the free flow of commerce along navigable waterways.

In Gibbons v. Ogden (S.Ct.1824), the Supreme Court held that a grant to Robert Fulton by the State of New York of an exclusive right to operate steamships on New York waterways was repugnant to the commerce clause of the United States Constitution. Chief Justice Marshall declared, "All America understands, and has uniformly understood, the word 'commerce' to comprehend navigation."

2. Modern Importance of the Navigation Power

Early cases used navigability as a means to determine whether congressional power extended over the subject matter of challenged legislation. Control of anything affecting navigation, because of its importance to commerce, was within the commerce power. Today navigability is rarely an issue in determining congressional power because it is generally understood that the commerce power is much broader than navigation. See Kaiser Aetna v. United States (S.Ct.1979).

The Supreme Court generally refuses to make an independent examination of whether the purpose of an act of Congress was in fact improvement of navigation. A congressional determination that it was necessary for navigation is usually conclusive evidence that it is within the commerce power. United States v. Chandler–Dunbar Water Power Co. (S.Ct.1913); United States v. Twin City Power Co. (S.Ct.1956). Even projects that arguably interfere with navigability have been upheld as proper exercises of the navigation power. In Arizona v. California I (S.Ct.1931), the Court rejected Arizona's contention that the recital of navigation as the purpose of the Boulder Canyon Project Act was a subterfuge because it provided for extensive damming and consumption of the water of the Colorado River. In an early case, the United States sought to enjoin a private irrigation project from diverting water from a non-navigable tributary because the diversions threatened navigability of the mainstream; the Supreme Court held that the navigation power extended to tributaries of navigable streams, upholding a federal statute prohibiting obstructions to the "navigable capacity" of United States waters. This established that depletions as well as conventional obstructions to navigation are subject to congressional control. United States v. Rio Grande Dam & Irrigation Co. (S.Ct.1899). Flood control projects on non-navigable tributaries have also been sustained as protecting navigable waters. Oklahoma *ex rel.* Phillips v. Guy F. Atkinson Co. (S.Ct.1941)(flood control was one of several stated purposes).

In only one case has the Court not obediently followed Congress's invocation of a navigation purpose for a federal project. In United States v. Gerlach Live Stock Co. (S.Ct.1950), the Court did not accept Congress's declaration in the Flood Control Acts of 1937 and 1940 that the entire Central Valley Project was "for the purposes of improving navigation...." Instead the Court found authority for the project under the constitutional power to spend for the general welfare (Article I, Sec. 8, cl. 1).

3. *Navigability for Title*

Today, the most important use of "navigability" is for determining title to streambeds. The definition is also used to determine whether compensation is required when land is taken by the United States along a stream (i.e., the existence of a navigation servitude).

Whether a waterway was navigable was early held to turn on whether it was "navigable in fact." E.g., The Daniel Ball (S.Ct.1870). It was not necessary that the waterway was actually used for navigation at a given time. If the stream once was navigable, navigability was not defeated by subsequent disuse. Although that case involved congressional power, the definition remains viable for determining title to streambeds. If the stream is navigable, title to the streambed is held to pass to the state at statehood. See Chapter Five, Section I A.

Congress has extended the definition of navigable waters to include waters that can be made navigable with reasonable improvements for purposes of the Federal Power Act. United States v. Appalachian Electric Power Co. (S.Ct.1940). It should be noted that states may develop their own definitions of navigability for allowing public uses on certain streams. See Chapter Five.

B. The Navigation Servitude

The navigation servitude should be distinguished from the navigation power and navigability for title. The navigation power is the source of congressional authority to legislate on matters relating to navigation under the commerce clause. Navigability for title determines riverbed ownership as between the United States and a state; the "navigation servitude," or rule of no compensation, is a concept that allows the federal government in special circumstances to affect private rights without compensation. When the federal government destroys or removes privately-owned structures in or near waterways, or when federal dams flood land adjoining a waterway or destroys the water power value of a private power plant by raising the water level, the affected lands may be damaged or destroyed without compensating the owners.

The fifth amendment to the Constitution prohibits the taking of private property rights for a public use without just compensation, but regulatory interference with use of private property is allowed without compensation up to the point all economically viable uses are destroyed. At that point, compensation is ordinarily due unless the limitations inhere in the nature of the property. Lucas v. South Carolina Coastal Council (S.Ct.1992). Of course the regulation must be a proper exercise of a congressional power enumerated in the Constitution. The Compensation claims arise when certain property rights in or on navigable waters are damaged or destroyed by the government. Presumably, property owners on or near navigable waters should expect to be subject to burdens resulting from the exercise of the navigation power.

1. Basis of the Navigation Servitude

Historically, navigation was an important public right. In England, the Crown held and could grant certain property rights in the beds of navigable waters. The rights granted were subordinate to the public right of free and unhindered passage of vessels for navigation, which was protected by the Crown; interference with the public right created a nuisance subject to abatement. The American colonies assumed the Crown's interests in waterways. The power to regulate commerce was then yielded to the United States government by the colonies through the commerce clause of the Constitution, but ownership of the beds was not ceded. The federal government thus controls the navigable capacity of waterways while the states own the beds.

Some decisions have attempted to justify the navigation servitude on a "notice" theory. Since investments in navigable waterways are made with knowledge of the paramount historical importance of navigation, investors can have no reasonable expectation of compensation for removal or destruction of a structure that obstructs travel on a navigable waterway. But the cases go well beyond this rationale. Courts have broadened the definition of navigability, and Congress has authorized some lands to be seized for use in multipurpose federal projects having only a nominal connection with navigation. The no compensation rule, as now applied, was criticized by the 1973 Report of the National Water Commission, which recommended legislation to provide for compensation in many navigation servitude cases.

2. *Extent of the Navigation Servitude*

Application of the navigation servitude depends on the location of the affected property and type of property rights involved. Ordinarily, the navigation servitude applies only to property located on, and property rights in, navigable streams. Takings of property on non-navigable tributaries must be compensated. United States v. Kansas City Life Insurance Co. (S.Ct.1950). However, this right of compensation can be defeated if Congress expressly states that its purpose is the improvement of navigation and there is a reasonable relation to a navigation purpose. On a waterway subject to the navigation servitude, the rule of no compensation extends to the ordinary high water mark of the stream. Noncompensability includes the streambed (including all land under the stream up to the ordinary high water mark) and structures within the stream.

a. *Obstructions to Navigation*

The earliest cases applying the navigation servitude concerned removal of obstructions to navigation. The first navigation servitude case to reach the Supreme Court involved condemnation of a toll-collecting franchise on the Monongahela River. Monongahela Navigation Co. v. United States (S.Ct. 1893). The condemnation was found compensable because the Court found the locks and dam had been constructed at the "implied invitation" of Congress. *Monongahela* has been repeatedly distinguished in later decisions as an estoppel case. It is uncertain what type of congressional "invitation" is sufficient to invoke estoppel, but more is required than, for example, issuance of a federal dredge and fill permit.

Subsequent cases dealing with obstructions to navigation held that obstructions are subject to the servitude. For instance, in Union Bridge Co. v. United States (1907), the government successfully utilized the 1899 Rivers and Harbors Act to force modifications of an obstructing bridge on the Allegheny River. Finding the loss noncompensable, the Court justified the servitude on a notice theory: the bridge company built the bridge with the knowledge that the federal government might someday use its navigation power.

b. *Damage to Property in Navigable Waterway*

An early case, United States v. Lynah (S.Ct.1903), held that flood damage to the land between a stream's low and high water marks caused by a federal dam was compensable. The decision, had it stood, might have given landowners on navigable streams a right to have the water level maintained in its natural condition. *Lynah* was overruled, however, by United States v. Chicago, Milwaukee, St. Paul & Pacific Railroad (S.Ct.1941). That case held that the navigation servitude extends to lands on a navigable stream up to the ordinary high water mark—an average of the high water marks over all seasons.

Everything within the navigable waterway is subject to the navigation servitude; thus, compensation has been denied for privately owned oyster beds destroyed by dredging Great South Bay in New York. Lewis Blue Point Oyster Cultivation Co. v. Briggs (S.Ct.1913).

c. Project on Navigable Stream Causing Damage to Property Rights on Non–Navigable Tributaries

When water backs up behind a dam on a navigable stream causing flooding or other damage to property on a non-navigable tributary, the damage is compensable unless Congress expressly invokes the navigation power to protect the navigable capacity of the mainstream. In United States v. Cress (S.Ct.1917), a government dam on a navigable mainstream raised the water level in tributaries, flooded lands along the tributaries, and destroyed the water power potential of a mill located on a tributary. The Supreme Court held that the injuries were compensable.

The *Cress* rule gives a landowner the right to maintain a tributary's stream level in its natural condition. The rule has been criticized because it makes the compensability of property turn upon its location: taking of property on a non-navigable tributary is compensable, yet an identical injury on a navigable stream is noncompensable under *Chicago*. The Court reaffirmed the *Cress* rule, awarding compensation in a case in which the soil on a farm became saturated because a dam on the Mississippi River caused an adjacent non-navigable tributary to flood. United States v. Kansas City Life Insurance Co. (S.Ct.1950).

In United States v. Willow River Power Co. (S.Ct. 1945), a dam on a navigable river raised water levels in both the mainstream and a tributary. This destroyed the water power value of a diversion through an artificial channel from a tributary into the mainstream. The Court denied compensation, finding that the affected property right was in the mainstream, not in the tributary as in *Cress*.

When flooding on a tributary is caused by a dam on the tributary, Congress can avoid compensation if it invokes the navigation power to protect the navigable capacity of the mainstream. United States v. Grand River Dam Auth. (S.Ct.1960).

d. Waters Rendered Navigable by Private Effort

If waters formerly non-navigable are rendered navigable by private activity, the government must pay compensation to assure public access to the newly navigable waterway. In Kaiser Aetna v. United States (S.Ct.1979), a developer deepened a pond and converted it into a marina by opening a channel to the ocean. The pond was navigable before the improvements though the only access

was across private land. The Supreme Court held
the navigation servitude inapplicable to the Army
Corps of Engineers' attempts to obtain a public
right of access to the marina. Although navigability was sufficient to invoke federal regulatory power
(i.e., to prevent activities interfering with navigation), condemnation of private property was required to obtain public access. A companion case,
Vaughn v. Vermilion Corp. (S.Ct.1979), also applied
the *Kaiser Aetna* reasoning to deny applicability of
the servitude to a system of human-made canals in
Louisiana that connect the Gulf of Mexico with an
inland waterway.

3. *Measure of Damages for Condemnation*

The taking of uplands (i.e., lands above the ordinary high-water mark) is compensable even if they
are located on a navigable stream. However, private rights that depend on the flow of a navigable
stream are subject to the servitude and are noncompensable. Such rights include water power value,
rights to consumptive use, and site value (i.e., value
added to the land by proximity to the waterway).

a. *Value of Water Power*

In United States v. Chandler–Dunbar Water Power Co. (S.Ct.1913), the United States condemned
both a power plant located in the river and the
adjacent uplands to preserve the navigability of the
St. Mary's River in upper Michigan. The Court
found the taking of the water power value attributable to rapids in the stream noncompensable not

only because the servitude allowed removal of structures from the river, but also because the claimed water power right was a form of right to the streamflow. The Court dismissed as "inconceivable" the idea that rights to the flow of running water in a navigable stream are capable of private ownership subject to compensation.

b. Site Value

Land adjacent to a waterway may be more valuable because of its usefulness as a hydroelectric power site, a recreational area, or a port or marina. When riparian lands above the ordinary high-water mark are condemned as part of a federal project, the question arises whether the condemnation award should include the site value. United States v. Twin City Power Co. (S.Ct.1956) involved land along the navigable Savannah River acquired by a power company as a possible reservoir site. The power site value was approximately seven times the agricultural value of the land. The owner argued that the lands did not fall within the navigation servitude since they were located above the high-water mark. The Court rejected the argument to the extent that it held the increment of value attributable to location on the stream was inherent in the flow of the stream and thus noncompensable under the rule of *Chandler–Dunbar*.

The decision in *Twin City Power Co.* does not modify the physical reach of the servitude as including only that part of the streambed bounded by the high-water mark. It does, however, exclude from compensability the portion of the value of uplands attributable to the streamflow. Although uplands are clearly compensable, their value may only include suitability for non-riparian purposes such as agriculture or mining.

In United States v. Rands (S.Ct.1967), Rands owned land along the Columbia River in Oregon, which the state had an option to buy for use as a port site. The land, which was about five times as valuable as a port site than for the next most valuable uses (sand, gravel and agriculture), was taken by the United States as part of a comprehensive plan for development of the Columbia River. The Court held that special values, such as port site value arising from access to a navigable waterway, are subject to the navigation servitude, thus denying any compensation attributable to such values. In addition, the Court held that the increase in value of lands remaining in Rands' ownership because of its new riparian location was a benefit to be deducted from the amount of any compensable harm.

The rule of *Rands* could have very harsh results, as illustrated in an example provided by the late Dean Trelease. Suppose a tract of land is worth $10,000 regardless of proximity to the water, but location on the waterfront adds a value of $5,000 to the portion of land on the water. If the half of the tract on the water is taken and flooded, the condemnation award should be only the nonriparian value (i.e., $5,000) since port site value is not considered. But value is added to the remaining land because it is now on the waterfront ($5,000) and this value is deducted from the award. Consequently the owner receives no compensation for the flooding of the lost land.

Because of the absurd effect of the *Rands* rule, pressure was brought to bear on Congress to expand compensability for condemned lands. In 1970, Congress passed § 111 of the Rivers and Harbors Act, 33 U.S.C.A. § 595(a), which provides that the compensation for real property taken for a navigation improvement project is the fair market value of the property in its highest and best use; the highest use may be based upon access to or utilization of navigable waters. Thus, an owner can recover waterfront value of land taken. The amount of actual recovery still must be reduced by the enhanced value of uplands now located on the water. In Trelease's hypothetical above, § 111 would give the landowner $10,000 for the flooded land (port site value included), but $5,000 would be deducted for appreciation of the remaining land for a net compensation of $5,000. Section 111 also limits compensability for depreciation of remaining (uncondemned) land that results from loss of access to navigable waters.

The rule that the value added to uplands by proximity to a navigable stream is noncompensable has also been judicially limited by allowing compensation if flowage easements are taken. A flowage easement is an interest in land that allows the holder to flood the land of another. In United States v. Virginia Elec. & Power Co. (S.Ct.1961), a power company planned to construct a reservoir for hydroelectric power purposes and bought a flowage easement to allow it to flood the land of another. The United States then decided to build a federal project on the same site. The power company conceded that potential hydropower value was noncompensable, but argued, and the Supreme Court agreed, that the flowage easement had other value not dependent upon streamflow. The Court's rationale was that the holder of a flowage easement has the right to destroy, by flooding, the value of the subservient fee. The fee owner, before sacrificing the use of the land for agriculture, timber, or grazing, would charge the easement holder the value of those uses. Thus, the easement has "... a marketability roughly commensurate with the marketability of the subservient fee." The Court limited the award of damages by discounting the easement's value to reflect the possibility of its non-exercise since a fee owner would sell a flowage easement for less if the holder of the easement were unable or unlikely to flood the land. The fact that the federal government had decided to build the project, however, was not to be included in the calculation of the "probability of the easement's exercise."

c. *Water Rights Created Under State Law*

Federal power may come into conflict with state-created water rights in a number of ways. If water use is regulated by a proper exercise of congressional power, there is no right to compensation. If a water right is taken or totally destroyed, the right to compensation will depend on whether the water right was subject to the navigation servitude.

The United States may regulate water use to carry out federal legislative purposes. In United States v. Rio Grande Dam & Irrigation Co. (S.Ct. 1899), the Supreme Court sustained the government's right to prevent the exercise of state-created water rights in order to carry out federal legislation protecting the navigable capacity of streams, as an exercise of regulatory authority and not a compensable taking. Congress may also authorize federal officials to distribute water from a federal project without regard to water rights priorities established under state law. See Arizona v. California (S.Ct. 1963). The only question for a court is whether Congress intended to override, or preempt, state law.

When a federal project makes it necessary to take or destroy a state-created water right, compensation must be paid unless the purpose of the project is for navigation, in which case the rights are subject to the navigation servitude. In United States v. Gerlach Live Stock Co. (S.Ct.1950), farmers in California's Central Valley irrigated their grasslands with the seasonal overflow of the Sacramento River. As part of the massive Central Valley Project, the government constructed Friant Dam, which eliminated the river's seasonal flooding, thus depriving downstream landowners of the overflow. The government contended that the loss was noncompensable since Congress had authorized the Central Valley Project for the control of navigation. The Court said the project was a reclamation project, not a navigation project, despite a general congressional declaration that the entire project was to improve navigation. Because the 1902 Reclamation Act expressed an intention that the federal government conform with state law in acquiring property for such projects, the water rights taken were held to be compensable.

II. FEDERAL LICENSING OF WATER POWER PROJECTS

A. Federal Power Act

The Federal Power Act of 1920 established a comprehensive national policy for hydroelectric power (hydropower) development. The Federal Power Commission, now the Federal Energy Regulatory Commission (FERC), was created as in independent agency to administer the Act. FERC has authority to license private hydropower facilities and to regulate interstate sale and transmission of electricity.

The Federal Power Act was the result of years of effort by conservationists, who had sought federal legislation to ensure comprehensive nationwide water power planning. One objective was to reconcile conflicting uses (e.g., navigation, irrigation, recreation, wildlife preservation, hydropower, and flood control) within the planning scheme.

The Act requires (in the absence of an existing, pre–1920 right-of-way) that a license be obtained from FERC for hydroelectric power facilities, including "dams, water conduits, reservoirs, power-houses, or other works incidental thereto," that cross, adjoin, or are located in navigable waters, public lands, or federal reservations. It also requires that permits be obtained for use of surplus water or water power from a government dam.

Facilities on non-navigable waters require licenses if the Commission finds the "interests of interstate or foreign commerce would be affected" by the proposed project. This language has led the courts to uphold broad extensions of the Commission's licensing jurisdiction. In Federal Power Commission v. Union Electric Co. (S.Ct.1965), a power company proposed to build a "pumped-storage" facility, in which water is pumped to a high reservoir, stored, and then released to generate power during periods of peak demand. The Supreme Court sustained a Commission decision to require a license for the project because the power generated would be transmitted across state lines. The Court added that if the project was not properly operated, timing of the flows of the navigable portion of the river downstream could be affected.

The Commission has declined to exercise jurisdiction in other situations in which electric power generation has a substantial effect on navigable waters and interstate commerce. Only if the project produces power by hydroelectric generation will the Commission require a license. The Supreme Court upheld the Commission's refusal to assert jurisdiction over several huge coal-fired power plants that would use large quantities of cooling water from the navigable Colorado River and would transmit power in interstate commerce throughout the Southwest. Chemehuevi Tribe v. Federal Power Comm'n (S.Ct.1975). The Court held that the plants were not "project works" requiring a license under the Act; nor did they use "surplus water" from a federal dam. The Court held that Congress only intended to license hydroelectric power plants, not plants that burn fossil fuels to make steam for power generation.

B. Conflict With State Law

Federal dams can dramatically affect the flow of streams, disrupting state water allocation. Although conflicts usually involve water laws, other state laws for the protection of fish habitat and the environment may also be affected. This is especially evident in states such as Oregon and Washington where large federal dams obstruct anadromous fish (e.g., salmon) spawning and migration.

The Federal Power Act has two provisions that appear to protect state law from federal encroachment. Section 9(b) requires license applicants to submit satisfactory evidence of compliance with state laws concerning hydropower development. Section 27 of the Act provides:

Nothing contained in this chapter shall be construed as affecting or intending to affect or in any way to interfere with the laws of the respective states relating to the control, appropriation, use, or distribution of water used in irrigation or for municipal or other uses, or any vested right acquired therein.

Both sections seem to preserve state law, but judicial interpretation has limited their effectiveness.

The Supreme Court held that § 9(b) does not give state governments a veto power over federal projects. First Iowa Hydro-Electric Coop. v. Federal Power Comm'n (S.Ct.1946). In *First Iowa*, the Commission granted a license to a hydropower cooperative to construct a dam on a tributary of the Iowa River. The Supreme Court held that where compliance with both state and federal permit requirements appeared impossible, subjecting the project to state law would frustrate the Act's purpose of comprehensive nationwide planning. The Court stated that § 9(b) is merely informational; if the Commission is itself satisfied with the degree of state law compliance, its decision is binding and a state permit need not be obtained.

The *First Iowa* rule was extended in California v. FERC (S.Ct.1990). California attempted to impose higher minimum flow requirements on a hydroelectric project than the rates set in the FERC license. Unlike *First Iowa*, where the issue was whether a state could effectively deny a permit to the project, the question was whether a state could determine the conditions on which water could be used by the project. The Supreme Court found that § 27 added nothing to the § 9(b) requirement of state law compliance as interpreted in *First Iowa*. The Court also distinguished its contrary interpretation of a provision nearly identical to § 27 which allowed state conditions on a water use permit for a federal Bureau of Reclamation project. See California v. United States (S.Ct.1978), Section C of this chapter. In California v. FERC, the Court said that the Federal Power Act "envisioned a considerably broader and more active federal oversight role in [private] hydropower development than did the Reclamation Act" in financing and building major federal water projects. Thus, § 27 is a general provision that cannot override the preemptive effect of specific provisions or the overall purpose of the Federal Power Act. It does require compensation to be paid, however, if state-created rights are taken by eminent domain. Portland General Electric Co. v. Federal Power Comm'n (9th Cir.1964); Scenic Hudson Preservation Conference v. Federal Power Comm'n (2d Cir.1971).

Where a congressional statute delegates responsibility for environmental protection to a state, however, FERC's exclusive authority may be qualified. The Clean Water Act, § 401, 33 U.S.C.A. § 1341, requires that before a federal permit or license is granted, the agency must obtain a certification that state water quality standards will not be violated by the permitted activity. The Supreme Court has upheld a state's imposition of minimum streamflow requirements deemed necessary to satisfy state water quality standards as a condition of certification for a FERC license. PUD No. 1 of Jefferson County v. Washington Dept. of Ecology (S.Ct.1994).

A hydropower license endows the licensee with certain preemptive powers of the federal government. In City of Tacoma v. Taxpayers (S.Ct.1958), the city applied for a FERC license to build a dam on a tributary of the Columbia River. The State of Washington opposed the project because the reservoir behind the dam would flood a state fish hatchery and state law forbade municipalities from condemning state property. Nonetheless, the Commission granted the license. The Supreme Court held that the license delegated to the city federal eminent domain power to condemn state property.

C. Protection for Fish and Wildlife

Hydroelectric power generating facilities can disrupt fish habitat and migration patterns. Columbia River harvests of salmon are now only about 8% of their size 100 years ago. The primary cause of the destruction of anadromous fisheries has been the construction of hydropower facilities on major rivers. Such facilities obstruct upstream spawning migration, alter water temperatures, and change the chemical composition of the water, thereby endangering the migrating fish.

Under the Federal Power Act, the Federal Energy Regulatory Commission must, prior to issuing project licenses, find that the proposed project is "best adapted to a comprehensive plan" for water development, navigation, water power, "and for other beneficial public uses, including recreational purposes." 16 U.S.C.A. § 803(a). The 1986 amendments to the Act expressly directed FERC to consider a project's effects on fish and wildlife. A court will examine a FERC refusal to develop a comprehensive plan to determine if the refusal can be supported by the record or is arbitrary and capricious. National Wildlife Fed'n v. Federal Energy Regulatory Comm'n (9th Cir.1986).

A number of federal environmental statutes require consideration of fish and wildlife values in projects constructed or licensed by the federal government. The National Environmental Policy Act (NEPA), 42 U.S.C.A. §§ 4331–44, requires preparation of an environmental impact statement identifying the environmental consequences of any proposal for a major federal action that may significantly affect the human environment. Other sections of the Act require the government to use "all practicable means" to achieve environmental protection goals by planning, interdepartmental coordination, and full consideration of environmental values in decision-making. Yet, the courts have been reluctant to enforce any provision of NEPA except the environmental impact statement requirement. That provision at least provides some assurance that decision makers are aware of the environmental effects of their actions.

The Fish and Wildlife Coordination Act, 16 U.S.C.A. §§ 661–666c, demands "equal consideration" for wildlife conservation in water resource development programs. It is extremely difficult in practice to give meaning to a requirement of parity between the values of the multiple purposes of

water projects on the one hand and fish and wildlife
values on the other. To help assure protection of
state interests in fish and wildlife, the Act also
requires coordination among the agency undertak-
ing or permitting a project, the U.S. Fish and Wildlife Service, and relevant state fish and wildlife
agencies before construction of a project .

Although not really an environmental statute, the
Pacific Northwest Electric Power Planning and
Conservation Act, 16 U.S.C.A. § 839, is a comprehensive act for allocating supplies and mitigating
impacts of federally produced hydropower. The Act
contains significant requirements for preserving
and restoring anadromous fish resources in the
Pacific Northwest, the region hardest hit by the
impacts of hydropower facilities. Under the Act, a
regional council develops a plan for protection, mitigation, and enhancement of fish and wildlife. Furthermore, managers of federal power facilities are
required to afford "equitable treatment" to fish and
wildlife, insuring that their operations do not subordinate fish and wildlife to other project objectives.
The Council's plans must be "tak[en] into account
at each relevant stage" of FERC proceedings. See
National Wildlife Fed'n v. Federal Energy Regulatory Comm'n (9th Cir.1986).

Another means of preventing water projects from
adversely affecting fish and wildlife exists when
Indian tribes have treaty fishing rights on the river
in question. Interference with river flows by diversion, impounding, or pollution of waters that damages fish habitat may reduce the ability of tribes to

take a meaningful share of fish as guaranteed in their treaties. If the federal government is responsible for such actions (directly or by licensing), it may be liable in damages for violating federal treaty obligations. Similarly, states are obligated to consider the effects of state controlled or authorized projects on Indian treaty rights.

III. FEDERAL RECLAMATION PROJECTS

A. Purposes

Congress sought to encourage settlement of the West by enacting legislation such as the Homestead Act to provide free or low cost land to settlers. Congress's purpose in allowing settlement on the public lands by self-sufficient family farmers was frustrated by fraud and abuse. Wealthy speculators (e.g., railroads and timber interests) were able to aggregate vast tracts of public lands under their ownership and control, making extravagant profits.

Much western public land was too arid to be used without irrigation. Settlers seldom had the capital required to construct dams and diversion works, so support grew for an increased federal role in financing and constructing irrigation projects.

In 1902, Congress passed the Reclamation Act, which established the Bureau of Reclamation in the Department of the Interior to administer the reclamation program. The stated purpose of the Act was to provide water for irrigation but it was intended to be part of a national policy of distributing public land without fueling the land speculation touched off by earlier public land programs and without enabling land monopolies. The clear intent of Congress was to promote the growth and well-being of small family farms in the West. Later legislation supplemented the purposes of reclamation projects to include hydropower, industrial, and municipal uses. Recreation, fish and wildlife protection, flood control, and navigation benefits are also provided pursuant to provisions establishing particular reclamation projects.

Early proposals for reclamation projects suggested that the program would be self-sustaining. But, a changed political conception of the program, in light of the meager repayment abilities of project beneficiaries and a belief that the nation generally would be benefited, led to a program of substantial subsidies. In recent years, however, greater concern for economic efficiency of reclamation projects has given impetus to requirements for detailed feasibility studies involving cost-benefit analysis and for repayment of project costs.

Enactments subsequent to the Reclamation Act authorized specific projects. For example, the Boulder Canyon Project Act, 43 U.S.C.A. § 617, passed in 1929, provided for construction of dams (including Hoover Dam) on the Colorado River as part of a comprehensive development plan. The Small Projects Act, 43 U.S.C.A. §§ 422 et seq., provided for expedited approval and partial federal funding of small projects, so long as the local government entity secures necessary water rights, easements, and land.

B. Congressional Powers

Several constitutional bases exist for congressional involvement in reclamation projects. Early cases based congressional authority on the property power, under which Congress may pass laws for the management of federal property. Kansas v. Colorado (1907). The power to tax and spend to promote the general welfare is another basis. United States v. Gerlach Live Stock Co. (S.Ct.1950).

C. Limitations on Beneficiaries of Projects

1. *Background and Policy*

The 1902 Reclamation Act included provisions to prevent speculation. Reclamation water was not to be used on more than 160 acres in single ownership, and the user of the water had to be a bona fide resident on or near the land to prevent absentee owners from reaping the benefits of the reclamation program. In addition, the Act required recipients of project waters to pay back a portion of construction costs over time, although without interest. These requirements, however, were often relaxed by amendments to the Act. Amendments were passed when the beneficiaries encountered hardship, and they allowed delay or forgiveness of payment obligations. The resulting subsidies were enormous.

2. *Acreage Limitation*

To help fulfill the Act's ideal of assisting only small family farmers, Section 5 prohibited the sale of reclamation water for lands in excess of 160 acres in common ownership. The acreage limitation (or "excess land" provisions) gave rise to more controversy and evasion than any other part of the reclamation law. Abuses led to an attempt at reform in the Omnibus Adjustment Act of 1926. Section 46 of that Act provided that excess lands could not continue to receive project water unless owners entered into a "recordable contract" to sell the excess land, with the price set by the Secretary based on pre-project values. Contracts typically gave the Secretary a power of attorney to sell the lands if the owner failed to sell them within ten years.

The 1926 Amendment also delegated responsibility for distributing water, in compliance with federal law, to local districts. The Department of the Interior entered long-term service contracts with the districts and the districts sub-contracted with water users.

Acreage limitations were successfully evaded by use of leases (since only common "ownership" was mentioned in the Act) as well as by various multiple ownership subterfuges that allowed a single operator to control thousands of acres. The Department of Interior failed to stop these abuses. In part, this was a recognition that, at least in some parts of the West, 160 acres was insufficient for a viable farming operation.

Congress also provided a variety of exemptions for specific projects. For such projects, the acreage ceiling was raised beyond 160 acres (480 acres, San Luis Valley Project) or the limitation was removed altogether (Colorado–Big Thompson Project) on the rationale that since the lands were already irrigated, reclamation water was merely "supplemental" and the risk of speculation was therefore diminished. Another type of exemption allowed landowners to avoid the recordable contract provisions (limiting the resale price) by agreeing to pay interest charges on the repayment obligation for water delivered to excess lands (Washoe Project). Hardship for large landowners in the Imperial Irrigation District caused by the 160–acre limitation was avoided by judicial interpretation: the Supreme Court held that the district was effectively exempted by the Boulder Canyon Project Act. Bryant v. Yellen (S.Ct.1980).

Finally, Congress took the excess acreage issue in hand. The 1983 Reclamation Reform Act increased the acreage that may be benefited from 160 to 960 acres and increased the charges for water. It also addressed leasing by setting an overall limit on ownership and leasing to 2080 acres. Excess lands are now subject to charges for the full cost of water delivery to those lands. Districts are given a choice of amending their contracts to conform with the new limitation or to begin paying full cost for excess acreage. Several districts in California's Central Valley challenged this "hammer clause" in the Reform Act as unconstitutional, arguing that it violates the due process and taking provisions of the fifth amendment. The Ninth Circuit ruled that there was no violation. It held that congressional silence concerning water service to leased lands conferred no vested right on the districts; such a right would be in conflict with the purpose of the Reclamation Act. Further, it held that Congress had never surrendered its sovereign right to regulate the quantity of subsidized water provided by the government. Peterson v. United States Department of Interior (9th Cir.1990).

The Reclamation Reform Act also repealed the residency requirement of Section 5 of the 1902 Act. That provision limited sales of reclamation water to bona fide residents on the land or in the neighborhood of the land, but had never been enforced by the Department.

D. Conflicts With State Water Law

Federal reclamation projects may come into conflict with a variety of state water laws (e.g., area-of-origin protection statutes or preference statutes). Like the Federal Power Act, the 1902 Reclamation Act contains provisions that appear to require federal compliance with state law. Section 8 provides that the Act is not to be construed as interfering with state laws "relating to the control, appropriation, use, or distribution of water used in irrigation ..., and the Secretary of the Interior, in carrying out the provisions of this Act, shall proceed in conformity with such laws...." Despite its broad language, the provision does not allow state law to override specific conflicting provisions of the reclamation law or legislation authorizing a particular project.

Until 1978, the Supreme Court interpreted § 8 to require observance of state law only to the extent of defining the property interest, if any, for which compensation must be made when a project is constructed. But in California v. United States (S.Ct. 1978) the Court announced that once rights are acquired, water from the federal project must be distributed by the United States according to state law except to the extent state law is directly in conflict with a provision of the federal reclamation law. The Court disapproved statements in its earlier decisions that had denied that states could impose conditions on water delivery and had read § 8 as requiring state water law to be observed in acquisition of water rights only to the extent that it defined water rights for which compensation must be paid. On remand, the court of appeals upheld virtually all permit conditions imposed on the project. United States v. California (9th Cir. 1982). Conditions that would prohibit water storage in order to protect fish, wildlife, and recreational uses were held permissible unless the government could prove that the storage was necessary to fulfill project purposes.

The decision in *California* did not purport to overrule earlier Supreme Court decisions recognizing extensive federal preemptive authority over state water laws in the operation of reclamation projects but it did narrow the effect of those decisions. The most important precedents were City of Fresno v. California (S.Ct. 1963); Ivanhoe Irrigation Dist. v. McCracken (S.Ct. 1958); and Arizona v.

California (S.Ct.1963). In *Fresno*, the city attempted to enforce state law preferences for domestic uses and uses in the watershed of origin. The Court said that § 8 did not require the Secretary to observe state law when it conflicted with § 9(c) of the Reclamation Act (giving preference to irrigation uses). *California* disapproved the Court's alternate ground—that under § 8, state law could not prevent the United States from exercising the power of eminent domain to acquire water rights.

In *Ivanhoe*, the Court held that the 160–acre limitation in § 5 of the 1902 Act applied to the Central Valley Project in spite of a state law doctrine imposing a public trust in favor of project water beneficiaries and requiring that adequate water be furnished to each regardless of the acreage they owned. The Supreme Court held that § 8 of the Reclamation Act did not override the express acreage limitation in § 5.

In Arizona v. California (S.Ct.1963), the Supreme Court held that provisions of the Boulder Canyon Project Act delegating discretion to the Secretary of the Interior to apportion project waters from the Colorado River were sufficient to override state water allocation laws. Although the Secretary could have followed state law in administering the river, as prescribed by § 8, the Court found that Congress did not intend the government's discretion to be so bridled in administering project waters. It cited *Fresno* and *Ivanhoe* as standing for the proposition that the United States is not bound by § 8 of the Reclamation Act to follow state law priorities in the delivery of project water. In California v. United States (S.Ct.1978), the Court disavowed its Arizona v. California (S.Ct.1963) interpretation of *Fresno* and *Ivanhoe*, suggesting that the decision could have rested on a direct conflict between state priorities and the operation of the federal project, though no actual conflicts were cited in *Arizona*.

In California v. FERC (S.Ct.1990), the Court determined that a state law saving provision, which was nearly identical to § 5, was ineffective in the face of the Federal Power Act's grant of licensing authority over private hydropower projects. See Section III B of this chapter. The Court found that the Federal Power Act's purpose of comprehensive river basin development required greater displacement of state law than was required by the Reclamation Act.

IV. ENVIRONMENTAL LEGISLATION

A. The Clean Water Act

The Clean Water Act was passed in 1972 to replace ineffective state regulation of pollution with a comprehensive national system involving federal-state sharing of responsibilities. 33 U.S.C.A. §§ 1251–1376 (Section numbers later in this chapter refer to the original legislation, not the code.) The goal of the Act was to eliminate discharge of pollutants by 1985 and to "restore and maintain the chemical, physical, and biological integrity of the Nation's waters ...," with an interim goal of swimmable, fishable waters by 1983. The Act allows enforcement by citizen suits, provides for monitoring and record-keeping, and subjects violators to criminal penalties and loss of government funding.

Pollution control standards under the Act are of two general types. Effluent standards limit the quantity of pollutants discharged from the source; ambient water quality standards limit the concentration of pollutants in the stream. Because it is often difficult to identify the exact source of pollution in applying water quality standards, the Clean Water Act utilizes effluent standards that are based on available control technology. The program's principal control mechanism is to place limits on discharge of pollutants from "point sources." The Act leaves non-point sources subject only to minimal controls, mostly through state programs that are not subject to any federal standards.

1. *NPDES Permitting System*

Section 402 of the Act establishes a pollution discharge permit system known as the National Pollutant Discharge Elimination System (NPDES). NPDES permits are required for discharge of pollutants from a point source into "navigable waters." A "point source" is a pipe, ditch, tunnel, floating vessel, well, container, concentrated feedlot operation, or other concentrated source of effluent and is distinguished from diffused sources such as runoff. The Act specifies that return flows from irrigated agriculture are not point sources. Navigable waters are broadly defined as "waters of the United States."

To obtain an NPDES permit, the applicant must comply with federal effluent standards. The effluent standards of § 301 originally required use of the best practicable technology currently available (BPT) by July 1, 1977 and use of the best available technology economically achievable (BAT) by July 1, 1983. The 1977 amendments to the Clean Water Act authorized extensions of the 1977 BPT deadline to as late as July 1, 1983, and of the 1983 BAT deadline to July 1, 1984. The 1987 amendments further extended deadlines for meeting BAT standards to March 31, 1989, but also broadened the coverage of the Act to include toxics and "nonconventional" pollutants. These amendments also created a new class of "conventional pollutants" (suspended solids, coliform bacteria, B.O.D., and acidity), for which best conventional control technology (BCT) must be achieved by the same date. Special effluent standards apply to new sources.

It is not clear whether the release of water from a dam is a point source discharge requiring a § 402 NPDES permit. The D.C. Circuit has ruled that "for dams to require NPDES permits, five elements must be present: (1) a pollutant must be (2) added (3) to navigable waters (4) from (5) a point source." National Wildlife Federation v. Gorsuch (D.C.Cir. 1982). But EPA has latitude to treat certain conditions (e.g., temperature, dissolved oxygen, and nitrogen supersaturation) as not constituting pollutants, to consider as pollutants only those that are introduced from the outside world, and not to consider a dam as a point source unless it is the point at which the pollutant first enters navigable waters (i.e., not when a dam merely holds back water inducing it to change chemically, then releases the already polluted water downstream). Thus, *Gorsuch* upheld EPA's general policy of treating dams as non-point sources. The Ninth Circuit has held that a dam used to collect mine drainage required a permit, finding that it met the *Gorsuch* criteria since it collects and channels human-caused pollutants that would not otherwise be in the river. Committee to Save Mokelumne River v. East Bay Municipal Utility Dist. (9th Cir.1993). It could also be argued that § 402 requires permits for certain transbasin diversions; the terminus of a pipeline may be construed as a "point source," and the imported water may contain "pollutants" (addition of material foreign to the importing region).

2. Water Quality Standards

Administration of water quality standards is left to the states, who are free to impose stricter controls than required by federal effluent limitations. States must designate uses (e.g., domestic, fishery, etc.) and develop water quality standards that are sufficient to support those uses. The states must then impose effluent limitations on NPDES permits in order to achieve the standards. This may prove virtually impossible where large amounts of pollutants are contributed by non-point sources. Some states adopted their own ambient water quality standards before passage of the Clean Water Act. Congress authorized the states to continue to promulgate water quality standards, but if they are inadequate in light of conditions and uses of the waterway, the Environmental Protection Agency (EPA) may impose its own standards.

Section 303 requires states to identify "water quality-limited" segments of streams (those where effluent limitations have proved inadequate to preserve water quality for the uses designated by the state) and to establish "total maximum daily loads" for each such pollutant, allocating among users the total allowable waste load. If the state fails to do so, the Environmental Protection Agency may establish stricter effluent limits on point sources (as described below) in order to maintain ambient water quality (e.g., where streamflows are insufficient to dilute the effluent).

Because the § 402 NPDES permit process also requires compliance with water quality standards, new water uses that degrade water quality (either by adding pollutants or reducing dilutive capacity of the stream by depleting flows) must comply with § 303 of the Act. Section 303 provides for the establishment of numerical water quality criteria (e.g., maximum dissolved solids concentrations). If maintenance of greater river flow is needed to ensure the requisite level of water quality, the state could condition an NPDES permit on a level of instream flow as well as limiting the input of pollutants.

Before a federal permit allowing water development may be issued, the federal agency must obtain a certification under § 401 that the project will not result in discharges that violate the state's water quality standards. This requirement can affect the quality of water used if the state's water quality standards impose minimum flow requirements. See PUD No. 1 of Jefferson County v. Washington Dept. of Ecology (S.Ct.1994), discussed in Section III B of this chapter.

3. *Planning Requirements*

Section 208 of the Clean Water Act provides for development of area-wide wastewater management plans. Areas with waste treatment problems are designated and local agencies formed to develop and oversee the local implementation of waste treatment plans. Plans must identify necessary treatment facilities and include siting recommendations. The EPA has combined plan requirements of §§ 208 and 303 into a single requirement for "water quality management plans." If a § 208 plan limits siting, noncompliance may result in withholding of federal construction funds or § 402 NPDES permits. Downstream water users who depend on effluent as their source of water supply may be affected by § 208 siting requirements if effluent from a new treatment facility enters the stream below their diversion point.

4. *Non-point Source Controls*

The largest uncontrolled cause of water pollution is from "non-point" sources. These include diffused sources such as urban and irrigation runoff, surface mining, and construction sites. They also include sources, like agricultural irrigation return flows, that are statutorily exempted from the definition of a point source. These sources were left outside Clean Water Act controls because they are numerous, difficult to regulate, and controls often are not cost-effective. In some cases (such as agricultural sources), control efforts encounter serious political opposition.

The management plans under §§ 208 and 303 are required to include an identification of procedures for controlling diffuse sources by use of "best management practices." This requirement was largely unsuccessful in motivating effective control on non-point sources. Absent more substantial directives states were reluctant to impose controls that might be costly to irrigators and could lead to limitations on water diversions. For instance, some water quality problems are caused by the amount and timing of diversions as well as the manner of use. Salts and other chemicals may pollute a stream when excessive water is diverted and leaches salts from the soils. Diverting too much water may also cause pollutants remaining in the stream to become concentrated.

The 1987 amendments to the Act (§ 319) require each state to address non-point source pollution by preparing: (1) an assessment of non-point sources and the best management practices (BMPs) necessary to control them and (2) a program to implement BMPs. If the program is not implemented there is no sanction except ineligibility for a sparsely funded program of related grants. Thus, control efforts remain rather ineffective in many states.

5. Dredge and Fill Permits

Section 404 of the Clean Water Act requires permits from the Army Corps of Engineers for discharge of dredge and fill materials into waters of the United States. Section 404 has greater reach than its terms suggest because of the territory and types of activities that are regulated and the strict federal requirements that can be imposed.

Clean Water Act jurisdiction extends not only to navigable waters, but also to tributaries and associated wetlands. Under the Act, navigable waters are "the waters of the United States." The Corps' § 404 regulations include any waterway involved in interstate commerce, including intrastate waterways used by interstate travellers for recreation. United States v. Byrd (7th Cir.1979). The definition further includes wetlands adjacent to these waters and has been extended to cover lands that support plant growth typical of wetlands (e.g., willow trees). This definition was upheld in United States v. Riverside Bayview Homes, Inc. (S.Ct. 1985). Thus, the areas regulated include thousands of acres of public and private lands far from any river.

The scope of activities covered by § 404 is far broader than traditional dredging and filling of ship channels. Regulated activities include, for example, the construction of bridges, dams, buildings, and

roads; flood control activities; and shellfish operations. There are exemptions for "normal farming,
silviculture, and ranching," and for irrigation and
drainage ditches. But, constructing a dike and
drainage system to enable bringing more land into
agriculture has been held to require a § 404 permit.
United States v. Akers (9th Cir.1986).

Once an activity falls under § 404, the Corps
must consider "all relevant factors" before permitting the project. There does not appear to be
another environmental statute that has such an
extensive coverage and vests such far-reaching dis-
cretionary powers in federal officials. Agency regulations list economics, cultural concerns, energy
needs, water supply, the needs and welfare of the
people, and a variety of environmental factors. Any
of these factors can lead the Corps to deny or
condition a permit. Once the Corps issues a permit, the permit can be reviewed and vetoed by the
EPA.

Section 404 also incorporates the full panoply of
federal environmental law by requiring imposition
of permit conditions to assure compliance with
these laws. Private projects thus may become "fed-
eralized" because they depend on a § 404 permit.
Since the Corps must comply with the Fish and
Wildlife Coordination Act, Endangered Species Act,
Wild and Scenic Rivers Act, Coastal Zone Management Act, National Environmental Policy Act, and
other laws that govern federal activities, the reach

of these laws is extended over all projects that require permits.

The Endangered Species Act (ESA) is one of the farthest-reaching environmental laws implicated by § 404. Section 7 of the ESA generally prohibits federal actions that would jeopardize the continued existence of any endangered species and requires the agency to consult with the U.S. Fish and Wildlife Service to determine the effects of a proposed action. For example, section 7 was invoked to deny a § 404 permit for Tellico Dam because the dam would affect the critical habitat of a tiny fish, the snail darter. Tennessee Valley Auth. v. Hill (S.Ct. 1978). The snail darter case raised such controversy that amendments created a process for exempting certain agency actions from Endangered Species Act requirements when a high level committee determines that: (1) no reasonable and prudent alternatives to the agency action exist, (2) benefits of the action clearly outweigh benefits of actions consistent with preserving the endangered species, and (3) the action is of regional or national significance.

Short of the elaborate exemption process, however, the Corps of Engineers must ensure endangered species protection when issuing § 404 permits. For instance, a court has upheld a permit condition requiring releases of water from a proposed dam in Colorado in order to protect critical whooping crane habitat downstream in Nebraska. Riverside Irrigation Dist. v. Andrews (1985).

B.　Impact on State–Created Water Rights

1.　*Wallop Amendment*

Concern with the potential effect of the Clean Water Act upon water uses led to the inclusion of language assuring that established water rights were not to be defeated. The Wallop Amendment, § 101(g), is a statement of congressional policy that the Clean Water Act should not be construed to abrogate, supersede, or impair state authority over water allocation or rights of states to water (e.g., under interstate compacts). The amendment's purpose, however, is not to prohibit "legitimate water quality measures" that affect individual water rights only "incidentally." See National Wildlife Fed'n v. Gorsuch (D.C.Cir.1982). Where necessary, this can result in curtailing depletions and consumptive use of water permitted under state water rights. Riverside Irrigation Dist. v. Andrews (10th Cir.1985).

2.　*Regulatory Takings*

Federal regulations that control the timing, quantity, or manner of water use often affect the value of water rights. Since the "property" is no more than a right to use the water for a defined beneficial purpose, controls that destroy the ability to make such a use are arguably regulatory takings requiring compensation under the U.S. Constitution. Examples of federal requirements under the Clean Water Act that may affect water use include water quality standards that demand releases of water to maintain flows in order to dilute pollution or protect fisheries, conditions in § 404 permits necessary to satisfy public interest concerns of the Corps, and prohibitions on diversions needed to avoid jeopardizing the existence of an endangered species. No court has held such limitations to be takings of property requiring compensation under the Fifth Amendment. Perhaps this is because the beneficial use doctrine implies the prevention of interference with the rights of others or of the public. As a result, there can be no property right to use water in a manner that causes harm. Furthermore, recent case law on regulatory takings under the Fifth Amendment does not entitle a person to compensation unless the regulation both: (1) destroys all economic use of the property, and (2) the owner would not necessarily expect the property to be so restricted by police power regulation. See Lucas v. South Carolina Coastal Council (S.Ct.1992).

3. *Effects on Common Law Remedies*

Section 505(e) says the Clean Water Act shall not restrict any statutory or common law rights to enforce effluent limitations "or to seek any other relief." Thus, remedies in nuisance and trespass may still be sought in state courts. Biddix v. Henredon Furniture Indus., Inc. (N.C.App.1985). Such actions may be brought by an affected party against a polluter in another state, but the suit must be judged by the law of the polluter's state. The Supreme Court has held that a contrary result would undermine the Act. It construed section 505 as allowing enforcement of additional state remedies only with respect to pollution caused by a party in the forum state. International Paper Co. v. Ouellette (S.Ct.1987).

C. Fish and Wildlife Coordination Act

The Fish and Wildlife Coordination Act requires federal agencies sponsoring or issuing permits for water projects to consult with the U.S. Fish and Wildlife Service "with a view to the conservation of wildlife resources" and requires mitigation measures to minimize adverse impacts. See Section III C of this chapter.

D. Wild and Scenic Rivers Act

The purpose of the Wild and Scenic Rivers Act is to preserve in a free-flowing condition certain rivers possessing outstanding "scenic, recreational, geologic, fish and wildlife, historic, cultural, and other similar values.... " Congress may designate rivers and states may recommend rivers for inclusion in the Wild and Scenic Rivers system subject to approval by the Secretary of the Interior. The Act provides for study of rivers by the Secretary of the Interior (or the Secretary of Agriculture if national forest lands are involved), who submits state and federal recommendations to Congress. As of 1996, 155 rivers were included in the system and 134 rivers were under study.

The Act prohibits the Federal Energy Regulatory Commission from licensing water projects "on or directly affecting" rivers included in the system and provides interim protection for rivers under study for inclusion by temporarily prohibiting project licensing on such rivers. One court has held that the prohibition applies only to federal study recommendations, not to a state recommendation. North Carolina v. Federal Power Commission (D.C.Cir. 1976).

V. INTERNATIONAL TREATIES

Water or aquifers accessible to more than one country usually are of vital importance to the affected countries. Historically, upstream nations, including the United States, have sought to control waters originating in their territory. The doctrine of "absolute territorial sovereignty," however, has given way to the practical necessity of dealing amicably with neighboring nations. Today, more flexible doctrines of limited territorial sovereignty and equitable apportionment generally govern the resolution of international water disputes, most often by means of treaties.

The United States is party to several water treaties with Canada, including the 1909 Boundary Waters Treaty, the Lake of the Woods Treaty, the Saint Lawrence Treaty, and the Columbia River Treaty. Treaties with Mexico include the 1906 Irrigation Convention and the 1944 Colorado River Treaty. Once the federal government enters into a treaty with another nation, it is the "Supreme Law of the Land;" under the Constitution, any inconsistent state laws are preempted. Thus, treaties affect the manner and extent to which state-defined rights may be exercised.

A. Examples of International Treaties

1. Mexico

The Mexican Treaty of 1944 was an effort to end years of disagreement between the United States and Mexico over the waters of the Lower Colorado River. The United States as the upstream nation, initially relied on the "Harmon Doctrine," which is based on a theory of absolute territorial sovereignty. However, pressures from Mexico to receive a share of water from the river grew as uses in Mexico increased. The 1922 Colorado River Compact among the seven states touching the river required the upper and lower basin states to contribute equally to supplying any future obligation to deliver water to Mexico.

The treaty with Mexico, signed in 1944, allocated to Mexico a guaranteed annual flow of 1.5 million acre feet of Colorado River water, to be reduced in the event of a serious drought in the U.S. The treaty is administered by an international commission. Negotiations were concluded in haste, and several troublesome ambiguities were glossed over. Most notably, the treaty mentioned nothing about water quality. Later, upstream development caused the river's salinity to increase as more water was consumed and large dams and storage reservoirs were created; less water in the river also meant greater evaporation from storage reservoirs and greater concentrations of salinity. Irrigators added to the problem by returning waters with high concentrations of dissolved solids.

The salinity problem lay dormant until 1961. In that year, the Wellton–Mohawk Irrigation District in Arizona began pumping drainage waters from beneath its lands, releasing the saline waters into the Colorado River just north of Mexico. Mexico protested to the U.S. in response. The U.S. and Mexico reached a series of interim agreements under which the U.S. consented to undertake salinity abatement measures. The final agreement, Minute 242 of the International Boundary Waters Commission, places a ceiling on the increase in the River's salinity below Imperial Dam.

The federal government assumed responsibility for meeting the salinity obligations of Minute 242. This is addressed by federal salinity abatement projects such as bypassing the Wellton–Mohawk return flows, a huge desalination plant, and construction projects that intercept various natural and human-made sources of salt. These federal projects are, in effect, an "insurance policy" against development constraints being imposed on the Colorado River basin states by the salinity control obligation.

However, many water problems with Mexico remain unsettled. For instance, there is currently no system for dividing transboundary groundwater. As unregulated pumping continues, border cities such as El Paso and Juarez find themselves competing for dwindling supplies. Thus, Minute 261 was negotiated to give the International Boundary Waters Commission increased authority over water quality in the border region.

2. *Canada*

Canada is both an upstream and a downstream nation because the Columbia river system meanders in and out of the two countries. Several issues have been negotiated.

One issue concerned storage responsibilities of the two nations and Canada's right to share the benefits obtained by the U.S. from storage in Canada. Large-scale storage was most feasible in Canada, but Canada had no incentive to build storage facilities. Initially, the U.S. simply offered to pay Canada compensation for any damages caused by the flooding of Canadian lands behind the U.S. dams. Canada instead sought a share of the far more valuable downstream benefits to the U.S. from storage, including increased hydroelectric power and protection from flood losses. After much debate over downstream benefit sharing, the two nations provided for an equal sharing of economic benefits in the Columbia River Treaty. The treaty specifies that Canada will provide 15.5 million acre feet of storage, the U.S. will operate dams to obtain maximum benefits from the Canadian storage, the U.S. may (for a price of $1.875 million per call plus hydropower losses) demand storage releases in emergencies despite Canadian hydropower needs, and Canada will not divert the Columbia River away from the U.S. and into the Fraser River.

B. Supremacy of Treaties Over State Water Law

Article I, Sections 8 and 9 of the U.S. Constitution give the President power to enter into treaties with the advice and consent of the Senate. State water law is thus subservient to international treaties. For example, in Sanitary Dist. of Chicago v. United States (S.Ct.1925), the Court enjoined the City of Chicago from diverting water out of Lake Michigan because the diversions lowered the water level of the lake and were in excess of amounts allowed under the 1909 Boundary Waters Treaty with Canada.

CHAPTER TEN

INTERSTATE ALLOCATION

Because state political boundaries generally do not correspond to the boundaries of river basins or aquifers, exercises of state police power often are inadequate to resolve disputes or to undertake desirable planning concerning water from a single source. As the demands for water within an interstate basin intensify, the need for interstate planning and management increases. This requires a reliable method of resolving disputes involving depletion and pollution of interstate waters. These disputes have been resolved by:

1. Judicial allocation (interstate litigation);

2. Compacts (interstate agreements); and

3. Legislative allocation (congressional apportionment).

I. ADJUDICATION

A. Litigation Between Private Parties

A typical interstate suit between private parties involves a downstream plaintiff alleging harm from diversions of an upstream defendant in another state. Some cases involve upstream pollution. The court in which the suit is brought must have jurisdiction over both parties and subject matter.

1. *Personal Jurisdiction*

Personal jurisdiction is usually obtained by personal service upon the defendant within the defendant's state of residence. Long-arm statutes, however, have removed the necessity of bringing suit in the defendant's state.

2. *Subject Matter Jurisdiction*

Private parties generally bring suit in the state courts of defendant's or plaintiff's state. Action may be brought in federal court if the suit meets the requirements of subject matter jurisdiction (i.e., diversity of citizenship and amount in controversy, or a federal question).

The ability of courts in one state to adjudicate water use in another state has been disputed. An early view of the problem was that since a water right is a form of real property, an action to establish water rights is in the nature of a quiet title action; the suit must therefore be brought in the state where the real property is situated. Conant v. Deep Creek & Curlew Valley Irrigation Co. (Utah 1901). Other courts adopted the more liberal view of jurisdiction that once a court obtains personal jurisdiction over a nonresident party, the decree need not operate directly upon the property; the court can enforce its decree by using the coercive effect of its contempt power. The Ninth Circuit used this personal jurisdiction-coercion theory in

Brooks v. United States (9th Cir.1941). *Brooks* involved water rights of Arizona and New Mexico users on the Gila River. Defendants had submitted to jurisdiction in Arizona and the court was held to have exclusive jurisdiction to adjudicate the matter although the rights of water users in the adjoining state had to be considered.

Problems of jurisdiction are magnified by the requirement that in a general stream adjudication, all affected users on a stream must be joined. If the United States has water rights on the stream, it too must be joined; a federal statute waives sovereign immunity and consents to state court jurisdiction to adjudicate its water rights in a general stream adjudication for this purpose. 43 U.S.C.A. § 666.

3. *Applicable Law*

Where individual water users in one state attempt to prevent interference with interstate waters by individual water users in another, substantial differences in the respective state laws can make it difficult to determine rights. For instance, if a downstream state follows riparian law and an upstream state follows appropriation law, can an individual in the downstream state insist on unimpeded flows, thereby defeating the established uses of upstream appropriators? It is a theoretically simpler matter, however, to integrate priorities of water users on a stream that crosses state lines when both are appropriation states. Thus, in an early case, the Supreme Court presumed that disputes among such users would be resolved in priority, as if no state boundary existed. Bean v. Morris (S.Ct.1911). The decision did not hold that either state is limited in how it defines or regulates rights to waters within its boundaries (absent federal legislation or an interstate adjudication). The idea that Congress conveyed public lands into private hands upon the condition that waters would be allocated by prior appropriation without regard to state lines has been argued, but not widely accepted. *E.g.*, Howell v. Johnson (C.C.Mont.1898).

Basic differences in state laws as well as jurisdictional and enforcement problems have led states to pursue litigation in which they represent their citizens collectively in *parens patriae*. This type of litigation has been commonly used on major interstate rivers where there is a multiplicity of parties, rather than litigation among individuals which may be feasible (though nonetheless complicated) on a small stream with few competing users, such as in Bean v. Morris (S.Ct.1911).

4. *Parens Patriae Suits*

A state may sue in its role of *parens patriae* to prevent harm to its citizens from actions of private parties in another state. In civil actions by a state against citizens of another state, the Supreme Court has original, but not exclusive, jurisdiction; there is concurrent federal district court jurisdiction. States have standing to sue in their *parens patriae* capacity under certain limited conditions: the state must have an interest independent of its individual citizens so the suit is not merely an attempt to act on behalf of individuals, and a substantial portion of the state's inhabitants must be adversely affected. This rule, expressed in Kansas v. Colorado (S.Ct. 1907), usually requires that the downstream state must be substantially affected by actions in an upstream state. A state suing in *parens patriae* is deemed to represent all its citizens, and each citizen is bound by the decree. Thus, private suits are often foreclosed once the state's rights are adjudicated. *Parens patriae* actions are further limited by the eleventh amendment, which states that the judicial power of the United States shall not be construed to extend to any suit brought by citizens of one state against another state. As interpreted by the Supreme Court, the amendment prevents a state from invoking the Court's original jurisdiction in a suit against another state, if the state is seeking a remedy for individual citizens (e.g., money damages) that would be prohibited in a suit brought directly by the individuals.

5. *Enforcement*

Decrees in private interstate suits raise serious enforcement problems since continuing supervision and modification of decrees is often required. For instance, in Lindsey v. McClure (10th Cir.1943), the New Mexico State Engineer's attempt to forbid Colorado uses of water from a New Mexico dam was held invalid. The court stated that the proper enforcement remedy was by judicial procedure, not orders of the state engineer. In one case, the

United States Supreme Court upheld a federal
court's enforcement of appropriation priorities
across state lines. Bean v. Morris (S.Ct.1911).

B. Litigation Between States

1. *Original Jurisdiction of Supreme Court*

The Supreme Court has original jurisdiction in all
cases in which a state is a party. As with private
interstate suits, the "case and controversy" requirement limits jurisdiction to "justiciable" disputes.
In suits between states, the Supreme Court serves
as a trial court. Procedurally, the action begins
with filing a complaint and hearings on motions
(e.g., to dismiss). If the complaint survives the
motions, the respondent state files an answer.
Typically, the Court appoints a special master to
hear and evaluate evidence, prepare findings of fact
and conclusions of law, and recommend a decree,
which the Court is free to follow or disregard.

The decree in an adjudication between states is
binding on all claimants to the water in question,
whether or not they were parties to the suit. Private users have no rights in excess of the state's
share of the stream because under the doctrine of
parens patriae the state is deemed to represent all
its citizens and each is bound by the decree. Private intervenors are not permitted unless the inter-
venor can show a compelling interest apart from
that of a citizen of the state.

The Court has been reluctant to take jurisdiction
in water allocation disputes for a number of rea-

sons, including: (1) the vagueness of standards of apportionment, (2) the need for continuing supervision and the Court's disinclination to play the role of referee, (3) the unmanageable mass of technical data introduced and the Court's lack of special expertise, and (4) the expense of litigation and of paying a special master. Even when it has taken jurisdiction, the Court has suggested that interstate compacts can lead to superior solutions.

2. *Justiciability*

Article III, § 2 of the Constitution confines federal court jurisdiction to "cases and controversies." Even if a court has both personal and subject matter jurisdiction, it may decline to adjudicate cases that are not "justiciable"—that is, in a form suited to judicial resolution. A suit may be rendered nonjusticiable if it is moot, collusive, not ripe, or a "political question" (i.e., would usurp executive or legislative authority). The issue of justiciability usually arises in water cases as a ripeness problem (e.g., there is no present "harm" to a downstream state claiming excessive use upstream, causing courts to find no case or controversy). Thus, the allocation of water rights for future development cannot be adjudicated. Further, the Supreme Court has said it will issue no declaratory decrees in interstate suits. The practical effect is often to deny plaintiffs relief and to perpetuate unbalanced development on an interstate stream since secure water rights are needed for investment financing and congressional authorization of water development projects.

3. *Sources of Law: The Doctrine of Equitable Apportionment*

Federal common law is applied in a narrow class of cases where there is a significant federal policy or interest that will not be effectuated by the application of state law. As such, the courts have a unique role in fashioning the rules of decision in cases involving state boundaries or shared resources like interstate rivers. The Supreme Court has developed common law to resolve disputes over allocation and pollution of interstate rivers.

If Congress speaks to such matters, the courts then decline to assert common law and defer to statutory law. After the Supreme Court took jurisdiction over a nuisance suit by two states charging Milwaukee with polluting Lake Michigan with sewer discharges, the Court found that federal common law had been displaced by the intervening enactment of amendments to the Clean Water Act. Milwaukee v. Illinois (S.Ct.1981). Moreover, the Court has upheld conditions the Environmental Protection Agency imposed on a pollutant discharge permit issued to a polluter in an upstream state, that demanded compliance with a downstream state's water quality standards. Arkansas v. Oklahoma (S.Ct.1992). In one instance, Congress entered the realm of interstate allocation of water, thereby displacing the courts. See Arizona v. California (S.Ct. 1963), discussed in section III of this chapter.

The Supreme Court has developed a comprehensive federal common law doctrine for interstate allocation of water by "equitable apportionment." The doctrine was announced in 1907 in Kansas v. Colorado (S.Ct.1907). A basic tenet of the doctrine is that "equality of right," not equality of amounts apportioned, should govern. "Equality of right" simply means that the states stand "on the same level," or "on an equal plane, . . . in point of power and right, under our constitutional system."

The Court will not be bound by the laws of the individual states. Thus, where strict application of riparian law would have prevented New York, an upstream state, from diverting water for use in New York City, the Court denied New Jersey's request for an injunction. Instead, it sought to balance equities to "achieve an equitable apportionment, without quibbling over formulas." New Jersey v. New York (S.Ct.1931). In a dispute between two appropriation states, the Court has applied the appropriation doctrine as the method of equitable apportionment. Wyoming v. Colorado (S.Ct.1922).

Application of the appropriation doctrine is, however, qualified in that protection of established uses may be more equitable than strict priority. Factors that inform equitable apportionment (and that might justify deviation from strict priority) include:

(1) Physical and climatic conditions;

(2) Consumptive use of water in the several sections of the river;

(3) Character and rate of return flows;

(4) Extent of established uses and economies built on them;

(5) Availability of storage water;

(6) Practical effect of wasteful uses on downstream areas;

(7) Damage to upstream areas compared to the benefits to downstream areas if upstream uses are curtailed.

See Nebraska v. Wyoming (S.Ct.1945).

In Colorado v. New Mexico (S.Ct.1982), the Court said it would not refuse to apply strict priorities between two appropriation states where the effect would have been to protect wasteful and inefficient downstream uses in New Mexico at the expense of newer, more efficient uses in Colorado. But in Colorado v. New Mexico II (S.Ct.1984), the Court refused to allocate waters to junior users in Colorado contrary to the interests of the inefficient appropriators in New Mexico because Colorado lacked a concrete, long-term plan for future water use.

The Supreme Court also deviates from strict priority among appropriators in two appropriation states by use of the "mass allocation" approach. Since the Court is reluctant to interject itself into intrastate allocations, it awards to each state a quantity of water to be distributed by the state's appropriation system. The Court may hold that certain specific diversions are within one state's share of the allocation, that a state may have a stated quantity of water, or that a state may have a given percentage of the flow, regardless of the mix of individual priorities within the state.

II. FORMATION OF COMPACT

Interstate compacts are used to effectuate a variety of objectives by mutual agreement of two or more states. They have been used to allocate interstate waters twenty-two times by an agreed "equitable apportionment" that otherwise might have required Supreme Court adjudication. See State *ex rel.* Dyer v. Sims (S.Ct.1951)(Eight-state compact to control pollution in the Ohio River.)

The availability of a judicial remedy encourages settlement of interstate disputes by compact. One great virtue of compacts over adjudication is that compacts avoid the justiciability problems encountered when the stream system in question is not yet over-appropriated. The compact allows parties to allocate unappropriated water, thus making a "present appropriation for future use." Ability to make these determinations in advance is crucial to long range water project planning. Compacts relating to interstate waters are formed for a variety of purposes besides allocation of water, including storage, flood control, pollution control, and comprehensive basin planning (principally by joint federal-state compacts).

A. Constitutional Authority

The basis for negotiating interstate compacts is found in article I, § 10, clause 3 of the Constitution, which states:

> No state shall, without the consent of Congress
> ... enter into any agreement or compact with
> another state, or with a foreign power....

The compact clause impliedly recognizes state power to negotiate and enter into agreements subject to congressional consent. In Hinderlider v. La Plata River & Cherry Creek Ditch Co. (S.Ct.1938), the Supreme Court stated: "the compact ... adapts to our Union of sovereign States the age-old treaty-making power of independent sovereign nations."

Typically, compact formation involves three steps. First, Congress authorizes negotiation of the compact, usually providing for a federal representative at the negotiations. Second, the compact is negotiated. Third, Congress consents to the compact.

Congress's consent determines whether the compact is a permissible agreement or a constitutionally prohibited "treaty, alliance, or confederation." Whether all interstate agreements require congressional consent is the subject of considerable debate. One view is that consent is required only for agreements that alter the political power of states, potentially upsetting the political balance of the union. Virginia v. Tennessee (S.Ct.1893). Others contend that consent is required for all interstate compacts, based on an implication in State *ex rel.* Dyer v. Sims (S.Ct.1951). Nevertheless, there is general agreement that compacts allocating interstate waters require congressional consent.

B. Administration and Enforcement of Compacts

Recent compacts uniformly call for creation of an administrative agency, typically a "compact commission," to make rules to carry out the compact and to collect information on physical circumstances (e.g., rate of river flow) for determining whether and to what extent the compact is applicable. The compact commissions are usually comprised of members appointed by the governors of the party states and a federal member with no vote or only a tie-breaking vote. Generally, states hesitate to vest substantial powers or prerogatives in a compact agency.

A state found to have violated a compact may be required to pay damages in cash rather than increased future water deliveries. Texas v. New Mexico (S.Ct.1987).

C. Legal Effect of Compacts

1. *Limitations on Private Water Users*

Apportionments of water by compact are binding upon the citizens of the compacting states whether or not individual citizens were parties to the negotiations. In Hinderlider v. La Plata River & Cherry Creek Ditch Co. (S.Ct.1938), New Mexico and Colorado had agreed to divide the flow of the La Plata River equally so each state would get the full flow of the river every other day. The plaintiff, a senior appropriator, sought to enjoin the rotation scheme as a violation of rights established under state law, but relief was denied.

The Court's rationale was that a water rights decree under state law cannot confer water rights in excess of the state's share of the waters. It also found that no compensable taking of vested property rights or violation of due process had occurred because the plaintiff had ample opportunity to object during the negotiations and there was no evidence of a defect in the compact's formation or of inequity or bad faith in the negotiations.

2. *Effect of Congressional Ratification*

State legislation that conflicts with terms of an interstate compact cannot prevent enforcement of the compact. State *ex rel.* Dyer v. Sims (S.Ct.1951). But there is some uncertainty over the extent to which Congress is bound by its ratification of compact terms. Although it cannot modify the terms of an agreement between states, Congress might condition its ratification upon agreement of the states to modify the compact. Congress also retains power to override a compact provision by explicit legislation.

State actions that interfere with interstate commerce are regularly held repugnant to the constitutional delegation to Congress of all power over commerce. But Congress has power to authorize states to regulate and impose burdens on commerce that would otherwise be unconstitutional. Thus, congressional consent to a compact may have the effect of immunizing state legislation from attack as an interference with interstate commerce. Intake Water Co. v. Yellowstone River Compact Comm'n

(D.Mont.1983). Once ratified, a compact has the
effect of a federal law and thus may be preemptive
of inconsistent state laws. The Supreme Court
made it clear in *Hinderlider*, supra, that to the
extent compact provisions are based on equitable
apportionment principles, they will preempt contrary state laws.

D. Interpretation of Compacts

The Supreme Court is the final arbiter of the
meaning of compacts. One guidepost is the Court's
own standard of equitable apportionment.

The Court's ultimate mission, however, is to determine the intent of the parties. The Pecos River
Compact said New Mexico would deliver water to
Texas based on "the 1947 conditions" of the river,
with those conditions being defined in a document
that used incorrect data. The compact commission
(with even representation from the two states)
deadlocked on whether to follow the document or to
base the allocation on actual river conditions. The
special master recommended that the commission
be restructured so it could resolve the matter, but
the Court said that to do so would change compact
terms. Instead, it ordered the special master to
resolve the matter using accurate data, which the
Court apparently believed to be the intention of the
parties. Texas v. New Mexico (S.Ct.1983). In
Oklahoma v. New Mexico (S.Ct.1991) the Court
probed into extrinsic evidence of the history of
negotiations of the Canadian River Compact to in-

terpret ambiguous terms consistently with the probable intent of the parties.

Whether lower federal courts have jurisdiction to interpret compacts depends upon whether the dispute is a federal question (*i.e.*, "arises under the Constitution, laws, or treaties of the United States"). Several federal district court cases have held that interstate compacts are not federal law, but the Ninth Circuit has found federal question jurisdiction to interpret interstate compact provisions. League to Save Lake Tahoe v. Tahoe Regional Planning Agency (9th Cir.1974).

III. LEGISLATIVE ALLOCATION

The lone example of legislative allocation of interstate waters concerns the Colorado River. The Supreme Court in Arizona v. California (S.Ct.1963) held that Congress, in passing the Boulder Canyon Project Act of 1928, intended to divide the waters of the river among the lower basin states. In so holding the Court recognized that Congress may act when the other apportionment mechanisms of compacts and judicial allocation have failed, are unavailable, or are not used.

Southern California early experienced rapid economic growth and a large population influx. Extensive irrigation water uses (especially in the Imperial Valley) were also established. Arizona had experienced more gradual expansion although the state anticipated future growth. Most Arizona uses were satisfied by pumping groundwater because geographical obstacles and lack of diversion facilities limited use of Colorado River water. Decline of Arizona water tables as a result of groundwater mining, however, made it clear that preserving the economy would eventually require resort to the waters of the Colorado. To do so, an elaborate diversion and transportation project was necessary. Later, the Central Arizona Project was planned to bring Colorado River water to the more populated parts of the state.

A compact commission in 1922 agreed to allocate the Colorado's annual flow (assumed to be well over fifteen million acre-feet (MAF)) approximately equally between the upper basin states (Colorado, New Mexico, Utah, and Wyoming) and the lower basin states (Arizona, California, and Nevada). Ratification of the compact was stalled by a long-standing dispute between Arizona and California over their respective shares in the 7.5 MAF allocated to the lower basin. Arizona feared the compact would solidify California's claim to most of the water and refused to ratify it.

Weary of the impasse, Congress enacted the Boulder Canyon Project Act in 1928, authorizing construction of Hoover Dam and a series of other storage reservoirs on the Colorado. It was opposed by Arizona. The Act was conditioned on acceptance of the compact arrangement by at least six of the seven states. California also had to agree to limit its allocation to 4.4 MAF plus half of any lower-basin surplus. The legislation further authorized a separate lower basin compact that would give Arizona 2.8 MAF and Nevada 300,000 AF. No such compact was negotiated. After several other attempts to stop construction of the Hoover dam failed in the Supreme Court, Arizona brought suit for an equitable apportionment of the waters of the lower Colorado. The suit was dismissed in 1936 because the United States, an indispensable party, refused to be joined. Arizona v. California (S.Ct. 1936). The U.S. later consented to suit, however, and after a three-year trial before a special master, the Supreme Court, approving most aspects of the master's report, held:

(1) Congress may, under its navigation and general welfare powers, apportion interstate streams by legislation.

(2) By enacting the Boulder Canyon Project Act, Congress exercised this power by "apportioning" 4.4 MAF to California in the limitation provision and specifying Arizona's and Nevada's shares through the authorization of a lower basin compact. Furthermore, Congress delegated to the Secretary of the Interior the power to contract for storage and delivery of project waters, and the Secretary then extended contracts reflecting the authorized shares.

(3) Federal law controls both the interstate and intrastate distribution of project waters, preempting state water law. (Note the contrast to the mass allocation approach, which leaves intrastate allocation to state law.) Therefore, the Secretary is empowered to allocate waters in times of short-

age by any reasonable method, although "present perfected rights" must be satisfied.

(4) Water from Arizona's tributaries (1.75 MAF) is not part of the allocation to be shared with California, but is available to Arizona in addition to its allocation of 2.8 MAF of mainstem water.

The opinion demonstrated that the Court prefers congressional allocations of interstate waters to playing the role of a trial court in complex litigation. The Court strained to find the federal power to allocate water among states and that it had been exercised.

IV. STATE RESTRICTIONS ON WATER EXPORT

The commerce clause of the United States Constitution, art. I, sec. 8, cl. 3, empowers Congress to regulate commerce among the states. The Constitution does not explicitly limit the ability of states to burden commerce, but courts have found "negative implications" from the grant of commerce power to Congress. This doctrine forbids states to discriminate against or unreasonably burden interstate commerce even if Congress has not legislated in the affected area. The doctrine is aimed at promoting free trade and preventing protectionism.

In evaluating state legislation for repugnance to the commerce clause courts consider whether: (1) the statute discriminates against nonresidents, (2) a legitimate state interest is present, (3) the state interest outweighs any competing national interest, and (4) less burdensome alternatives are available to accomplish the state's purpose. The test is essentially one of reasonableness of the state regulation in light of competing state and federal interests.

In Sporhase v. Nebraska *ex rel.* Douglas (S.Ct. 1982), the Supreme Court held that Nebraska groundwater is an article of commerce and that a Nebraska statute restricting lawful water exports to states that allowed the reciprocal privilege of export to Nebraska was unconstitutional on its face. The *Sporhase* opinion reviewed two earlier decisions, Hudson County Water Co. v. McCarter (S.Ct. 1908)(New Jersey statute could prohibit interstate transfer of water because water is in public ownership and, therefore, subject to state control free of the commerce clause) and City of Altus v. Carr (W.D.Tex.1966)(Texas law could not prohibit export of groundwater which, under other Texas law, is an article of commerce). It said that the state public ownership theory of *Hudson County* had been rejected in a case involving wildlife and that it was simply shorthand for expressing the importance to the state of regulating and preserving important public resources.

Whether state statutes violate the commerce clause depends partly on the nature of the interests the state is seeking to protect. Arid western states, in which water is scarce, have a strong conservation interest. Only even-handed state restrictions that are equivalent to the state's efforts to conserve water resources within the state will be upheld. In order for the court to find that there is no alternative restriction less burdensome upon commerce than an embargo, a state would have to prove water scarcity and maximum efforts to deal with the problem by in-state conservation measures.

New Mexico has had difficulties preventing El Paso, Texas from developing and using waters from an aquifer in New Mexico. The New Mexico statute banning interstate export of groundwater was held unconstitutional. A revised statute was held constitutional insofar as it subjected exports to review under "conservation" and "public welfare" standards because public interest review applied to instate uses as well. But other provisions giving priority in the State Engineer's considerations to the interests of New Mexico citizens discriminated against interstate commerce and did not pass constitutional muster. El Paso v. Reynolds (D.N.M. 1984).

Colorado requires that any waters diverted into another state must be credited to Colorado's obligation to deliver water to the importing state under any applicable compact or other allocation. To the extent that this is seen as carrying out a congressionally approved allocation it should be upheld. Other devices to protect state interests may also be tried, such as comprehensive statewide water planning, economic pricing of water, and innovative taxation schemes.

CHAPTER ELEVEN

WATER SERVICE AND SUPPLY ORGANIZATIONS

The company or city agency that provides water for domestic, municipal, and industrial uses is the most widely known entity involved in supplying water. Most private water companies are investor owned; a few are "mutuals," owned by the water users. However, water companies usually are public utilities regulated by a state agency. They, and not their customers, are holders of water rights. In the eastern states, where riparian rights prevail, it was necessary to pass special laws granting authority to companies and even to municipalities selling water to their residents to take water for use on non-riparian lands.

Although nearly everyone is served by a domestic water service utility, the organizations and agencies that distribute the largest quantity of water are those that supply agricultural irrigation water in the West. Many of them also supply water for municipal and industrial purposes.

The scarcity of available water was a barrier to settlement of the arid West. The first public lands utilized were near streams where water was readily accessible for mining and agriculture. The 1866

Mining Act validated the use of public land for building facilities to transport water to more distant lands, but construction and maintenance costs were a substantial obstacle. Crude, inefficient ditches were built to distribute irrigation water to river bottom lands, but the growing numbers of farmers soon exhausted the easily irrigable lands. Bringing water to benchlands over considerable distances required cooperative effort for those unable to pay the cost of building their own ditches. A main canal could be constructed with lateral ditches to distribute water to several farmers, and storage facilities assured availability of water during times of limited supply and high demand.

The Pueblo Indians and the early Spanish settlements of the Southwest used communal ditches to irrigate their lands, providing models for cooperative irrigation efforts. Some of these ancient community ditches, known as *acequias*, still operate today in New Mexico. At first, many individualistic settlers resisted organizing sufficiently to build large facilities, and such efforts failed. The earliest settlers to accept and use cooperative methods were the Mormon pioneers in Utah; their strong social organization facilitated successful irrigated agriculture in the dry, inhospitable Utah Territory.

The early settlers' enterprises evolved into a variety of organizations that deliver water. Water users' organizations can be divided into public and private entities. Private water distribution companies include for-profit ("carrier ditch companies" and water utilities) and non-profit ("mutual companies"). Private companies are usually organized as corporations, but may take other business forms. Few irrigation water supply organizations are totally private, for-profit companies today; most enjoy the benefits of tax exemption or other public subsidies.

Public water organizations can be roughly divided into regulatory bodies and water supply organizations. Regulatory bodies, such as groundwater management districts, engage in administration of water laws and conservation planning. Water supply organizations, such as irrigation and conservancy districts, are formed primarily to raise revenue (by property taxation and bond sales) to construct and operate irrigation projects. Some contract with the federal government to administer government-financed reclamation projects.

I. PRIVATE ORGANIZATIONS

A. Water Utilities

Water utilities are private companies having rights to take water and divert, store, and distribute it to customers by means of owned facilities. They may be corporations, partnerships, or sole proprietorships. The water is usually sold as a commodity, the company having reduced it to possession. Many western states (e.g., Colorado) consider the water to be the property of the state and the company's charges to be for the service of water delivery. Water companies are made public utilities by statute in nearly every state. In exchange for an exclusive franchise or monopoly to serve an area, they are subjected to public regulation by a state commission, board, or municipal government. Typical regulations require delivery of water to all within a defined service area, non-discrimination among users, and submission of major transactions (e.g., sale of assets, mergers, dissolutions, or acquisitions) for approval. The most significant form of control is rate regulation. As with other types of utilities (e.g., electric, telephone, gas), rates are fixed to allow a reasonable profit. A consumer owns no water right as such, but has rights defined under state public utility law.

B. Mutual Water Companies

Mutual water companies exist to serve their shareholders. Some states regulate them as public utilities, but most do not because, as nonprofit corporations or associations owned by the water users themselves, regulation is less necessary. Mutuals are not usually permitted to sell water to other than their own shareholders, nor may they be compelled to do so. Water rights of a mutual company are generally owned by the shareholders themselves, the quantity of rights being evidenced by shares of stock. Much of the discussion below of mutual ditch companies applies to mutual water companies.

C. Carrier Ditch Companies

Private, for-profit companies, known as carrier ditch companies, achieved an early popularity during settlement of the West. Carrier ditch companies backed by profit-seeking investors financed construction of irrigation works to deliver water to which individual users held rights. Nearly all such companies failed either because of infeasibility or because projected uses did not materialize as farmers opted for "free" groundwater, or chose to do dry-land farming rather than pay for water delivery. Many of these companies were subsequently reorganized as irrigation districts or non-profit mutual ditch companies; investors recouped some of their money by selling out to these entities. A few carrier ditch companies still operate in Arizona, Texas, and elsewhere.

D. Mutual Ditch and Irrigation Companies

Irrigation companies provided a means for organizing water users, usually as corporations, to finance and maintain facilities to transport, store, and distribute water to shareholders. Irrigation companies that are non-profit organizations may be exempt from both state and federal income taxes, but they are subject to the Fair Labor Standards Act and to unemployment compensation laws.

Formation of mutual ditch (or irrigation) companies was authorized by special state laws as early as the 1860s. Mutuals were formed in several ways, including: by holders of water rights who transferred their rights to the newly formed companies in exchange for stock; by joint owners of a ditch who traded their interests for stock, expanded the facilities and sold stock to others; by land developers who conveyed a share of stock along with each acre sold; and by local water users after bankruptcy of for-profit companies serving the area. Thus, shares of mutuals may not be considered subject to state securities laws since they are essentially a contractual arrangement among shareholders for distribution and use of jointly owned water rather than a medium of investment in an entity organized for profit. Bylaws usually restrict the shareholders to asserting and changing their water rights through the company. East Jordan Irrig. Co. v. Morgan (Utah 1993).

The greatest growth of mutual ditch companies occurred after western state constitutions (Arizona, Colorado, New Mexico, Utah, and Wyoming) exempted ditches, canals and the associated works owned by mutuals from state property taxation. Some mutual ditch companies were formed to contract with the federal government for reclamation project water and are still in operation for that purpose. Now, however, this purpose is most often served by irrigation districts, as described below.

A number of private irrigation corporations were formed under the 1894 Carey Act, 43 U.S.C.A. § 641, which awarded one million acres of arid federal lands to any western state that would cause the land to be irrigated and settled. Often this was done by encouraging formation of companies to build irrigation works. The lands were then sold by the state to individuals who bought shares in a mutual ditch or irrigation company formed to operate the irrigation works. Like carrier companies, many Carey Act corporations failed because they could not repay capital costs; some reorganized as irrigation districts.

1. *Financing*

Irrigation companies secure revenue almost exclusively from water users (i.e., by user fees and stock assessments), but some issue bonds secured by irrigation works or shareholders' lands. Assessments of stock (to pay operating costs and bond amortization) may be enforced by withholding water for non-payment.   Henderson v. Kirby Ditch Co. (Wyo.1962).

2. *Ownership of Rights*

Irrigation companies typically issue shares of stock that represent the quantum of the shareholder's right to receive water.   There is no obligation to serve members of the public in the service area that are not shareholders in the company.   Thayer v. California Development Co. (Cal.1912).   The company holds legal title to the water rights and represents its users against other appropriators. But each shareholder is beneficial owner of the individual water rights which are evidenced by the shares (contra, Texas).   Jacobucci v. District Court (Colo.1975)(shareholders in a mutual ditch company are real parties in interest and should be joined in an action to condemn water rights of the company, although company holds legal title).   Courts will protect private water rights of shareholders against abuses by the company.

3. Transfers

Holding water rights as shares of ditch company stock facilitates transfers. Stock issuance may have to comply with federal securities laws and state blue-sky laws. The Uniform Stock Transfer Act provides that transfer of title to shares requires either personal delivery by the owner or a written power of attorney. Stock in mutual companies is commonly considered appurtenant to (and thus passes with) land which is described on the face of the stock certificate. In fact, no paper shares exist in some small companies because "shares" simply pass with the land. Contrary presumptions may be imposed by statute. For example, a Utah statute provides that water company stock does not pass with the land without an express declaration by the transferor that the stock is appurtenant.

To protect the company against having to make uneconomical water deliveries to distant users, shares may be made inseverably appurtenant to land or transfers may be subject to approval under provisions in the articles of incorporation or bylaws. The company itself may restrict transferability (e.g., by requiring the company's consent, Riverside Land Co. v. Jarvis (Cal.1917)). California has recognized the right of companies to prohibit transfers to another ditch. Consolidated People's Ditch Co. v. Foothill Ditch Co. (Cal.1928). Although Colorado has allowed transfers if the transferor continues to bear a proper share of maintenance costs (Wadsworth Ditch Co. v. Brown (Colo.1907)), a bylaw limitation on changing the place of use to lands within a single county has been upheld. Fort Lyon Canal Co. v. Catlin Canal Co. (Colo.1982). If a change in the place or type of use results in harm to others, however, the transfer may be restricted. See City of Boulder v. Boulder and Left Hand Ditch Co. (Colo.1976); Chapter Three, Section IX. State laws relating to the transfer of water rights may also apply.

4. Priorities

As a rule, no priorities exist among shareholders with a proportionate interest in the same water supply even when supplies are insufficient for all users. But if users convey rights to a mutual company with different priority dates, the company can issue different classes of stock related to the priorities and with different burdens and privileges. Thus, a holder of shares evidencing a high priority may be assessed at a higher rate because the high priority confers greater benefits. Robinson v. Booth-Orchard Grove Ditch Co. (Colo.1934).

5. Regulation

A company may be treated as a public utility subject to regulation. This usually results if water service is provided to other than shareholders. E.g., Yucaipa Water Co. No. 1 v. Public Utilities Comm'n (Cal.1960) (company delivered water to lessees of shares of stock).

II. PUBLIC ORGANIZATIONS

A. Regulatory and Planning Bodies

Some public entities regulate present water uses while others plan for future uses. For example, the Colorado Water Quality Control Commission promulgates water quality standards under the Colorado Water Pollution Control Act and assists in administering water pollution control measures. The Water Conservation Board engages in joint federal-state water project and water use planning, and is involved in financing public and private irrigation projects. The Groundwater Commission determines rights and regulates water use in designated groundwater basins. Within designated basins, groundwater management districts may be formed (having both use-regulation and taxing powers) to assist the Groundwater Commission in regulating groundwater use. Types and activities of such regulatory bodies vary from state to state.

B. Municipalities

Laws of most states recognize the authority of cities to distribute water to their residents. State statutes or constitutions often authorize municipalities to avoid certain restraints in water law to carry out their water service responsibilities. For example, riparian states may allow municipalities (which are not riparians) to obtain and use rights to water on nonriparian lands; in appropriation jurisdictions, municipalities may be able to appropriate water in ways and for purposes not available to other users.   Thornton v. Farmers Reservoir &

Irrigation Co. (Colo.1978)(state legislation could not limit city's constitutional powers by restricting condemnation of water rights to those needed for 15 years in the future).

A municipality that serves its citizens generally may be considered a public utility subject to regulation. Under many state laws, however, municipalities are exempted from public utility regulation, even when they may be serving consumers beyond municipal boundaries. Board of County Comm'rs of Arapahoe County v. Denver Bd. of Water Comm'rs (Colo.1986)(city is a public utility, but is statutorily exempt from Public Utilities Commission regulation).

A city can deny or withhold water service on grounds reasonably related to public health and safety. Refusal to serve must not be arbitrary or malicious. If it is not rationally related to the public entity's legitimate interests (such as limited supply), denial of service that leaves land with no economically viable use could theoretically result in a regulatory taking of property that is compensable under the Constitution. Lockary v. Kayfetz (9th Cir.1990). Such a finding would depend, however, on rather difficult proof that the plaintiff's land had no economically viable use without the water service, not simply that there was a reduction in property value. No court has so held. *Lockary* was a test case, and after establishing the principle stated above, the plaintiffs dropped the suit.

Municipalities do not have a duty to serve consumers outside their boundaries, however. Fulghum v. Town of Selma (N.C.1953). But if they regularly do so, they probably will be required to provide service in a nondiscriminatory manner. See Robinson v. City of Boulder (Colo.1976)(city held itself out as ready to serve the public in the area to the extent of its capacity). This does not mean the same rates must be charged. There is a split of authority on whether nonresident customers have a right to be supplied with water from the municipality at "reasonable" rates. Compare Hansen v. City of Buenaventura (Cal.1986)(duty to provide service at reasonable rates) with Southgate Water District v. Denver (Colo.App.1992)(no judicial review of reasonableness charges).

C. Irrigation Districts

Irrigation districts exist under several names, including conservancy district, conservation district, reclamation district, water control district, and fresh water supply district. Although they have many different organizational forms and powers, the distribution of irrigation water is common to each. Some also perform functions such as electric power generation, drainage, and flood control. Irrigation districts are formed under special provisions of state law and enjoy a governmental or quasi-governmental status; yet most have a certain degree of legal autonomy that exempts them from taxation and public accountability. Irrigation districts distribute about half of all water used in the

West, giving them economic power and political influence.

1. Formation of Districts

Beginning with California's Wright Act in 1887, all western states passed laws authorizing formation of irrigation districts. The statutes define the organizational form, powers, and purposes of the districts. Typically, they provide for formation upon petition of local landowners or electors. The petition sometimes can be acted upon by a state court after a hearing; often, an election is required. Some types of districts may be formed by act of the legislature without voter or landowner consent.

Reluctant property owners can be forced to participate in a district project for the benefit of an area when the project is feasible only with full participation. Objecting landowners have been uniformly unsuccessful in challenging formation of districts. E.g., People *ex rel.* Rogers v. Letford (Colo. 1938) (inclusion and taxation of nonirrigable lands with an adequate water supply and within incorporated cities did not violate due process clause); Fallbrook Irrig. Dist. v. Bradley (S.Ct.1896)(upholding the constitutionality of Wright Act over due process objections).

2. Benefits of Districts

Possessing power to levy assessments against all property within their boundaries, irrigation districts historically provided an effective way to finance irrigation works. They helped solve problems of capital formation that had beset agriculture in much of the arid West. Benefits of being a governmental entity, such as tax exemption and the ability to raise capital by selling tax exempt bonds motivated people to form districts. However, where a district is formed for a governmental purpose, such as irrigation supply, and then engages in other economic activities, it may lose tax exempt status. A water district (or city) may also lack governmental immunity from suit on the ground that water supply is essentially a proprietary role.

The most powerful motive behind the creation of most irrigation districts was to provide a vehicle for participation in federal reclamation projects. The federal reclamation program began around the turn of the century. It has subsidized water projects benefiting much of the irrigated agriculture of the western United States. See Chapter Nine, Section IV. At first, the government intended to operate the projects directly, but a 1922 statute authorized contracts with irrigation districts to manage, operate, and maintain federal projects upon their completion and to distribute the water from them. The districts usually must agree to repay project costs directly attributable to irrigation benefits, which is accomplished by imposing assessments and user charges.

3. *Ownership of Water Rights*

Irrigation districts, not their constituents, own the water rights they exercise. The users' rights are essentially contractual. But see Bryant v. Yellen (S.Ct.1980)(Boulder Canyon Project Act requiring satisfaction of "present perfected rights" preserved individual users' rights under state law).

4. Election of Boards

Board members of irrigation districts are usually elected. Some types of districts in some states (e.g., "conservancy districts") provide for the appointment of members. The right to vote in a district election may be in each elector, each landowner, or weighted according to the amount of acreage owned.

Irrigation district voting has been held not subject to the one-person, one-vote principle established under the equal protection clause of the fourteenth amendment to the Constitution. Ball v. James (S.Ct.1981). In *Ball*, a multipurpose district limited voting privileges to landowners and allowed one vote per acre of owned land. The plaintiffs, who each owned less than one acre of land, alleged that the district's broad powers (to condemn property and sell tax-exempt bonds) and nonirrigation purposes (providing hydroelectric power to metropolitan Phoenix) affected non-landowning voters sufficiently to require that they be given voting rights. The Court disagreed, following the rule of Salyer Land Co. v. Tulare Lake Basin Water Storage District (S.Ct.1973) that certain districts may limit the voting franchise to landowners. If a district has a limited purpose and its activities disproportionately affect landowners, the Court in *Ball* said, the voting limitation bears the required "reasonable relationship" to statutory objectives. As a result, a few large landowners can control decision-making in some districts.

Ball and *Salyer* have been distinguished. A state law disenfranchising non-landowner residents was held unconstitutional because a substantial number of residents were concerned with and pay for the district's provision of water and sanitation services. Bjornestad v. Hulse (Cal.App.1991).

5. *Financial Aspects*

Irrigation districts may be empowered to raise revenues by assessing property, imposing taxes, charging users for water, and marketing other services. Revenue raising powers of districts depend on the state laws that authorize their creation. For instance, in Colorado "conservancy districts" may tax all lands in their boundaries, but "irrigation districts" are limited to taxing irrigable lands. It is not necessary that taxes be in proportion to the benefits received.   Millis v. Board of County Comm'rs of Larimer County (Colo.1981). State laws may allow assessments to be levied upon all land in a district based upon the value of the land or upon land classifications (e.g., tract size or type of soil). Some districts impose a flat assessment for each acre of land. Bonds may be issued by virtually all irrigation districts; it is this governmental authority that led to formation of most early districts. Sullivan v. Blakesley (Wyo.1926).

User fees are sometimes charged for water actually used. These charges may be in addition to taxes and assessments.

6. *Functions*

Irrigation districts began as rather simple organizations whose sole purpose was to deliver irrigation water, but today many districts are involved in other activities such as hydroelectric power generation, operation of recreation facilities, drainage, flood control, sanitation, and municipal and industrial water supply. An example is the Salt River Project Agricultural Improvement and Power District, serving metropolitan Phoenix, Arizona, which derives ninety-eight percent of its total revenue from power sales. Multiple purposes complicate administration of irrigation districts and may lead to conflicts among different constituencies, however. Irrigation users may feel, with some justification, that their interests are subordinated in disregard to the original legislative purpose of creating irrigation districts.

Although irrigation districts are commonly spoken of as "political subdivisions of state government," they have both public and private attributes, enjoying many benefits of both. Their public character gives them tax-exempt status, the power to tax, and freedom from regulatory agency interference, yet their private character allows them entrepreneurial flexibility and a degree of independence from regulators or electors. In *Ball*, supra, the Supreme Court recognized that the Salt River Project Agricultural Improvement and Power District was a "governmental entity," but also was a "business enterprise" in its dealings with power consumers. As the federal government's willingness to finance costly reclamation projects declines and the functions of irrigation districts move farther from their original purposes, many state legislatures may reappraise the place of the districts in political and economic life.

D. Municipal Water Districts

Some states authorize creation of several special types of districts that deal with problems of procuring water supply not necessarily related to irrigation. They are akin to "irrigation districts" that develop and transport water, and then distribute it to a number of water companies, municipalities, and large consumers. California has passed enabling legislation for the creation of special districts, known as municipal water districts and replenishment districts, to manage imported surface waters and local groundwater resources by administering rights determined in basin-wide adjudications, controlling pumping to safe annual yield rates, importing supplies, and preventing salt water intrusion. See Chapter Six, Section V B.

*

INDEX

References are to Pages

ABANDONMENT
Foreign Waters, 112
Prior appropriation rights, 176–178
Riparian rights, 66–67

ACCRETION AND AVULSION
Loss of riparian rights, 66–67

ARTIFICIAL WATERCOURSES
Defined, 27–29
Right to remove, 28–29

BENEFICIAL USE
See Prior Appropriation

CALIFORNIA DOCTRINE
See Hybrid Systems

CIVIL LAW SYSTEM
Louisiana, 212–214

CLEAN WATER ACT
Generally, 379
Dredge and fill permits, 302, 386–388
Effluent limitations, 382–383
Interstate pollution, 404
Management plans, 385–386
National Pollution Discharge Elimination Systems, permits, 380–384

CLEAN WATER ACT—Cont'd
Non-point source control, 384–386
Purpose, 379
Wallop Amendment, 389

CLOUD-SEEDING
Rights in precipitation, 110–111, 306

COLORADO DOCTRINE
See Prior Appropriation

COLORADO RIVER
Boulder Canyon Project Act, 349, 372, 378, 412, 413–415
Compact of 1922, 413
Legislative apportionment, 412–415
Mexican Treaty of 1944, 392, 393–395
Reserved rights, 321–322, 323, 324
Transbasin diversions, 160

COMMERCE CLAUSE
See also Marketing Water
Federal Power Act, 365–366
Interstate exports, 415–417
Navigation, 223, 348–351
Reserved rights, 314
Water as article of commerce, 84

DAMS
See Federal Power Act, Reclamation Act, Storage

DESERT LAND ACT OF 1877
Prior appropriation recognized, 21–22, 80–81,
Text, 196

DIFFUSED SURFACE WATER
Generally, 10–11, 291, 293
Capture of, 303–304
Damage from surface flows, 293–295
Defined, 293
Drainage projects, 301–303
Liability for drainage,
Civil law rule, 297–299
Common enemy rule, 295–297
Reasonable use, 294, 299–301
Reservoirs, 294–295
Restatement (Second) of Torts rules, 299
Tail water, 294

DIFFUSED SURFACE WATER—Cont'd
Regulation of use, 303–307
Rights in, 303–307
Springs, 26,
Subject to appropriation, 305–307
Watercourses distinguished, 23–29, 292
Wetlands protection, 301–302

DISTRICTS
See Service and Supply Organizations

DITCH RIGHTS
See Rights of Way; Service and Supply Organizations

DRAINAGE
See Diffused Surface Water

FEDERAL ACTIVITIES
    Generally, 13–14, 346–347
Hydroelectric power licensing, 363–368
International treaties, 392–396
Interstate allocation,
    Compact formation, 407–412
    Legislation, 412–415
Navigation, 347–351
Pollution control, 379–388
Reclamation projects, 371–379
Separation of Powers, 139
Water projects,
    See Hydroelectric power licensing and Reclamation projects,
        this topic
Wild and Scenic Rivers Act, 391–392
Wildlife protection, 368–371

FEDERAL AND INDIAN LANDS
See Reserved Rights

FEDERAL POWER ACT
    Generally, 40
Congressional power to enact, 363–365
Fish and wildlife protection, 368–371
Regulatory jurisdiction under,
State law conflicts, 365–368
Wild and Scenic Rivers Act, 391–392

FISH AND WILDLIFE
    See also, Instream Flow

FISH AND WILDLIFE—Cont'd
Endangered Species Act, 388
Fish and Wildlife Coordination Act, 369–370, 391
Hydroelectric power development, 368
Indian treaty rights, 370–371
Pacific Northwest Electric Power Planning and Conservation
Act, 370

FLOWAGE RIGHTS
Condemnation, 362–363
Liability for flooding, 294–295
Prescription, 28

FOREIGN WATERS
Defined, 27, 110–113
Developed water, 110–111
Imported water, 111–112
Ownership, 27
Reuse, 110–113, 134
Riparian rights, 27

FORFEITURE
Prior appropriation, 178–179
Riparian rights, 73

GROUNDWATER
Generally, 8–10
Artesian water, 239
Aquifers, 239–241
See also Tributary, this topic
Common pool resource, 245, 247
Conjunctive use,
Generally, 271–272
Augmentation, 282–283
Hydrologically connected sources, 272–280
Imported water, 280–281
Contamination, 247, 285–290
Correlative rights, 249–251, 275–278
English rule, 248
Federal interests, 325–326, 394, 417
Hydrology, 237–242, 274–275
Liability rules,
Generally, 247, 254
Correlative rights, 249–251
Economic analysis of, 258–262
Economic reach, 258–259

GROUNDWATER—Cont'd
Liability rules—Cont'd
   Junior liable, 255
   No liability, 254–255
   Reasonable use, 255–256
   Restatement (Second) of Torts, 256–258
Louisiana, 213
Mining and overdraft, 241, 245–246, 267–268
Nature of rights,
      See also, Liability rules, Permit systems, this topic
   Generally, 247–248
   Absolute ownership, 248–249
   Correlative rights, 249–251, 256
   Economic analysis of rules, 259–262
   Prior appropriation, 251–253
   Public resource subject to police power, 253–254
Optimum yield, 245–246
Organizations and districts, 245, 268–271, 285–287, 435
Percolating waters, 237–238, 242
Permit systems,
   Generally, 262–264
   Critical areas, 269–271
   Pre-existing uses, 251–252, 266–267
   Pumping limits, 265–271
   Water right, 264–265
   Wells, 264
Pollution,
   See Contamination, this topic
Prescription, 250–251
Pueblo rights, 214–216
Pumping costs, 242–246, 259–262, 266–267
   See also, Liability rules, this topic
Pumping regulation,
   Mining, 267–268
   Protection of quality, 269–271
   Protection of rights, 266–267
   Tributary to surface water, 278–280
Reasonable use, 255–256
Reserved rights, federal and Indian, 325–326
Safe yield, 240, 268
   See also, Mining and overdraft, Optimum yield, this topic
Springs, 240
State judicial remedies, 289–290
Storage, 281–284
Subsidence of land, 244–245, 249

GROUNDWATER—Cont'd
Tributary, 241, 274–280
Underground watercourses, 26–27, 237–242
Wells, 242–246, 263–265

HAWAIIAN LAW
Water rights, 8, 206–212

HYBRID SYSTEMS
Generally, 7–8, 190–191
Adjudication of unused riparian rights, 203–204
Administration, 201–206
Disputes between riparians and appropriators, 202–203
Division of land,
See also, Riparian rights, Riparian lands
Source of Title rule, 31–32
Hawaii, 206–212
History, 20–22, 191–196
Limits on riparian rights, 196–201
Loss of rights, 66–67, 73, 198–201, 203–206
Louisiana, 212–214
Non-riparian uses, 54, 204–206
Prescription, 204–206
Pueblo water rights, 214–216
Riparian rights modified, 85–88, 197–201
States applying, 8, 190
Takings, 201

HYDROELECTRIC GENERATION
See also Federal Power Act
Federal licensing, 363–368
Pacific Northwest Electric Power Planning and Conservation
Act, 370
Riparian rights, 40–41
Wild and Scenic Rivers Act, 391–392

INDIAN WATER RIGHTS
See Reserved Rights

INSTREAM FLOW
Pollution control, 379–388
Prior appropriation,
Diversion requirement, 92–97
Reservations from appropriation, 116–117
Reserved rights, federal and Indian, 311–313, 321
Wild and Scenic Rivers Act, 115, 387, 391–392
Wildlife protection, 387, 391

INTERSTATE ALLOCATION
Generally, 14, 397
Adjudication,
Equitable apportionment, 404–407
Interstate, 402–407
Jurisdiction, 398–399
Parens patriae, 400–401
Private parties, 397–402
States as parties, 402–407
Commerce clause limits on states, 415–417
Compacts,
Colorado River, 412–415
Constitutional authority, 407–408
Enforcement, 409
Preferred over adjudication, 407
Conflicts with state law, 410–411, 416–417
Federal legislation, 412–415
State export restrictions, 415–416

LAKES AND PONDS
Artificial, 27–29
See also, Watercourses
Minimum lake levels, 113–114
See also, Instream Flow
Navigability, 25–26, 45–47
Public rights, 45–47, 226, 232
Public Trust Doctrine, 224–226
Riparian rights, 235

LITTORAL RIGHTS
See Riparian Rights

LOSS OF RIGHTS
See Abandonment; Forfeiture

LOUISIANA
Generally, 8, 212–214
Code, 212–213
Groundwater, 213
Pollution, 213

MARKETING WATER
See Prior Appropriation, Transfers

MINING ACTS OF 1866 AND 1870
Recognition of prior appropriation, 79–80, 180–181, 194, 202
Rights of way, 180–181, 202

MINING ACTS OF 1866 AND 1870—Cont'd
Text, 194

MUNICIPAL USE
    See also, Service and Supply Organizations
Distribution of water, 420–421
Groundwater, 251
Louisiana, 213
Prior appropriation, 92, 100, 104, 156
Pueblo rights, 214–216
Riparian rights, 36–38

NATIONAL ENVIRONMENTAL POLICY ACT
Hydroelectric power projects, 369

NAVIGABILITY
Definitions, 45–47, 219–222, 350–351
Federal navigation power, 219–222, 347–351, 364
Lakes, 25–26, 45–47
Navigation servitude,
        Generally, 220, 351–352
    Access,
        For surface use, 229–233
        Formerly non-navigable waters, 356–357
    Condemnation damages, 357–361
    Obstructions to navigation, 353–354
    Property in navigable waterway damaged, 354–355
    Property on non-navigable tributary damaged, 355–356
    Site value, 358–361
    Takings, 351
    Water power value, 357–358
    Water rights, 361–363
Public rights to surface use, 223–224
Public Trust Doctrine, 224–226
Recreation, 223
State navigability, 222–223
Title of beds of navigable waterways, 45–46, 222, 352

POLLUTION
Clean Water Act, 302–303, 379–391, 404
Diffused surface water causing, 384–385
Groundwater, 247, 285–290
International, 393–394
Interstate, 404
Prior appropriation, 103, 117
Riparian rights, 36, 42–44

POLLUTION—Cont'd
State regulation, 273–275, 390–391, 402–403

PRESCRIPTIVE RIGHTS
Flowage easements, 28
Groundwater, 250–251
Hybrid systems, 205–206
Non-riparian uses, 54–55
Prior appropriation rights, 179–180
Riparian rights, 54–55, 69–72

PRIOR APPROPRIATION
Generally, 6–7, 74–77
Abandonment,
    Generally, 176–178
Access to water sources, 180–185
Adjudication and administration, 149–151
    See also, Procedures, this topic
Adverse possession, 179–180
Appurtenance to land, 156–157, 185
Augmentation, 188
Beneficial use, 97–100, 118–120
    Efficiency, 99, 120–128
    Measure of the right, 118–120
    Non-navigable waters, 226–229
    Public interest, 145–149
    Seepage, 129–134
    State laws, 98
    Waste not permitted, 103
Change of use,
    Diversion point, 164–168
    Foreign waters, 110–112
    Historical use limitation, 120, 173–175
    Limits, 173–176
    Manner of use, 172–173
    No harm rule, 159, 161–162
    Place of use, 168–169
    Procedures, 162–164
    Purpose of use, 169–170
    Quality protected, 175
    Return point, 171–172
    Salvaged water, 112–113
    Storage, 171
    Time of use, 170–171
Colorado system, 152–155
Condemnation of rights, 105–106

PRIOR APPROPRIATION—Cont'd
Conditional rights, 91–92
Conjunctive use of groundwater, 275–278
Conservation, 129
Diffused surface waters, 108, 304–306
Diversion requirement,
    Conditional rights, 93–95
    Due diligence, 93–95
    Exceptions, 95–97
    Means of, 123–128
    Physical diversions, 92–93
    Storage, 185
Duty of water, 121, 122–123
Efficiency,
    See also, Beneficial use, Inefficiencies, this topic
    Limit on right, 122–129
    Means of diversion, 118–129
    Reuse, 112–113
Elements,
    Generally, 74–75, 88–89
    Beneficial use, 97–100
    Diversion, 92–97
    Intent, 89–92
Extent of right,
    Generally, 117–118
    Beneficial use, 118–120
    Continuation of stream conditions, 161–164
    Duty of water limitations, 121, 122–123
    Efficient means of diversion, 123–128
    Quantity, 118–120
Federal control,
    See also, Reserved rights, this topic
    Commerce power, 415–417
    Condemnation, 357–363, 365–367
    Hydroelectric power development, 363–368
    Interstate allocation, 357–367, 376–379, 407–415
    Navigation, 347–351
    Pollution, 379–388
    Reclamation projects, 371–379
    Wildlife protection, 387–388, 391
Federal recognition, 193–196
Foreign waters, 110–112
Forfeiture, 178–179
Futile call, 104, 278–279
Groundwater, 241, 251–253, 274–280

PRIOR APPROPRIATION—Cont'd
History,
     Generally, 6–7, 77–79
   Early systems, 135–138
   English precedents, 17–18, 39
   Hybrid systems, 82, 191–196
   Modern systems, 81–82
   Public lands, 21–22, 78–81, 180–181, 193–196
   Riparian doctrine repudiated, 20–22, 81, 196–201
Hybrid states,
   See Hybrid Systems
Inefficiencies, 97–100, 103, 112–113, 123–128, 155–156
Initiation of rights,
   See also, Procedures, this topic
Instream flows, 96–97, 113–116
Intent to appropriate, 89–92
Interstate allocation 405–407
Limitations on right,
     See also, Change of use, Federal control, Reuse, this topic
   Beneficial use, 120–122
   Decreed right, 130–132
   Duty of water, 121, 122–123
   Efficient means of diversion, 123–128
   Hybrid state, 197–201
   Interstate allocations, 405–407
   Pollution, 103, 117
   Public interest, 145–149
   Statutory criteria, 144–145
Loss of rights, 176–180
Measure of right, 118–120
Municipal use, 98, 100, 104, 156
No harm rule, 159, 161–162
   See also, Change of use, this topic
Nonuse, 176–178
Perfection of rights,
   See also, Procedures, this topic
Permits,
   Constitutionality of statutes, 138–141
   Criteria, 144–145
   Procedures, 141–149
   Review of agency decisions, 150, 152
   Storage, 186–187
Place of use,
   See also, Change of use, this topic
Preferences, 104–106

PRIOR APPROPRIATION—Cont'd
Prescription, 179–180
Priority, 101–106
      See also, Relation back doctrine, this topic
   Enforcement, 103–104
   Quality rights, 103
   Qualification of senior right, 102–103
Procedures,
   Administration and enforcement, 151–152
   Change of use, 162–164
   Colorado system, 152–155
   Constitutional issues, 138–141
   Disputes among water users, 150–151
   Early systems, 135–138
   General stream adjudications, 149–150
   Permitting, 141–149
   Purpose, 138
   Review of agency decisions, 150
Property concepts, 2, 7, 82–85
Public Interest,
   See Beneficial use, Permits, Public trust doctrine, this topic
Public "ownership" and state police power, 74–75, 82–85
Public trust doctrine, 148–149
Purpose of use, 169–170
   See also Change of use, this topic
Quality,
      See also Pollution
   Change of use, 173
   Public interest, 145–149
   Right to, 102, 117
Quantity, 120–129
Regulation, 151–152
Relation back doctrine, 89, 90, 143
Reservations by states for future uses, 116–117
Reserved rights, 113–116, 316–317
   See also, Reserved Rights
Reuse,
      Generally, 129–135
   Foreign waters, 110–113
   Limitations, 134–135
   Salvaged water, 112–113, 133–134
Rights of way, 180–185
Riparian landowners' rights, 33
States applying, 7
Storage, 169, 185–189

PRIOR APPROPRIATION—Cont'd
Surface use, 223–224
Takings, 122, 141
Time of use,
   See also, Change of use, this topic
Transfers,
       See also Change of use, this topic
   Generally, 155–161
   Conveyance of land, 156–158
   Foreign water, 110–112
   Impediments, 99–100
   Interstate, 415–417
   Severed from the land, 156–158
   Stock in ditch or irrigation companies, 424–426
   Transbasin diversion, 110–112, 158–161
Waste,
   See Beneficial use, Efficiency, Inefficiencies, this topic
Waters subject to,
       See also, Public "ownership" and state police power,
          this topic
   Generally, 106
   Foreign waters, 110–112
   Groundwater, 241, 251–253, 274–280
   Instream flows, 113–116
   Lakes and ponds, 109
   Reserved rights, 113–116, 316–317
      See also Reserved Rights
   Salvaged water, 112–113, 133–134
   Springs, 109–110
   Streams, 107–109
   Tributary water,
      See groundwater, this topic
   Watercourses, 106–110
   Waters withdrawn from appropriation, 113–117

PUBLIC LANDS
   See also Reserved Rights
Acquisition of water rights, 308–318, 344–345
Appropriation doctrine, 20–22, 78–81, 180–181, 193–196
Public interest, 2, 7, 11, 145
Rights of way, 180–181

PUBLIC RIGHTS
       See also, Prior Appropriation, Permits, Public "owner-
         ship" and state police power, and Surface Use
   Generally, 2, 11–12

PUBLIC RIGHTS—Cont'd
Groundwater, 253–254
Navigable waters, 45–46, 223–224
Non-navigable waters, 226–229, 232–233
State laws, 85

PUEBLO RIGHTS, 214–216

QUALITY
See Pollution

RECLAMATION ACT
Acreage limitation, 373–376
Congressional power to enact, 373
Districts, 423, 429–435
History, 371–376
Residency requirement, 376
State law deferred to, 340–341, 365, 376–379

RESERVED RIGHTS
Generally, 12–13, 308
Aboriginal Indian rights, 319
Appurtenance, 325
Hawaiian water rights analogized, 206–212
Indian allotments, 327–329
Instream flow, 113–116, 323, 340
"Non-reserved" rights, 344–345
Origins, 308–311
Power to create,
Generally, 313
Commerce clause, 313, 314
Exercise, 314–315
Property clause, 314
Treaty clause, 313–315
Prior appropriation system, 316–317
Priority, 318–319
Public lands, 311–313
Pueblo rights analogized, 216
Quantification,
Generally, 330–344
Adjudication, 332–338
Legislation, 339
McCarran Amendment, 334–338
Negotiation, 338–339
Practicably irrigable acreage, Indian lands, 321–322
Purpose of reserving land, 319–323

RESERVED RIGHTS—Cont'd
Quantification—Cont'd
    Sovereign immunity, 334–338
Regulation of, 339–341
    State law, 339–341
    Tribal, 341–344
Riparian rights system, 317–318
State reservations for future uses, 116–117
State water law inferior, 315–318
Transfer,
    Indian allotments, 327–329
    Leases, public and tribal lands, 326–327
Use of, 329–330
Waters reserved,
    Groundwater, 325–326
    Outside reservations, 324–325
    Streams on or bordering reservation, 323

RESTATEMENT (SECOND) OF TORTS
Sections 822–831, p. 299
Section 826, p. 43
Section 833, p. 299
Section 843, p. 23
Section 846, p. 293
Section 850, p. 48–49
Section 850A, pp. 49–51, 201
Section 855, pp. 52–53
Section 858, pp. 256–259

RIGHTS OF WAY
Appurtenant to water rights, 185
Condemnation, 184–185
Public lands, 180–181
Purchase, 183–184
Trespassers, 182–183

RIPARIAN RIGHTS
    Generally, 4–6
Abandonment, 67
Abrogation by state law, 85–88
Appurtenance, 30–32, 59, 68
Artificial uses,
    Natural uses distinguished, 34–35
Artificial watercourses, 27–29
Conveyance of land,
    Appurtenance, 30

RIPARIAN RIGHTS—Cont'd
Diffused surface water, 306–307
Discharge of waste, 42–44
Domestic use,
    See also, Natural uses, this topic
Extent,
    Appurtenance to land, 30–32
    Watershed limitation, 29–30
Foreign waters, 27
Forfeiture, 73
Gravel recovery, 41–42
Hawaiian water rights, 207–212
History,
    American precedents, 18–20
    English precedents, 15–16, 17–18
    French precedents, 16–17
    Repudiation, western states, 20–22
Hybrid systems,
    See Hybrid Systems
Industrial uses, 35–36
Irrigation, 35–36
Littoral rights, 24–26
Loss, 67–73, 197–201
    Avulsion and accretion, 68–69
    Forfeiture, 73
    Legislation, 72–73
    Nonuse, 67
    Permit systems, 72
    Prescription, 69–72
Mining, 35–36
Modifications,
        See also, Reasonable use, Statutes limiting, this topic
    Hybrid systems, 192–193, 196, 197–201
Municipal uses, 36–38, 418, 427
Natural flow,
        Generally, 18, 19–20
    Preference for natural uses, 34–35
Natural uses, 34–35
Nature of rights and duties,
    Common law, 33–34
    Irrigation, industrial, and mining, 35–36
    Natural uses, 34–35
Non-riparian uses, 51–56
Nonuse, effect of, 67
Ownership of beds and waterbodies, 220–222

RIPARIAN RIGHTS—Cont'd
Permit systems,
        See also, Hybrid Systems
     Generally, 56–59
   Criteria, 57–58
   Exemptions, 56–57
   Modification of existing rights, 72–73
   Non-riparian uses, 54
   Provisions, 58–59
   States with, 56, 57
Pollution, 36, 42–44
Power, 39–41
Prescription, 54–55, 69–72, 204–206
Public rights,
   Navigable waters, 45–46
   Non-navigable waters, 46, 226–229, 232–233
   Reasonable use rule, 232–233
Reasonable use,
     Generally, 18–20, 48–52
   Economic analysis, 55–56
   Gravel recovery, 41–42
   Harm to plaintiff, 53–54
   Hybrid systems, 197–198
   Hydroelectric generation, 40–41
   Irrigation, industrial, and mining uses, 35–36
   Municipal use, 36–38
   Non-riparian uses, 51–56
   Permit systems, applicability to, 48
   Pollution, 36, 42–44
   Preference for natural uses, 34–35
   Prescription, 69–72
   Restatement (Second) of Torts rules, 48–53
   Storage, 38–39
Reciprocal rights, 44–45
Reserved rights, 317–318
   See also, Reserved Rights
Riparian lands,
     See also, Surface Use
   Avulsion and accretion, 68–69
   Defined, 23
   Division,
     Grants and reservations, 59–65
     Partition, 30
     Source of title rule, 31–32
     Unity of title rule, 30–31

RIPARIAN RIGHTS—Cont'd
Riparian lands—Cont'd
    Division—Cont'd
        Watershed limitation, 63–65
      Owners' rights, 34–44, 233–236
      Use of water limited to, 51–56
      Watercourses, 23–29
Source of title rule, 31–32
Springs, 26
States applying, 5
Statutes limiting, 72–73, 81–83, 85–88, 193–201
Storage rights, 38–39
Surface use, 44–47
Takings, 201
Transfer,
    Appurtenance, 55, 59
    Grants and reservations, 59–65
Underground watercourses, 26–27
Unity of title rule, 30–31
Use restricted to riparian land, 16–17
Waste discharges, 42–44
Watershed limitation, 29–30, 51–52, 63–65

SALVAGED WATER
Recapture and reuse by appropriator, 112–113, 132–135

SERVICE AND SUPPLY ORGANIZATIONS
    Generally, 418–420
Carrier ditch companies, 421
Conservancy districts,
    See also, Irrigation districts, this topic
Drainage, 301–303
Groundwater, 280–281, 435
Irrigation companies, 424–426
Irrigation districts, 429–435
Louisiana, 213
Metropolitan Water District, 280–281
Municipal water districts, 435
Municipalities, 427–429
Mutual ditch companies, 422–424
Mutual water companies, 421
Planning bodies, 427
Reclamation projects, 423, 431
Utilities, 420–421, 426, 427–428

SPRINGS
See also, Groundwater
Definition, 26
Diffuse surface water, 293
Ownership, 26
Subject to appropriation, 110

STORAGE
Groundwater, 281–284
Liability for releases, 38–39, 289–290
Prior appropriation, 169, 185–189
Riparian rights, 38–39

STREAMS
See Watercourses

SURFACE FLOW
See Diffused Surface Water

SURFACE USE
Generally, 217–218
Access to waterways, 229–233
    Condemnation, 230
    Implied right of access, 230–233
Public rights in navigable waterways, 218–223
    Federal definition, 219–222
    State definition, 222–223
    Title to beds, 220–222
Public rights in non-navigable waterways, 226–229
Public Trust doctrine, 11, 224–226
Rights of riparian owners, 233–236

TAKINGS
Hybrid systems, 201
Navigation servitude, 351
Prior appropriation, 122, 141
Riparian rights, 201

TITLE TO BEDS OF STREAMS AND LAKES
See Navigability, Surface Use

TRANSBASIN DIVERSIONS
Interstate, 415–417
Restrictions on, 158–161

TREATIES
Indian,
    Congressional power, 313–315

TREATIES—Cont'd
Indian—Cont'd
    Fishing rights, 370–371
    reservation purposes, 308, 321–322, 330–332
International, 392–396
    Canada, 392, 395, 396
    Mexico, Colorado River, 393–395
    Supremacy, 396

UNDERGROUND WATERCOURSES
    See also, Groundwater
Definition, 26–27

WATER INSTITUTIONS
See Service and Supply Organizations

WATERCOURSES
Artificial, 27–29
Defined, 23–29, 106–110
Diffused surface waters distinguished, 23, 106, 108, 293
Great ponds, 25
Lakes and ponds, 24–25, 109
Ownership of beds, 220–222
Public uses,
    See Surface Use
Springs, 26, 109–110
Streams, 24, 107–109
Subject to appropriation, 106–110

WEATHER MODIFICATION
See Cloud-seeding

WELLS
    See also, Groundwater
Depletion effects, 243–245
Drilling and pumping, 240–243
Optimum yield, 245–246
Permits, 262–264

WETLANDS
Drainage, 301–303

WILD AND SCENIC RIVERS ACT
    Generally, 391–392
Clean Water Act, § 404, p. 387
Hydroelectric facilities, 391–392
Instream flow, 115, 287, 391–392

†